THE JUDGE'S WIFE

The Judge's Wife

Memoirs of a British Columbia Pioneer

Eunice M.L. Harrison

Introduction by
Jean Barman

Edited by Ronald B. Hatch
Annotations by Louise Wilson

Ronsdale Press

THE JUDGE'S WIFE
Copyright © 2002 Louise Wilson

RONSDALE PRESS
3350 West 21st Avenue
Vancouver, B.C., Canada
V6S 1G7

Set in New Baskerville: 11 pt on 15
Typesetting: Julie Cochrane
Printing: Hignell Printing, Winnipeg, Manitoba
Cover Photo & Frontispiece: Eunice M.L. Harrison at age sixty-two
Cover Design: Julie Cochrane

Ronsdale Press wishes to thank the Canada Council for the Arts, the Government of Canada through the Book Publishing Industry Development Program (BPIDP), and the Province of British Columbia through the British Columbia Arts Council for their support of its publishing program.

National Library of Canada Cataloguing in Publication Data

Harrison, Eunice M. L., 1860–1950
   The judge's wife

   ISBN 0-921870-92-2

   I. Harrison, Eunice M. L., 1860–1950   2. Pioneers — British Columbia — Biography. 3. British Columbia — History — 19th century.
I. Title.
FC3822.1.H37A3 2002   971.1'02'0922   C2001-911600-4
F1088.H37 2002

Contents

Introduction

I first encountered "the judge's wife" a dozen years ago. Eunice Harrison's granddaughter Louise Wilson was a student in a course to which I gave a guest lecture at Malaspina College in Nanaimo. She kindly alerted me to the existence of her grandmother's memoir and arranged for me to see a copy. Its pages transported me back to a time and place almost as if I became the judge's wife. I introduced Eunice Harrison's voice into my British Columbia history *The West beyond the West*, regretting I could include only glimpses of her life.

It is therefore a special pleasure to welcome *The Judge's Wife* into print. The memoir is one of very few by the first generation of newcomer women to British Columbia.[1] Shortly after Eunice Seabrook's birth on 15 June 1860 into a well established family in London, Ontario, her father was caught up in the Cariboo gold rush. Unlike most men who soon returned home grateful to be there, Seabrook came back only long enough to gather up his wife and daughter so they could share in this new adventure.[2]

Arriving in British Columbia in 1864, the family first lived in New Westminster. Four years later they moved to Victoria, where Roades Seabrook joined the shipping firm of Rithet's and also got involved with sealing. The children attended private school, Eunice Seabrook completing her education at Mrs. Fellows' Finishing School. Victoria was in those days a very small place, meaning that everyone who mattered, or rather considered they did so, knew everyone else who mattered, at least in their eyes. Its newcomer population at the time the British colony of British Columbia joined the Canadian Confederation in 1871 was under 2,500. The entire province contained about 10,000 non-Aboriginal persons. Of these 1,500 were Chinese and 500 African American, people who did not much count in the eyes of the few other newcomer families.

For a brief moment in her youth, Eunice Seabrook became her own person. As her memoir recounts, she delighted in summer trips to the raw lumber town of Granville, site of the future Vancouver. Hitching rides with family friends running tugboats or other watercraft, she spent considerable time there freed from the constraints of genteel Victoria. The "Indian war dance" she attended is described in her memoir. So is the bathing beauty contest she not only entered but won, much to her parents' chagrin.

Almost inevitably, Eunice Seabrook soon succumbed to societal expectations for young women of her time. In 1880 she married promising lawyer Eli Harrison. A decade her senior in age, he had arrived in Victoria from San Francisco with his equally respectable family in 1858. After their marriage his career figures almost as prominently in the memoir as her own doings. Part of the reason is the durability of the marriage, the other part the expectation of the day that a wife would merge her life into that of her husband. Named a County Court Judge for Cariboo and Lillooet shortly after the marriage, Eli Harrison continued to maintain his residence in Victoria. Eunice Harrison includes her husband's descriptions of his extensive travels by diverse means through the interior. She also recalls her own trip with him on one of his circuits. On being made a judge in Nanaimo in 1889, the family obligingly following him there. Returned to Victoria, they had a new house built for them by well-known architect Samuel Maclure, a process and product described in some detail. Called "Oakwood" for the old oaks on its acre of grounds, the house was very appropriately located on Harrison Street, named in honour of the judge, by now a man of considerable prominence.

Eunice Harrison's evocative and anecdotal account contains vignettes of individuals as diverse as colonial governor James Douglas and his family, Queen Victoria, various robbers, and what she terms "a very, very long train of Chinese servants coming and going through the decades (mostly going)" (74). She incorporates, as a matter of course, the numerous Aboriginal peoples whose lives were interwoven with hers, a useful reminder of the contribution that both Aboriginal and Chinese people made during these years to all aspects of British Columbia.

Eunice Harrison's memoir is perhaps most revealing for its fine portrait of married women's lives during the late nineteenth century. As befit the judge's wife, she was expected to enliven Victoria society. At its heart was Government House, home to the monarch's representative, the Lieutenant Governor. She knew what were the expectations and how to play the game. She could do so in part because she was privy to the rules, including the consequences of transgressing them. The approved wording on a lady's visiting card, when and where it should be left, the placement of gloves by a gentleman making a social call, the minutiae of wedding gift giving — all of these niceties Eunice Harrison understood as a matter of course and shares with readers of her memoir.

The ease with which Eunice Harrison fulfilled her role as the judge's wife was because both she and her husband had learned, through their private education in Victoria, how to do so. They took for granted the colonial character of social practices and considered it essential that their children also do so. Her descriptions of Collegiate School and Corrig College, which the four Harrison sons attended, indicate more clearly than any official account these institutions' primary allegiance to the colonial center that was Britain. Students were taught as if they lived at the heart of Empire as opposed to residing in a distant outpost. The two Harrison daughters were sent to Angela College in Victoria and also to All Hallows at Yale, interestingly enough just after the future King George V and his wife visited the school, perhaps for that very reason.

Many of the events Eunice Harrison chooses to record may seem commonplace to us today, but underline how restricted were women's opportunities for adventure and achievement. Her spare time was occupied by burning patterns on wood or leather, painting china, and playing various musical instruments. She sometimes sought to give extraordinary meanings to everyday incidents, in part, I expect, to counter their monotony. Amateur theatricals and summer camping holidays on the beach, both highly fashionable and thereby permissible, gave particular pleasure. So too did small, unexpected delights. She tells us how, on his circuits, Eli Harrison discovered melons growing near Lytton as early as 1870, almost all of Lillooet's houses built of sun-dried adobe, and Quesnel Forks to be "quite a village, with houses, stores, men, women and children, but all Chinese" (138). There are excellent descriptions of the gold rush town of Barkerville, the judge's Chinese court interpreter Ah Quan, and the sealing industry out of Victoria.

Eunice Harrison also possessed the capacity for reflection. Living vicariously through her husband, she took enormous pride in his successful career. She was at the same time well aware of her sheltered existence as the judge's wife, or indeed any man's wife. She noted sadly how one of her husband's visitors was, long years later, still a mystery to her because "in those days, ladies, especially wives, were not often told things" (123). Persuaded for health reasons to take her two youngest children on a holiday to California in 1906, she had to tread carefully, for "it was 'not the thing' for ladies to travel alone" (209). The trio was in San Francisco when the earthquake and subsequent fire struck. Eunice Harrison's harrowing description of the events into which they were plunged and her tenacity in getting back to Victoria speak to her resourcefulness.

Because, "from 1906 forward, the times can hardly be called pioneer" (241), Eunice Harrison ended her memoir with the California earthquake. She was perceptive. By then the province's non-Aboriginal population approached a quarter of a million. Victoria had grown tenfold from the days of her childhood to 25,000, Vancouver to twice that size. The British Columbia to which she came as a child was no more.

With the passage of time Eunice Harrison grew more independent. The struggle for female suffrage was the most visible manifestation of a broader shift whereby, during the first decades of the new century, growing numbers of women made their lives on their own terms. The colonial proprieties that once entrapped the judge's wife lost their force. Arthritis had prompted her first trip to California, whose hot, dry climate was more conducive to her well-being than rainy damp British Columbia. From 1908 she and her youngest son Herschel, with whom she was particularly close, began to take annual winter trips south. She stayed there longer each year after 1913 when, on completing his schooling in Victoria, Herschel decided to study and then practice law in California. Her summers she spent with her husband in their Victoria home. By then her other children were on their own, daughters wed and three older sons following in their father's footsteps as members of the bar in British Columbia. Claude was a longtime City Prosecutor in Victoria, Paul Phillips an MLA for Comox elected in 1924. Their brother Victor ran unsuccessfully in 1928 in Nanaimo, where he served as mayor.

Eunice Harrison's life took another turn in 1928, when her husband became ill. She together with Herschel and his American bride moved into "Oakwood," the family home in Victoria, to take care of him and remained there following Eli Harrison's death in 1930. The Depression brought economic difficulties. Unable to keep up mortgage payments, Eunice Harrison lost "Oakwood." In 1939 she moved up island with her son and daughter-in-law and their three young children; there they rented a hundred-acre farm outside of Duncan in order to be more self-sufficient.

It was there in the spring and summer of 1945 that Eunice Harrison constructed her memoir. In doing so, she drew on diaries she had kept over the years, her husband's writings, and other materials. She dictated it to Herschel who did the typing, according to her granddaughter Louise Wilson. He sent the typescript to several publishers, but to no avail up to Eunice Harrison's death on 25 January 1950 aged almost ninety.[3] A year later Herschel sent sample chapters to the editors of *Northwest Digest,* an outdoor adventure magazine published at Quesnel in the British Columbia central interior. They accepted it with enthusiasm, and it ran there as a serial between 1951 and 1953.[4] A decade later Eunice Harrison's son lodged the original typescript, used for this edition, in the National Archives in Ottawa.[5]

Eunice Harrison reflected shortly before her death in 1950 on the enormous changes she had seen during her lifetime. "As we race forward with the streamlined age, the past recedes with ever increasing momentum and my eighty years of life and adventure in this land well might have been eight hundred years ago." Watching "the boats of the local yacht club sporting in the bay," she observed how "it seems but yesterday that I saw the same waters teeming with Indian craft." We who follow are fortunate indeed that Eunice Harrison understood the importance of memory, of, as she put it, "venturing to add my own testimony to that of some other pioneers as to life in the early days" (14). Her words draw women, on their own terms, into British Columbia history.

The Why of This Book

Vancouver Island is about 290 miles long and 50 to 80 miles wide, the total area being about 20,000 square miles. It is, therefore, almost half the area of England and three times that of Wales; or more than half the size of Ireland or Scotland.

Even now in 1945 there is no road going the full length, either on the East or West coast; the centre is mountainous.

Large areas are practically unknown if barely explored. The settled sections, however, are, for the West, old, and have a population of about 150,000.

Vancouver Island, mountainous and heavily wooded with evergreens, is the largest of the many islands which lie off the coast of British Columbia, Canada's most Western province.

It is separated from the mainland and its great mountain ranges, by Haro, Georgia, Johnstone, and Broughton Straits and Queen Charlotte Sound, from the American Olympic mountains to the South by the Strait of Juan de Fuca.

Vancouver Island was, at first, a separate colony established in 1849 and governed from England.

The mainland of British Columbia is very large, rugged and contains vast unexplored regions. It is said to be larger in area than the United Kingdom of Great Britain, France, Holland and Denmark combined.

The mainland colony was established in 1858 and had its capital at New Westminster, built in 1859 the year of the Gold Rush. Both colonies were united in 1866 but it was not until five years had passed that the colony entered the Dominion of Canada, in 1871.

Although the total population of British Columbia is now nearing one million, mostly in a few coastal cities like Vancouver on the mainland, established as late as 1886, and which now has about 400,000 people, it is on the whole very sparsely settled, with vast tracts of land and virgin forests. There are thousands of lakes, thousands of wooded islands, many rivers and great ranges of high mountains.

When I turn from glimpsing the white pyramids of some of the mainland mountains, gleaming through the golden-blue haze across the straits and watch the boats of the local yacht club sporting in the bay, it seems but yesterday that I saw the same waters teeming with Indian craft.

It seems as though it was only the day before yesterday that there was no pale face in the territory and it had lain a land of mystery for hundreds, if not for thousands, of years.

As we race forward with the streamlined age, the past recedes with ever increasing momentum and my eighty years of life and adventure in this land well might have been eight hundred years ago — so quickly have the inhabited areas in British Columbia gone forward.

The bygone days are growing more mythical and few of the earlier pioneers remain.

I am therefore venturing to add my testimony to that of some other pioneers as to life in the early days.

Reliance has not been placed on memory only; the draft was carefully checked by personal diaries and old family letters, documents and the like.

EUNICE M. L. HARRISON
"Kent Place,"
Duncan, Vancouver Island,
B.C., Canada
November 1, 1945.

CHAPTER 1

Red Jackets

The tall, pleasant man wearing burnsides and dressed in a scarlet coat, laughingly lifted me up several times and set me down amidst a pack of hounds with question-mark tails that swarmed about the hall door urging him out.

I watched the old gentleman leave the house and mount a black-maned, red horse held by a groom.

The rider was my paternal grandfather Joseph Seabrook, Esquire,[1] fond of his hounds and horses which he had brought out with him from England in 1832 to Caradoc, London, Ontario.

My grandfather had set up, in 230 wooded acres, a residence in 1833 as much like an English country house as could be in a new country. The place name was "Stowe."

There I was born a few months before the firing on Fort Sumpter[2] started the United States Civil War.

My mother Louise Annette, was a daughter of Dr. Alfred Holloway through whom I was the great granddaughter of Vice Admiral

Vice-Admiral John Holloway of the Red Squadron, the great grandfather of Eunice Harrison. Courtesy of L. Wilson.

John Holloway of the Red Squadron (who, when a junior officer, had been at the battle of Trafalgar) and had married my father, Roads Seabrook, in Ontario in 1859. My father was my grandfather's youngest son and had also been born at Stowe, where we were all living.

My maternal grandfather I remember through an unpleasant circumstance.

I was see-sawing with a youthful nurse maid in the orchard at Stowe, when she suddenly got off and the jar threw my face violently against the board. The cries of the maid brought my mother out and she said that she found I had a badly sprained ankle and, worse, the bridge of my nose was broken; in fact the nose was flat on my face.

A servant on a galloping horse soon brought Dr. Holloway and he put my nose in a sort of plaster cast. My mother said that every day she had to (in some way not quite clear to me) encourage the bridge to rise again.

Certainly I have since had quite a bridge to my nose but perhaps it was never again a "family" nose although assiduously repaired by a maternal grandfather.

Among my paternal grandfather's intimate friends at Stowe in Ontario were Dr. Starr, who had served in the British army under Wellington against Napoleon in Spain, Major Somers and Captain Agassiz. Captain Agassiz of the early pioneers (after whom Agassiz, B.C. was named) greatly excited my father's interest in British Columbia, and when my father was in his twenties he went out alone to look over the Cariboo gold fields.

On father's return in 1864, he decided to take my mother and me to pioneer in the West.

I vividly recall the bustle of packing and how the several men and women servants came up from the servant's hall and stood in a row to bid us farewell.

Father, mother and I went off in a carriage driven by one of the servants whose big double-breasted great coat, with its large buttons, attracted my childish fancy as much as did the fore-arm grasping a cross which dangled as a crest from my grandfather's gold watch chain.

Looking back, I saw my grandmother (who was a Roads, sometimes spelled Rhodes or Roades) and servants crying, with the women holding their aprons to their eyes, but I could not understand why, since I felt thrilled to be off with my parents on adventure.

I never saw my grandparents, Stowe or Ontario again. My grandfather died a few years later and the large old house at Stowe was burned down in 1868.

Of course no one then made the trip to the Pacific coast across Canada and we set out for British Columbia by ship that took an interminable amount of time. At the Isthmus of Panama I watched the natives dive for pennies thrown to them by my mother and other passengers. That was long before the locks at Panama and we went overland across the Isthmus to take the *Brother Jonathan* on the Pacific side for British Columbia.

San Francisco was our first port of call and we received news of the Civil War which was still raging.

San Francisco, with somewhat more than 60,000 population, was even then a picturesque city. Little did it enter my child's mind, as our vessel resumed its journey through the Golden Gate that I should some day nearly lose my life there and leave the port amidst scenes of tragedy.

The *Brother Jonathan* proceeded slowly up the coast, passing Washington State which then had less than 24,000 people; after touching at Victoria, the ship proceeded to New Westminster, then having a little over 1,000 whites.

New Westminster stands on a rather steep hill, overlooking the muddy, swirling Fraser River, and, as there was no Vancouver then, it was the largest city on the mainland. The whole country thereabouts seemed to swarm with Indians. Many children, native and white, were drowned in the currents of the river near New Westminster.

My father had received an excellent education in Ontario at Squire Livingstone's private academy, a select boarding school but of an unpleasantly Spartan sort. The Merediths and others prominent in Eastern Canada had been school fellows, but my father acquired no profession.

He always remembered the harshness of an early teacher and it killed in him any taste for the dry learning required for the Bar or other learned professions. Livingstone Academy was later burned down by a "corrected" pupil.

As my father was a modest, retiring sort of man it was clear that, without business push or a learned profession he would have a hard time.

This in fact proved to be the case for awhile; he tried prospecting, and a bit of ranching on the mainland, and without the timely arrival of a remittance from Stowe or relatives in England, he would have been in a bad way.

In morals he was a strict puritan, with a knowledge of mathematics and a conscientious disposition. He became a member of the staff of Rithets, a large shipping company, of which he later became a Vice President.

CHAPTER 2

"Ick Clune"

"*Ick Clune*"[1] said the large old Indian grinning, as he approached me on the verandah, holding out to me a bundle of gum stick.[2] He wore a red blanket with black bands, held together by a big bone skewer. I was rather fascinated by the Indian's queer hat — like an inverted basket — which many of them then wore.[3]

But my wonder turned to fear when I saw the awful, sinister sores on his face and hands. He pressed the gumstick into my hands and motioned me to take it in to my mother. I told mother how he looked and, after a swift glance through the window, she cried "Smallpox!"[4] It was then raging in the Indian rancheries near New Westminster.

My father at once went to Dr. Black and he said that he would come and see me in nine days. When he came later, he said I had developed smallpox in its very worst form — black smallpox — and he put a sign on the house.

I was five years old and it is one of my earliest memories. To keep

Songhees Indian with "inverted basket" hat. RBCM, PN5933.

me warm I was wrapped like a mummy and slept between my parents in their double bed.

Strange to say, they never caught the disease and neither did a couple and their two children who were our guests in the house at the time. In fact my parents never caught smallpox at any time and were never vaccinated.

My father was so opposed to vaccination for any purpose that he slept with a revolver under his pillow, when the authorities were forcibly vaccinating people. Father said that no one was going to force him against his will.

In the Sixties and somewhat beyond, the pioneers still looked to firearms for self-protection, although the English system of laws had been adopted on November 19, 1858.

My parents and I went through many subsequent epidemics of several kinds; none of us were ever vaccinated and none of the others ever contracted any of the infectious diseases.

The nine days of observation and twenty-one days with the worst kind of smallpox gave my mother time to obtain advice from her father Dr. Holloway. It was simple — Keep my hands tied so as not to cause pox marks by scratching and keep light from my eyes. Thanks to this advice I had no noticeable pox marks.

CHAPTER 3

Victoria and School Days

We left New Westminster in 1868 aboard the *Enterprise*[1] for Victoria (population 2,000); it would be hard to recognize to-day.[2]

Quite a forest surrounded Beacon Hill, and the now old residential section of James Bay had not even started building.

The ancient outer wharves did not then jut from the seashore, and of course there was no breakwater, no grain elevator, no cold storage warehouse or woollen mills.

The *Enterprise* passed through a crowd of Indian canoes and war canoes paddling back and forth from the Songhees village[3] which lay at the left entrance to the inner harbour. The Songhees were flat-heads and had quite a thriving community there. The drum of tom-toms intrigued our interest, but the effluvia from dead salmon and fish nets drying on the low roofs of Indian shacks almost lifted us from the deck.

Then a turn of the wind brought compensating fragrance from

Old Songhees reserve, c. 1880. BC Archives, F-09955.

the sweet-smelling pines and the strong salt of wharves, warehouses and ship chandlers.

To the right we saw picturesque wooden parliament buildings facing the inner harbour, and their unique design, suggestive of the Orient, invited the friendly nick-name of "bird cages."

To their left, an arm of the sea undulated under a wooden bridge (later replaced by a stone causeway), over the site of the Empress Hotel, and almost up to the grounds of the present Reformed Episcopal Church.[4]

The *Enterprise* cautiously continued its way to a little wharf at the foot of Yates Street. After we had disembarked, and while my parents were attending to the baggage on the wharf crowded with colonials eager to watch the ship's arrival, I glanced at them again:

My mother, Annette Seabrook, serious blue-gray eyes; black wavy hair, shaded with a bonnet and parasol; her shapely erect figure, not over five feet three inches; exceptionally small feet in two and one-half shoes. Her pink complexion had the natural freshness of one still in her twenties although she had had several children, of whom the youngest, my baby sister Annette, was then in her arms.

My father, Roads Seabrook, very deep blue steady eyes; fair hair; bewhiskered but not heavily; shapely hands. He stood not over a straight five feet eight and one-half inches and was that day wearing a double-breasted blue serge which enhanced the width of rather broad shoulders.

As we walked up a wooden sidewalk looking for a hotel, I was holding the hands of my young brothers Bagster Roads and Joseph Ivan (both born on the mainland of B.C.), when we were startled by a wooden Turk, ten feet high, painted blue, white and red, and smoking a large cigar, which he in fact was advertising. This wooden figure was one of the best known of Victoria's old landmarks.

We registered at the St. Nicholas Hotel,[5] on Yates Street, near Government. It was a wooden building, and, at that time, the best hotel in town. (Years later, another St. Nicholas Hotel came near to being my death.)

The principal streets of the little town of 2,000 were Government, Douglas, Yates and Fort, as they are now, but then they did not go far without running into the woods. Fort Street started at the harbour, passed the Fort — which I saw many times; it resembled in appearance the bastion still preserved in Nanaimo, B.C. — and straggled on out of town for about a mile, laterally up hill.

Interspersed amongst the many fine oaks on the higher part of the road were a few homes. Father took a bungalow next to the Ellas,[6] and on the site of the brick house later built by the late Lieutenant-Governor Paterson.[7]

There were no street lights and at night lanterns were carried to find our house.

*The so-called "Birdcages," the old Legislative Buidings, Victoria, 1859.
BC Archives, G-05987.*

Dolly and I ran in. It was a large light room. An elderly gentleman
over six feet in height rose from his seat by a writing table and met
us. "Who is this little lady, Dolly?" "My school chum Eunice Seabrook." "Then she must be my chum too," he said gaily. Placing a
hand on each of our shoulders, he marched us across to a thin
elderly lady who was doing some fancy work by a far window. He
introduced me to Lady Douglas who showed me the fancy work she
was engaged on. She spoke to me in French, probably to see if I
understood. I did not, but it led me to start my French lessons the
next week.

Lady Douglas then said, in rather foreign English, to go and play
and "Ask Aimee to give you cookies." Their cook always had a fresh
daily supply which Aimee dispensed.

Then we played at a favourite spot down by the hazelnut tree.

This was my first meeting with the first Governor of B.C., Sir
James Douglas and his wife Lady Douglas,[8] through their grand-
daughter the late Dolly Helmcken,[9] my fellow pupil at St. Ann's
Academy.[10]

That visit was followed by countless other playtimes at the
Douglas and Helmcken homes which adjoined,[11] and at our place.

I saw Sir James often and Lady Douglas also; they were always friendly and charming to a little girl, as was their son-in-law the Hon. John Sebastian Helmcken, M.D.,[12] who, in addition, was full of joking remarks.

~⌒

After school hours at St. Ann's, "Skookum"[13] was my companion whenever mother sent me on errands. He was part Great Dane — jet black with a tiny white star on his chest.

One late afternoon in November I had to pass down Douglas Street on a section where it was a country dirt road. There was a wooden sidewalk but I preferred the centre of the road when it ran past a tavern always full of sailors.

Suddenly Skookum's hair bristled and he made a low growl while looking towards a clump of bushes. From it came the voices of several tipsy sailors. "Here comes a girl, m'lads!"

But as they frolicked into the road, their merry self-confidence suddenly turned to dismay. Skookum was quietly waiting for them with a row of gleaming teeth, bristling hairs on his back and throaty growls. "*Shay*, I don't like the looks of this, m'lads; gals shouldn't have 'em. Lets 'ave 'nother drink," and they reeled back towards the tavern.

Skookum and his friend, our big, black fighting cat (that scratched dogs as they passed our fence), often proved excellent house guards.

CHAPTER 4

"Teignmouth"

Although the philosophical old timer must needs let his regret pass with the general change, one sorrowfully lingers over the memory of the old homes. And this thought occurs: Why didn't some authority preserve a few for the study of future generations?

When someone does decide to do this in an isolated instance, only the ugly shell is usually found to be standing. At best, like a well-preserved top hat but without its brim. For most of the charm has gone from a house after successive municipal councils or others have gouged away the original grounds which, for decades, had given distinction to the place.

"Teignmouth,"[1] the home of my parents, is an instance. Repeated street widenings, "improvements" and adjoining land sales, slashed it up out of all recognition.

It was not such an unattractive place in the Seventies, the Eighties, Nineties and even for some distance into the twentieth century.

A while after we had come to Victoria, my father and mother bought an acre of land near what is now Douglas Street and Hillside Avenue. It was rather unpromising at first, and he and mother had a free hand to lay out a drive, flower gardens and a lawn-tennis court.

Many trees were brought in from the forests and a large rockery was set out in about the middle of the front grounds, a fir in the centre surrounded by moss and ice plants. Entering what is now Douglas Street, the drive wound past the house and out on Douglas Street again.

My parents designed and built a one and a half storey house much in the style of a Swiss chalet. The rooms downstairs were eleven feet high; ten feet upstairs. It was finished in 1874 and we took possession in that year.

The complex and growing traffic problem was the city fathers' headache then, as now. Temperamental horses and drivers, uncertain lights and oozing mud, made it, perhaps, somewhat worse than in motor days.

Our stables were on the side of the property (now Hillside Avenue) and housed a carriage and, later, my sister's high dog cart; also one, and sometimes two, horses at a time. The best of these was "Jacob," a rangy fellow with plenty of get-away in his long legs. Jacob, in fact, was the only one of four of our horses that would not stubbornly object to being attached to my sister's high-swung dog cart.

We could all ride or drive. It was lucky for father that he could. He often said that he had been set on a horse when he was six and had been at home there ever since, adding, with a smile, that it had put something of a permanent (through really very slight) bend in his legs. Skill in riding probably saved his life.

He rushed into the house one day in desperate search of a towel or other cloth. I ceased to wonder when I saw his bloody arm, from a session with an axe in the garden. Quickly swathing the arm with a towel, he leaped on a horse bare-back and raced out of the place.

When he all but dropped in the surgery of Dr. Helmcken, Sr., the noted practitioner emphatically said that he had got there just in time. Father saved his arm as well as his life, but the arm was in a sling for a long time.

In Victoria I attended Mrs. Newman's and Mrs. Attwood's private schools; then St. Ann's Academy; Mrs. Wilson Brown's (the present Y.W.C.A annex is part of the building); Mrs. Cridge's (her husband was later Bishop Cridge of the Reformed Episcopal Church) and finally Mrs. Fellows' finishing school (head mistress, Miss Morgan).[2]

Most of my teachers were English gentlewomen of the old school. Among other school chums I recall, besides Miss Dolly Helmcken already mentioned, were Bertha and Laura Bloomingdale, Sarah Todd (Mr. Todd who owned so much land near Cadboro Bay), the Cooper girls and Mabel Hope Charles whose father was prominent in the Hudson's Bay Company. She married the Hon. D. MacEwen Eberts, later a Justice of the Supreme Court of B.C.

CHAPTER 5

A Summer in Granville

One day, shortly after "finishing" at Mrs. Fellows' I came in from an afternoon ride. I had scarcely jumped from a tall horse from Bowman's stables[1] (for we only had carriage horses in our own at the time) and tossed the reins to Bowman's hostler who had ridden up to take the horse back, when father came forward smiling.

"You can manage those long drapes pretty well, Loulie," he said, indicating the old style woman's riding habit I was wearing, "but how about your 'sea legs'?"

"You remember the *Etta White*[2] you were admiring in the harbour the other day? Well, I was speaking to Captain Smith yesterday and he said that Mrs. Smith and he would be happy to give you a trip to Granville."[3]

I was delighted. The *Etta White* with its trim lines and new coat of green and white paint, had caught my fancy.

Mother demurred a bit. Whoever heard of a young lady going on

Granville, c. 1884. CVA Dist. P. 30.

a tug boat to visit friends? Father smoothed it over by glowing accounts of Captain and Mrs. Smith.

Captain Smith proved to be no ordinary swaggering seafaring man. He was quiet in manner, blue eyed, dark, lean, and six feet tall. His wife was little, if any, shorter. Both were rather handsome and very nice mannered English. Mrs. Smith told me that she had often accompanied her husband on the tugboat, and he was happy for it, since she kept things spick and span.

They assigned me a tiny but very clean stateroom. The cook served Mrs. Smith and me a sumptuous lunch, and the trip was all too short.

This tug boat trip to Vancouver in 1877 was more pleasant than any later trip by water — whether by canoe, row boat, launch, yacht or steamer. We steamed straight through Vancouver harbour to Moodyville.[4] There a row boat was waiting to take me over to Granville (later called Vancouver).

In Granville, we young people formed a small private orchestra of girls and young men: piccolo, flute, flageolet, two violins, piano, a 'cello and a small drum.

I played the piano and led. We practised and played for amusement in a small house on what was then called Hastings Street. Whenever I went to see my friend Mrs. Alexander[5] (her husband ran the large mill and was a magistrate) I had to pass Manning's saloon, but never noticed the least disturbance from the place.

While we played many of the opera pieces in our little orchestra we also used some of the pieces then considered on the "music hall" side, such as "Champagne Charlie."

We engaged in a good deal of boating on Burrard Inlet and we girls (Carrie Havelock was one; she later went back to England) arranged boating contests as to who could cross the inlet first. It was then that the first bathing beauty contest was held on the coast, if not in the whole of Canada. Of course it wasn't called that and it wasn't open to the public. Mrs. Dietz from San Francisco, who was known for her pleasant foibles and wealth, engineered a contest and got a young doctor from Moodyville to examine and measure the girls, who numbered about fifty. They had assembled there from the various districts on a holiday.

I surmised that my parents in Victoria would rather object to my taking part in such a novel diversion, but I could see no harm in it. A friend finally persuaded me to enter. The physician lined us up and measured us from head to toe, amidst much merriment, in which the inevitable chaperone heartily joined.

I was very surprised when I was declared the winner, and more so when awarded a handsome gold prize worth about fifty dollars, for no one knew that a prize was to be awarded.

When I told my parents they were extremely annoyed and made me promise to never engage in such things again.

CHAPTER 6

The Man in the Woods

While on this trip to Vancouver, I had left the home of Mrs. Alexander at Hastings,[1] and had taken the two-plank sidewalk through the thick forest which then had to be traversed to reach Granville.

When about half way, I was stopped short by a shriek followed by a loud, mirthless laugh.

Glancing anxiously at the shadows cast by the fir trees, sharply defined by the newly risen moon, I thought I saw the form of a man. He had a hatchet in his hand and was viciously striking to right and left, while threatening in bad language some unseen enemy.

It must be George, I thought. I had heard about George. He had arrived in Hastings from Australia a few years before, with a past. It shadowed his whole life.

George's full name was never known, but he often spoke aloud to himself of revenge on some enemies and he sometimes accompanied his wild talk with a pantomime of killing.

I was very frightened at meeting George in such a lonely spot at that time of late afternoon, but I managed a bold tone and called out as loudly and firmly as I could: "George, I'm glad you've got a hatchet, as I want you to escort me to Granville where I am going to play 'Her Bright Smile Haunts me Still'."[2] That at once brought George out of his mood, and with pathetic eagerness he went ahead of me as a bodyguard.

Whenever I was in Granville, George would sit in the street within hearing distance and if I didn't play "Her Bright Smile Haunts me Still," during my practice, he would timidly knock at the door and beg me, in respectful and pathetic terms, to play it.

I have often wondered what happened to George who, notwithstanding his unpleasant aberration, was deemed harmless enough among an easy-going pioneer people. From his random remarks pieced together, people concluded that he had been party to some tragedy in Australia in which a young woman and men had figured, and that the shock and dwelling on thoughts of revenge had partly unhinged his mind.

While in Burrard[3] I also purchased a Canadian pony named "Boots,"[4] of strawberry colour and with a very black mane. I kept him in a stable on False Creek Road before you get to the bridge, a couple of blocks from the house I was staying at, which was built on piles right over the waters of Burrard Inlet, Granville side.

One evening, just after dusk, we saw unusual smoke arising, evidently from a fire in Hastings. My friend Miss Miller and others, saddled their ponies or took gigs to ride to investigate, for in those days all turned out if a fire occurred within riding or walking distance.

There was so much excitement that, although I had not as yet purchased a saddle, I took my pony and mounted him bare-back, and, of course, riding side saddle as all girls had to do at that time. All went well until I got close enough to the fire to see that it was the mill and for Boots to clearly understand what was going forward, when he abruptly turned tail and raced back to his stable on False

Creek Road. I was much surprised as he was an amiable and trac-
table horse, but I found out later that, when a colt, he had been
burned in a stable fire and had learned his lesson.

After the fire was over, my host and hostess told me that, before I
returned to Victoria, I should really see an Indian war dance.[5]
"They don't hold them as often as they used to," they added.

"But they wouldn't let me in," I objected.

"They will if I say so," he said. "I was made a chief awhile ago for
some service they esteemed."

"Do go!" urged his wife. "You will be quite safe; it's a rare
chance."

The dance was to be held in the deep woods on the waterfront
near Hastings. As our buggy approached on the road nearest to the
gathering, I saw great clouds of smoke and sparks pouring out of an
immense bark tent about the size of a circus tent. Chanting, moaning and drumming came from within. The only light which could
be seen was from the chinks in the bark slabs, as there were no windows.

The proceedings were not open to the public but a few friends
had been invited and a few buggies were parked in the woods when
we arrived. When we entered the door-way, the first sight that met
our gaze was a huge bonfire on the earthen floor, in the middle of
the place; sparks, cinders and smoke continually went up through
an aperture in the roof.

Gaily dressed squaws, wearing voluminous coloured skirts, coloured bands or handkerchiefs around their heads, braided hair
hanging down their backs, some also wearing hammered silver
bracelets or anklets, were chanting a monotonous and weird
sound, the while softly clapping their hands to the time.

Some of the braves were naked save for a loin cloth; others wore
beaded leather costumes or gaily trimmed leather trousers only;
and others had coloured feather headgear with a row of feathers
hanging down their backs.

Natives dancing by the E&N Railway trestle with many spectators.
RBCM, PN6492B.

Hideous masks were worn by some or they had their faces fierce-ly painted; all wore beaded moccasins.

Most common was the traditional costume at that time: scarlet and black or variegated Indian blankets, fastened with a bone or hammered silver skewer, and a feather or two in their hair.

Soon began a hum-drumming, made by thumping on benches between their knees while others used brightly painted all-skin Indian drums.

Suddenly an old woman stepped out from the side and com-menced a moaning chant and, stooping over, did a sort of slow hop and muttered chant around the bonfire; another joined her, with the chanting from the crowded walls an ever-growing crescendo.

Then men began to join in, one by one, dancing in a crouching

Natives in full regalia. RBCM, PN 16761.

posture, until the excitement grew to a high pitch and the squaws retired but continued their moaning chant.

The men, now the sole performers, waving torches and spears, worked themselves into a frenzy, while the Indians around the walls, seated on planks laid on log rounds, made more and more noise.

Finally the Indian dancers jumped in and out of the fire and war-whooped more wildly than ever. They kept up the dancing until they began to drop, one by one, apparently exhausted.

One old man who wore no mask, but had a painted face, remained, and he kept jumping in and out of the fire for a long time alone, until finally he started to walk to his seat, but collapsed before reaching it and some of the Indians carried him out.

The Indians then dispersed, lighting their way with torches. Most of them embarked in war canoes for the vicinity of New Westminster; others riding off on ponies.

Indian women wearing blankets and a mixture of dress.
RBCM, PN 8849.

No Indian spoke to us or to the few other whites — before, during or after the performance — nor did we see any refreshments served at any time.

"You see um fire dance, uh?" asked the old Indian washer woman at Teignmouth when I returned home to Victoria.

"Yes," I said, surprised that she knew. "You like it?" "Yes." "Uh-hah. Good for you," she leered as she waddled off to tend the clothes soaking in the wooden tubs in the wash house.

The Chinese cook in the kitchen had been intently listening. "Chune-amuck-a-Hi" he grumbled in comment as she moved out of hearing. "Him heap *no good!*" he commented with spirit about the dance as he caught my eye when I passed through the kitchen.

CHAPTER 7

A Strange Party on the *Matilda*

O n another occasion I took the *Enterprise* for a lengthy stay on the mainland. The *Enterprise* was a side-wheel steamer and, because of the rough seas, had to lay up for two days and two nights in Active Pass.

During the several months I spent in Burrard, I never tired of the sight of the beautiful harbour of Vancouver. Then, as now, it was full of shipping. But in 1878 sailing ships were the main feature, the majority of course, engaged in the lumber trade.[1] One day I rode again on the *Etta White* as it piloted a large Australian ship into the harbour. Two Norwegian craft were particularly magnificent: one was painted pale green with white masts and the other was all shining white. As they sailed into Vancouver harbour they seemed more majestic than any of the others.

Men-of-war of the Royal Navy occasionally came in. And many were the entertainments we attended on board. I recall particularly those on *H.M.S. Shah*.[2]

R. Maynard's photo of sailing ships being loaded at Moodyville on the north shore of Burrard Inlet in 1888. BC Archives, A-03315.

But an exciting night on the barque *Matilda*[3] left the most vivid impression on my mind. The ship was anchored in mid-stream ready for departure, and Mr. and Mrs. Alexander, a few others and myself had been invited to attend the captain's parting dinner.

Sailors rowed us out. While dessert was being served I was surprised at the hurried and nervous way the dishes were brought on, and in a few moments sounds of a struggle could be heard.

The captain was speaking to me when the noise reached him; he paused and looked very concerned. The noise increased and he had half risen to go, with a word of excuse, when a crowd of fighting men broke into the dining saloon.

Without a moment's thought, I slipped under the table and clung to the centre beam, while the long tablecloth further concealed my presence. The struggle continued for some time, until the sound of boats against the ship's side told me that men had come from the shore. They were soon aboard and after a sharp tussle, subdued the fighting members of the crew.

Meanwhile my host and his wife at Burrard were almost frantic as to my safety. They had put out in a boat to go on board themselves, and at once commenced a search for me. Great was their relief and amusement to find me clinging to the beam under the table. I was told that some of the crew violently objected to making another voyage in the *Matilda*.

Only a few hours later the ship sailed and foundered off Cape Flattery with the loss of all hands. It was said that the bottom had fallen out, and I was told that the ship had been condemned, but the captain (or the owner) was determined to try just one more voyage.

CHAPTER 8

The Fugitive

D ancing and little parties were the chief diversion during my stay in Burrard, but dances were not held more frequently than once a fortnight. Now and then, however, there was a ball, and the dancers came from New Westminster, Moodyville and surrounding settlements.

One evening, I was waiting for the sleigh to go to a dance, when Clara L., one of the young ladies visiting at Granville, (from Seattle) came into the drawing room to show me her new dress. She was a tall pretty brunette and the heavy blue silk trimmed with a good shade of red, really became her. I was dressed in white and my ornaments were coral earrings, necklace and double bracelets. They were of unusual Oriental design and colour and had been given to me about two years earlier by Captain Means and his wife, who had come to Burrard from India.

My friend had no ornaments, and, as she admired mine greatly I suggested that she try them on. She showed so much pleasure that

I loaned them to her for the evening; then her sleigh came and off she went in high glee.

My host and his wife were an hour late in arriving from New Westminster, where they had gone for the day, and I had to wait for them. Home at last, after a hasty snack, they were hurriedly dressing for the ball when a loud knock was heard at the front door. My host exclaimed: "Who could that be at this late hour?"

He went to the door and returned with a small parcel addressed to me and urged me to open it before going out. I replied: "Oh, we'd better hurry; I'll open it when we return."

My host and his wife evidently suspected something, for they urged me not to put off opening it. I then tore open the package and there to my amazement was a heavy rope necklet of yellow gold with an oblong gold locket, set with pearls, attached. There was no name or other indication of the giver. Just a scrap of paper: "To the most unselfish girl I know — Do wear this in place of the corals."

I never learned who sent it, but only suppose it came from someone who had been dancing or talking with Clara and, admiring the red corals, had been told by her that they had been loaned by me. I had a number of friends in Burrard but could not be sure of the one who had bought such a gift at a jewellers (there was no early closing then) and had sent it in such haste. No one I knew ever admitted sending it — and it remains one of the little mysteries we all meet with in life.

There was another mysterious happening while I was living in Burrard that was of a more sombre hue. It was about two o'clock in the afternoon. I was alone in the house and was commencing to practise on the piano. The children of the house had not yet returned from school.

Came an unusual knock on the street door; it was quick, nervous, furtive. Being broad daylight I had no hesitation about opening the door. There stood a slightly built young man, aged apparently in his early twenties; he had dark hair and dark eyes.

"I am pursued," he gasped, breathless and excited, as he slipped unceremoniously into the music room, closing the door after him. His tone was suppliant and not in any way menacing.

"I have done no wrong, I swear it," he earnestly pleaded in answer to the doubt he must have seen in my eyes. "I am pursued; do hide me."

"What have you done?" I asked.

"Nothing, absolutely nothing. Do hide me; it is of the utmost importance, and can I," he faltered a bit, "have the loan of ten dollars? There is a ship out there," he added, as if it explained everything, pointing to where a number of vessels lay at anchor in the harbour, "and after I have shaken them from my trail, I will get on board and be off to Australia."

He said all this with the most deadly earnestness, and between gasps. Then listened intently by the front door.

What he heard seemed to quicken his anxiety. "For God's sake, hide me! I have done no wrong, I swear it on my soul!" he pleaded.

I fully realized that he was asking me to run a great risk in more ways than one, but I could not refuse such an earnest, and very evidently, wholly honest appeal from one in such strange distress. Off the music room was a small cupboard in which the children of the house hung their cloaks. Into that closet I pushed him, thrusting in after him a ten dollar bill (the exact sum I happened to have with me at the time, curiously enough). Then I hurried to the piano and proceeded with practice exercises with sustained vigour.

Whoever was chasing the intruder, never came to the door of the house. After I had practised an hour or two, I went to the door of the cupboard and called out: "You had better go now!"

There was no response. I peered in; there was no one there. He had evidently slipped out during my piano practice.

When I went to town I made discreet enquiries, but never learned a thing, not even the least clue as to the young man's identity or as to whom his pursuers could have been.

I had quite forgotten the incident, when seven years later, almost to a day, I received an envelope without return address. It was postmarked in Australia at some place unknown to me; within was the English equivalent of ten dollars, and a note, undated and un-signed, the handwriting I thought like too many U's: straight up and down. It read — "I return this with much gratitude to the little lady who had faith in one appealing for help."

I have never heard anything further of the matter.

CHAPTER 9

Romances and Tragedies

When I was attending dancing school in Victoria, I met and
became acquainted with a young girl, Miss Fanny Palmer,[1]
who was the daughter of a local music teacher.

She was a petite, blue-eyed blonde with pretty ways. On the stage
at the local opera house was a professional singer, a very nice gentlemanly young man, to whom Miss Palmer introduced me. He
made a great hit in the then new comic sea song "The Capital
Ship."[2] Perhaps one might call him an old fashioned Eddie Cantor,
if that can be imagined.

The two fell madly in love and all their friends and acquain-
tances thought it an ideal match. He left for San Francisco on the
North Pacific[3] to fill a theatrical engagement, and, whether by accident or design, Fanny Palmer went south on the same steamship.
Also on the vessel was S.P. Moody[4] after whom Moodyville (now
part of Vancouver) was named.

Fanny came back in a few days. The waves laid her on the sand by
Dallas Road, Victoria, with seaweed in her golden hair. The ship

Victor Harrison, age twenty-seven, second son of Eunice and Eli Harrison. Victor was successful in bringing Brother XII to trial. He was later mayor of Nanaimo. Courtesy of L. Wilson.

had sunk off Cape Flattery with the loss of about three hundred lives.

Strange to say Fanny's body came all the way home on the waters of the straits. Another drowned passenger, also with seaweed in her hair, was laid out beside Fanny in the old Fort, prior to burial. There were only two survivors of the shipwreck who managed to keep afloat on a raft for three days, when they were picked up. One died and the other, a Mr. Jelly,[5] in a very weak state, survived and lived for many years.

The Schooley murder mystery also occurred in this period. The murder of an old man was traced to his son-in-law, a Mr. Schooley.[6] Mr. Schooley was a well-to-do citizen who was fond of riding a white horse. Schooley was tried in the Supreme Court, then held in the old Legislative buildings across James Bay, replaced in the Nineties by the stone pile of Parliament buildings.

Mr. Justice Gray, to whom I will refer later, sentenced him to death. A member of my family, Victor Harrison who attended a private school with the convicted man's son, witnessed the hanging. The execution took place in the old Bastion Fort where the Law Courts in Victoria now stand. The Fort had high walls and on each corner a guard tower. Schooley broke down completely, and even though he was a murderer who had shot his father-in-law, many of the public were sorry for him.

Victoria and Burrard Inlet (Vancouver) might be said to be at the cross-roads of the Pacific, where thousands of very interesting travellers from the seven seas have sojourned through the years.

I do not believe that any other places this side of the Pacific have been the temporary stopping place of so many strange travellers. I recall many, some of whom I personally knew.

For instance, while I was still unmarried, I became acquainted with an old English gentleman who, for a long time, had been a globe-trotter. He had sailed to India often and one day we fell to talking about things in that mysterious land.

"I know a proficient in the magic arts," he said. "Not a common juggler, who can, of course, be easily met with. But this is a man of high character and a deep philosopher. I did some small favour for him, which he rated much more highly than it deserved, it seemed to me. One day before I sailed, he gave me a curious gold ornament and said, very solemnly, that it would bring good luck in money matters to whomever it was given."

"Would you like to see it?" the old chap suddenly asked.

"Of course!" I answered with much eagerness.

He opened a leather case which he kept in a sea chest and drew out of it a solid bit of gold.

"Why," I exclaimed, "it's a gold nugget!"

"Yes. No goldsmith has worked this. But doesn't it suggest something?"

I had already thought of it. "Africa!" For its natural shape was just like that continent, at least as it appeared in geographies.

"Yes, doesn't it look like Africa? But it is pure, raw gold of India." Then my friend corrected his statement a bit. "A jeweller did add this," and he indicated a small ring soldered to the top of the broadest part of Africa. "And through it I have run this short, meshed, gold chain."

After some further conversation, my friend insisted on giving me the keepsake, as he said he was not coming out to the American continent again.

I kept "Africa" from India for some years, then shortly after the building of the second Harrison Street house, I gave it to my elder daughter on her wedding. More than forty years have rolled away and she has been consistently lucky financially, even during the Depression, and is today. Probably a coincidence, but that's what happened.

CHAPTER 10

A Lantern Journey
and its Sequel

M y visits and several months' sojourn in what later became the city of Vancouver, had been much in the nature of a musical and boating lark, and then I returned for awhile to our home, Teignmouth.

In Victoria the social activities of the girls who had "finished" at Mrs. Fellows' academy were regarded much more seriously. Society was highly conventional, as befitted an older and rather conservative place. Masonic and Naval balls were most fashionable at that time and at one of them I formally "came out." At such affairs I met Governor Nelson[1] and others who became good friends, one of whom sent me a solid gold pin designed like a feather; it was made from the gold discovered in the survey for the C.P.R. and was marked 1877.

Dancing, driving and occasional horse-back riding filled my Victoria days. Sometimes I also attended Mrs. Palmer's select dancing academy, where the latest dances from England were practised.

Others attending included Frank Barnard[2] (later Lieutenant-Governor Sir Frank Barnard, who died a few years ago), Jack,[3] Pontie and Florrie Gray, children of Mr. Justice Gray[4] of the Supreme Court of B.C. and "Jimmie" Douglas,[5] son of Governor Douglas, who later went to live in England.

At one of the Masonic balls I met Eli Harrison, then a young lawyer in his twenties, who was becoming known as a Crown Prosecutor. I sometimes went horseback riding with him and managed quite nicely to clear three-bar fences on one of the colony's old historic farms. My companion did the same, not without apprehension.

Some months later, in a severe winter in the late Seventies, when Eli Harrison was Crown Prosecutor in New Westminster he was involved in the case of a miner who had been killed in a brawl. The case dragged on to a late hour. A belated dinner made it later. But late as it was and bad as was the weather, he determined to reach Granville — some twelve miles distant — that very night.

He hired a special stage. Two or three miles before he reached Hastings, a great dip in the road broke the axle. A sudden thaw was making the road almost impossible, but he waded through the mud and slush to Hastings. After that, there remained but a mile more to Granville over a raised wooden sidewalk, two boards wide, but through a thick forest in the pitch dark. That late the only lantern he could borrow at Hastings was an Indian's.

Eli set off, but was astonished to find that he was being shadowed. Prosecuting criminals sometimes leads to attacks on the prosecutor away from the Court House. Yet he had always been fair, he reasoned. Indeed he was of the old English legal school of thought that prized civil liberties above all.

He waited for his "shadow." It ambled up. It was the Indian. "Me make sure lantern come back me — sure." Eli laughed. "All right, follow on. Make sure."

And the dour Indian doggedly followed the lantern he had loaned until it was safely in his possession again.

Playing croquet on the lawn of "Fairfield," the house of Cariboo Road bridge builder, Joseph Trutch. BC Archives, C-05218.

Reaching a certain house at two in the morning, the counsellor awakened the owner to see if he couldn't obtain an interview with a certain party. This certain party was I. And the question put by the ardent advocate received an affirmative answer. We were to be married.

He then trudged back to the broken-down stage, and there met another stage which his driver had, in the interim, brought up. By hard driving and extra pay, they were just in time to reach the steamer for Yale.

Eli's satisfaction turned to horror, however, when he discovered about half way to Yale that his barrister's wig was not on board. In his excitement he must have left it in New Westminster. What to do?

*Eli Harrison, Jr., age thirty-three, in his judge's wig
and gown. Courtesy of L. Wilson.*

Court dress imperatively required that an advocate appear dressed
in wig and gown.

The captain put back the ship, much to the annoyance of some
of the passengers. When the vessel docked, there was the hotel
keeper waiting at the wharf holding out the wig in its snug little

metal box. He well knew the barrister's custom of travelling with wig and gown, surmised his dilemma when he saw the wig box, and guessed what the sight of the returning steamer meant.

Young Eli Harrison,[6] my husband-to-be, was one of the earliest arrivals on the coast. He had come out in the covered wagons and had later reached Vancouver Island in 1858 while Vancouver Island was a separate Crown Colony. In 1866 the colony of Vancouver Island united with the mainland colony and were one colony until in 1871, when the united colonies of B.C. joined the Dominion of Canada.

In the next chapter I will take up the story of Eli Harrison.

CHAPTER 11

With the Covered Wagons

The burning heat at last was lessening. The monotonous creak of the heavy axles and dried-out harness with the jangling little chains would soon commence again. For the prairie schooners[1] must on to their unknown destiny.

Thank heavens the Sioux band[2] that had appeared from nowhere had been unaccountably friendly to the little party and had actually smoked a pipe of peace with them.[3]

The leader gathered up the reins, but White Cloud, the Sioux chief, made no attempt to ride off from the caravan he had been detaining. Instead, he moved his wild-eyed piebald horse nearer to the leader.

What could the taciturn chief want?

At last White Cloud broke the solemn silence. Pointing to the curly, yellow-haired little boy whose hazel eyes looked fearlessly into his, he said: "White Cloud want-um papoose. Make him big chief."

The little fellow drew closer to his mother's knee, while his blue-eyed, sturdy English father, reins in hand, answered with a forced smile: "You speak high, good words to us, Big Chief—but you make laugh. For all we pale faces go Wake-si-ah."[4]

How much of it would the Sioux understand? He would certainly understand "Wake-si-ah," which meant "we were going on a distant journey." However, White Cloud was accustomed to having his slightest wish obeyed.

The deep lines above the chief's aquiline nose deepened as he frowned. "No make laugh, Paleface. Want-um boy — make-um chief," he repeated.

But when he noted that the white father was adamant, he wasted no further words. Pointing to the western sun, he said: "Follow him — Palefaces. Papoose — some day — big chief."

Abruptly turning his pony, he whirled away with his braves in a cloud of alkali dust.

That was the oft-told story by the parents of Eli Harrison, the young B.C. barrister, and so it was told to me. (I will call him Eli II and his father Eli I.)

Shortly after Eli II was born in Missouri in 1852, his parents started on the long trek across the Mississippi, the endless prairies and over the Sierra Nevada Mountains to San Francisco.

After parting with White Cloud, anxious days continued, especially on account of fighting between Box Elder, a shaman-warrior, and the Mormons. The rumour was that Box Elder was about to attack Fort Bridger.[5] (A substantial part of the Bridger stockade is still preserved as a historical monument).

Eli I's little party was drawn into the fighting when they neared Fort Bridger, for the attack had started. They passed through without personal hurt except that the family papers were stolen, a precious bundle of parchment documents and letters.

These papers were at the root of Eli I's adventurous career. I will give, in brief outline, the rather romantic story as it was told to me by the parties concerned and also as shown by the many family papers in my possession.

Family legend says that in the time of the Commonwealth,[6] the Harrisons split into Republican and Royalist branches. General Harrison, whom so many Royalist writers scornfully refer to as the Butcher Regicide,[7] was either an ancestor of the former or the close collateral of an ancestor. Some of them went out to the West Indies and thence to the James River, Virginia.

There they prospered, maintaining for generations the mansions and plantations of Westover, Berkeley and Brandon.[8] Daniel Webster, for one, refers to their places in describing his trip on the James River. The Harrison rampant demi-lion crest appears in at least one tombstone there and on some silver at Brandon.[9]

One tombstone of colonial days alludes to a deceased Harrison as having been loyal to his king, as if to infer that he was an exception. At any rate, Benjamin Harrison[10] was one of the signers of the Declaration of Independence. That line produced, also, two Presidents of the U.S., William Henry Harrison[11] and Benjamin Harrison.

The former wrote to Eli I, referring to their relationship. By one of those curious, often inexplicable and frequently unmeaning coincidences of life, one of my English people sent me from England a silk election flag used by William Henry Harrison or by a campaign manager for his 1840 presidential election. It has his picture reproduced (probably by stencil) in the fly with the words "General William H. Harrison, the Hero of Tippecanoe."[12]

Just how and why it got to England is a matter for speculation. My correspondent only knew that it had been in the family long before her time.

The Royalist Harrisons had much landed property in England, and one was closely concerned in bringing over William of Orange.[13] Eli I had a Court sword[14] bearing the arms of the House of Orange on the guard and the motto "I will maintain it."

This sword Eli I received as a significant family heirloom; he had it with him in the covered wagon and in fact throughout all his adventures. Near to his death he gave it to me, along with a queer sword from India, and it is in a fine state of preservation.

At the time Eli I was born in 1824, their immediate family had been broken up. This was due to the family property having been "leased" for 99 years and/or for the "lives" of certain close relatives, whichever is the longer. After that the estate reverts to the grantors or their heirs. (This, I believe, is called in old English property law an estate *pur autre vie.*)

The property adjoined one of Lord How's several estates — the How and Harrison coats-of-arms are in the same church where there is also a vault to William Henry Harrison. The legend says that the Lord How of that time jovially said that, if help were needed for the purpose, his heirs would help the Harrison heirs establish their right to the estate when the time had expired.

One of the "lives" implied in the lease was an English army offi-

The Harrison coat of arms. Courtesy of L. Wilson.

cer who sold his commission and went to South America where he was quite successful and became a general. The surname was localized to Del Haro. He married a wealthy South American and returned to England on a visit and tried to buy up the lessees' interest, but they refused to sell. As his wife did not like England he returned to South America, dying without heirs.

After schooling, Eli I impulsively joined the army and his commission was bought out by a relative. He then sailed for India where, he told me, he had many strange adventures. He showed me the queer Indian sword and tassel, the blade still stained with old blood. That sword he also carefully kept.

He had some natural talent for art and later, while in Rome, studied the specialty of painting church murals and ceilings. In this he became quite skilled, both in design and execution. When remittances failed to arrive from England, he could always get high pay for very little effort in this specialty.

Many English liberals at that time (as shown, for instance, in Jane Welsh Carlyle's letters[15]) ardently sympathized with the free Italian patriots like Mazzini and Garibaldi.[16]

Eli I met Garibaldi in some of his worst days of struggle and grew to know him intimately.

Eli I's sister Ann, married Count Julian Poranskinsky, a Russian Pole who became a political refugee. They clubbed and lived together awhile. Later, after Garibaldi came into power, he wrote to Eli I again, urging him to come to Italy where he would give him the title of Count and an excellent official position, but Eli I was too English to accept.

In 1847, Eli I was again in England and there married Elizabeth Warburton of the ancient Warburton family of county Cheshire. Soon after, about 1850, they sailed for America to seek his father who had gone to visit the American Harrisons.

In America, Eli I's father purchased a mile square tract of land in Arkansas and put it in charge of an overseer, a former bailiff or constable by the name of Stubbs, for the use of Eli I and his brother.

Elizabeth Harrison, neé Warburton, wife of Eli Harrison, Sr.
Courtesy of L. Wilson.

The father then went to New Orleans to meet the boys by appointment. One brother, Thomas Harrison, said he waited six months at Red River in 1848 but the father never came. Later it was learned that he was either killed by Indians or drowned on his way up the Mississippi to Little Rock, Arkansas about 1847.

In 1850 Eli I went with his wife to the U.S. to try and get particulars of his father's death — his father also being one of the named "lives" in the estate. He visited various places in the Old South and stayed at some of the Harrison plantations; he also stayed in Macon, Georgia a short while.

In 1852 Eli I travelled to Arkansas and found that his brother Thomas, along with a few slaves, was living on the large tract of land their father had bought. Thomas was an obstinate man. Going to an election poll, he was challenged because he was not an American citizen. "I own much land and pay taxes." "That makes no difference." "Perhaps this does," said Thomas as he smoothed the butt of his rifle. He was at once allowed to vote.

Having failed to find his father, or to overcome Thomas's stubborn streak, which made him refuse to return to England to deal with the property, Eli I determined to go West.

Eli II was born February 22, 1852 in St. Louis, Missouri. When the boy was old enough they started on the trek West with a prairie schooner, four oxen and two cows. Eli I was then about twenty-nine years of age; his wife twenty-one.

They later fell in with a Mormon caravan, the St. Louis Company of Saints,[17] so-called, which had left Nebraska in June 1853. After a hazardous trip, they reached Salt Lake City August 19, 1853.

According to a letter received during the compilation of this book, from Heber J. Grant,[18] President of the Mormon Church, their historian asserts that there is mention of Eli I's arrival, a description of his party, equipment, etc., and a record that in January 12, 1854 he was a member of the 37th Quorum of Seventy[19] in Salt Lake City.

As is well known, Garibaldi was a member of a secret society and he was something of a mystic. Eli I was also rather inclined that way. The Mormons were impressed with this and his skill in painting various religious figures and symbols and treated him as a rather privileged person.

That is, until they found out his ideas. Like my father and quite a few other pioneers, Eli I was a very strict puritan, in theory and practice, and he could not accept some of the doctrines the Mormons held, especially as to marriage. An old letter gives that as his main reason for pushing farther West.

They left Utah with two prairie schooners and outfits, and after some difficult going, they were met by White Cloud's band of braves as I have already described.

CHAPTER 12

Mr. & Mrs. Eli Harrison, Sr., in San Francisco, 1854-1858

The Harrisons' covered wagons finally reached California after many more hardships but without further incidents of particular interest.

The San Francisco of 1852 was the well organized metropolis of the Pacific coast with a population of 34,776. However, there were many turbulent, lawless characters and during the Vigilante days the Harrisons had an exciting time when, with British and French residents, they were celebrating the British and French victories in the Crimean War against Russia. Rough-necks attacked the Franco-British party, but they were repelled and the mob forced to disperse.

An old letter from one of Eli I's people says: "In 1849 I sailed from Liverpool, eleven of us in a brig to the Pacific to search for the sum of thirteen tons of gold and silver on Cocos Island.[1] We sailed into Panama and sold the brig and cargo. Captain Gladstone,[2] brother of the Rt. Hon. W.E. Gladstone, the late retiring Prime

Minister of England, then crossed the Isthmus at Darien and returned to England. I went up to Mexico and from there to California, worked in the gold mines in the summer and wintered in Mexico. In 1853 I went to the Sandwich Islands, Samoa, New Zealand, discovered gold, went to Australia and back to Tahiti, calling at a great number of islands and came to the claims in California."

Arriving in California, he joined Eli I for awhile and they successfully mined a good deal of gold on the Feather or American river which ran into San Francisco Bay. He then went on a two years' voyage, leaving his partner John Tillinghurst in charge of their mine.

When he returned, Tillinghurst said to him: "Shoot me! You are entitled to do so. I got into a bargain in regard to the gold mine and lost the claims." They had deposited what money they had with the Adams Express Company. When it failed, the Company owed Eli I a considerable sum of money.

John Harrison, Eli's younger brother, who had been with the covered wagons, commenced the study of medicine but before long died in Amadore County, California.

In 1858 Eli I, his wife and Eli II, sailed for Vancouver's Island on the steamship *Brother Jonathan*.

The population of various Northwest centres at that time was as follows: "Washington (1850) 11,594, New Westminster (1861) 164 males, Victoria (1853) 254 whites (in 1860) 608 whites. And the whole of B.C. by 1870 had only 13,247 whites.

So that when Eli I and II arrived in Victoria its population was probably not more than 500 whites.

CHAPTER 13

Marriage and a Royal Wedding Gift

I married Eli II in 1880 in the little corrugated-iron St. John's Anglican Church[1] which, some years previously, had been brought out in parts from England and re-assembled in Victoria where the Hudson's Bay Department Store is to-day. The Reverend Percival Jenns officiated.[2]

The most valued of my wedding presents was an opera bag from H.M. Queen Victoria,[3] sent to me through my great-grandmother in England. The Royal wedding gift came about in a rather unusual way. My maternal great grandmother Mrs. Eunice Bagster[4] had incidentally acquired a considerable fortune through the Bagster Publishing House which specialized in bibles.

It is true that the office of King's Printer and the two Universities of Oxford and Cambridge alone had the legal right to publish the bible, but it occurred to Mr. Bagster[5] that the monopoly did not extend to a bible with notes, and he therefore decided to supply one.

Photograph of the opera bag sent by Queen Victoria to Eunice Harrison,
now in the Victoria and Albert Museum. Courtesy of L. Wilson.

Obtaining fine paper from John Dickinson (who later became
famous in that field) and writing up the notes himself, Bagster's
firm produced a unique bible in 1812, known as the Ruby Foolscap
Octavo. He then sponsored other fine editions of unusual character and quality. These pleased King George IV so much that he

invited Mr. Bagster to Court and offered to confer a knighthood upon him as had been done in the case of Sir David Hunter Blair who held the Royal monopoly of bible publishing in Scotland. But Bagster had entered on his work through spiritual convictions and felt that he should not accept worldly recognition.

He started his work over again when a disastrous fire[6] destroyed his plant, and made an even greater success, issuing the first bible in flexible binding; the first on India paper, in 1828; the first with "yapp" edges;[7] and the first facsimile edition. In fact, he introduced the facsimile idea, which has been extensively used, and for this he was acclaimed "the benefactor of both hemispheres."

Mrs. Birch Bagster became a quite noted philanthropist. For instance, as an old account stated: "In the reign of George IV a number of Chippewa Indians from Eastern Canada visited England to hold a council with that monarch and present their grievances for redress. Mrs. Bagster became warmly interested in their welfare. Many a war dance was performed in her drawing rooms before invited guests. When the Indians were ready to leave, numerous presents were given them by the King and some others. Foremost among them were Mrs. Bagster's, whose gifts included the largest sugaring kettle to be found in all London's foundries and it was received by the Indians with great satisfaction.

"However one who was present said that he was disappointed that on taking leave, the Indians stood like 'a row of stoics'; I felt disappointed that they were so unmoved. But after they had left I altered my opinion, for on going outside I found them all leaning against a wall, their faces veiled with their sleeves, giving vent to their pent-up feelings. Though contrary to their Indian habit to show grief . . . they expressed it privately when alone."

Queen Victoria soon heard of Mrs. Bagster's benefactions and began calling upon her. On one of the Queen's visits, when Mrs. Bagster was nearing one hundred years of age, she noted that the aged lady had just laid aside a fine lace cambric handkerchief she was making which she kept in an opera bag she had also made.[8]

Mrs. Bagster, philanthropist, in 1877, at age one hundred.
Courtesy of L. Wilson.

The Queen asked about the fancy work. Mrs. Bagster replied that she was making a handkerchief and opera bag as a wedding present for her great-granddaughter Eunice Harrison in a distant colony.

Her Majesty asked, "What colony?" and Mrs. Bagster answered, "Vancouver's Island." The Queen's interest seemed to even increase and, after a moment of thought, she asked Mrs. Bagster how would the great granddaughter like a bag made of the Royal household silk? Mrs. Bagster's answer can be imagined.

Queen Victoria then asked that Mrs. Bagster write to her great granddaughter Eunice and tell her that the Queen sent her the Royal household silk as a wedding gift.

Several days later the young Princess Beatrice brought to Mrs. Bagster some Royal household silk embroidered or woven with the Crown, the Royal arms, the Queen's likeness, etc., (A remarkable early example of art in silk.) The rich colourings are still unfaded. Mrs. Bagster made it into a neat bag, and with the bag she had made and the handkerchief sent it to me with the Queen's felicitations.

Excerpts from the London *Times*, the *Windsor & Eton Express* and the *Vineland Independent*[9] of the time all mention the Queen's friendship for and visits to Mrs. Bagster.

I might add the following further item, albeit rather reluctantly as it may be received with incredulity by some. An old letter from a quite unimpeachable source says that the Queen regarded Mrs. Bagster as a wise and saintly character and on one occasion the Queen asked for her blessing and knelt to receive it. As Her Majesty left the room where the one hundred-year-old lady sat, it was noted that the Queen was weeping.

If intimate, ribald stories can be told of the Stuarts, why not one of the piety and humility of Victoria?

CHAPTER 14

Housekeeping

My husband Eli and I commenced housekeeping in a cottage which my husband had rented on Bird Cage Walk to be near the government offices where he was a lawyer associated in the Attorney-General's Department.

We occupied the house for some months. The location of our first family hearth in that house is in the basement of the present museum building,[1] Parliament Square, which, I am informed, was built over it.

I was practising on the piano in the drawing room one day when halted by the distant sounds of rapid, profuse and varied Chinese expletives proceeding from the direction of the kitchen. They were instantly followed by hurried foot-steps down hall. But they were of the four-footed kind.

Skookum burst in with his ears back with pleasure;[2] his large body, not to mention his tail, wriggling all over as he proudly brought in his mouth to me a package from mother. He had come all the way from the other end of Douglas Street.

A Chinese houseboy in Victoria. BC Archives, B-02583.

He was coolly oblivious of the expostulating Chinaman fizzing at his heels. This the first (since I had set up my own house) of what was to prove to be a very, very long train of Chinese servants coming and going through the decades (mostly going). He had the curious name of "Hee."

"How for — What for — That dog. What you call 'em Missa Hallison?" "Him come in — fool 'im my good new — clean floor."

Skookum had quickly learned, after a couple of my visits with mother, just where my new abode was in relation to his at Teign-mouth, and mother, with a light parcel, had sent him on his way rejoicing.

Impetuous informality Skookum thought a virtue — and with great cheerfulness he had dashed across the glistening clean floor with his fat, muddy feet.

When I laughed, Hee faintly smiled and silently returned to his quarters. This was literally so, because cooks and houseboys wore noiseless Chinese satin slippers, in addition to blue trousers, a long white starched apron and a starched white Oriental coat, with its high collar. They had an abundant supply of these uniforms and always kept them spotlessly clean and stiffly starched. Now and then I would have a cook who concealed his queue under a tall, starched cook's hat, but generally my Chinese simply had their queues braided around their heads, until the year came when all queues disappeared because of the political changes in China.

Skookum soon began calling on me whenever the fancy struck him, without waiting for instructions. He unhesitatingly threaded his way through the congested traffic on the small, shaky, wooden bridge that preceded the present embankment and concrete causeway in front of the Empress Hotel.

Quite a few herdics, painted a light shade of oak, took passengers for some distance in town, in a few directions. They were a curious, toy-like street car, very low slung, with two parallel seats the length of the herdic, at right angles to the driver, one row of passengers thus facing the other. The motor power was one horse to a herdic. Herdics did not last long, for Victoria took to small dinky electric street cars at a rather early date.[3]

In July 1881 my husband was Crown prosecutor at the Assizes in the Cariboo, as he was again in October 1881. In his absence I returned to Teignmouth on a visit.

One of the cases on the docket related to the sensational Pool murder mystery.

CHAPTER 15

The Tom Pool Murder
Mystery & Old Scandals

Tom Pool,[1] of unknown antecedents, kept a store at Half-way house between Seaton and Anderson lakes in the Cariboo. He lived with a squaw and had two young half-breed children.

On a day in 1879, some passing Indians reported that they had found the place burned down. Investigation disclosed the charred bodies of Pool and the two children, and that Pool had been shot through the chest, probably from behind.

Suspicion rested fleetingly on a band of Chilcotin Indians,[2] and there was some talk of their anger with Pool over his squaw. It then fixed more definitely on one of the two Scottish neighbours, cattle raisers in a small way, nearby. One of them, James "Scotty" Halliday,[3] had passed the store with an Indian packer the day before and admitted having called in. However, he denied all knowledge of the tragedy and threw suspicion on one Black Jim, a rather notorious Indian. Black Jim was arrested but, having a strong alibi, was acquitted at the preliminary hearing.

There was some talk that when Halliday returned home on the day of the murder, he had asked his Indian wife to wash blood stains from his shirt — due to a wound on his arm, he said.

With a little more circumstantial evidence against him, Halliday was arrested. Then some twenty dollar gold pieces were found in his cottage and it was recalled that Pool was known to have had quite a stock of gold pieces, none of which was found in the ruins of his place. On the other hand, Halliday explained that he got his gold pieces from one Budwig, a Lillooet money-lender.

While Halliday was in jail, a certain Jerry Woods[4] got talking with him and told him that another neighbour in that vicinity, named Carey,[5] had testified against him, thus leading to his arrest. This casual bit of information made Halliday very indignant and with many an oath he growled "Why the **** cut the children's throats himself." On the strength of that, Carey was arrested, sent up for trial and acquitted.

Then Halliday was tried. The strongest evidence against him was the inference to be drawn from his oral admission to Jerry Woods. But against the veracity of Woods was the fact that he stood to gain a $500 reward. The jury could not agree on a verdict and the case was moved to another Assizes. Next on the record is a motion by my husband that Halliday be allowed out on quite heavy bail until a later sitting of the Court. At that later sitting, again through my husband, Halliday was released, along with the bail money.

This did not satisfy the local folk, and Halliday was arrested again on a charge of having murdered one of the two children. At the preliminary hearing before a Justice of the Peace he was held for trial. But when that later took place, the jury acquitted him. Halliday is said to have lived until 1898 when he died in Clinton.

Tom Pool's was only one of many unsolved mysteries and unusual scandals. No one would dare to frankly write a book of the latter extending over eight decades in a small colony. Nor would one have the heart to do so, in most cases.

Some of the true stories, however, would tax the ingenuity of a fictioneer.

Monsieur A came out from Quebec. In modern slang he was "a city slicker." Unfortunately, in the early days there were red light districts[6] in B.C. with literal red lanterns hanging from gates. Monsieur A continued the unfortunate habit he had acquired in Montreal and went on visiting one such house in particular, although he was engaged to a young lady visiting from the South of France.

He married her and they made the Continental grand tour, but visited B.C. once more before settling in Europe.

The woman of the *demi monde* had not forgotten him. While he was sauntering by her house on his last trip to B.C., just before returning to Europe, a revolver shot rang out in broad daylight and he fell dead in front of her gate, shot through the back. She escaped and the young widow went back overseas alone.

Mr. B was hounded by a heavy debt; perhaps his few friends were not so sorry when the papers announced his premature death and burial. Some years later, my husband's friend, the early B.C. architect Mr. Tiedmann, was walking down Broadway, New York, when he ran into Mr. B.

"But — but, you're *dead*," he stuttered. "Never mind that, Mr. Tiedmann," was the calm reply. "Come in here and have lunch with a living dead man."

"It was like this," said Mr. B, as Mr. Tiedmann could scarce eat the food the waiter placed before him, for staring at Mr. B. "My most pressing creditor — that is, the really vicious one — was going to have me arrested for debt. I had heard that that could be done under certain circumstances. There was a smallpox epidemic in the district, very bad where I was living. Indians who had had the disease were employed to bury the dead. It was easy for me to pass off on the Indians the body of my neighbour whom I had discovered just dead of smallpox, and put up the death flag.[7] I was desperate. I took a chance. In hiding, I watched my dead body carried out of my cottage to a large-scale smallpox burial, by Indians who thought of nothing but firewater. I disguised myself simply, and got over to the U.S. and here I am and doing well."

"No," he added, as if reading honest Mr. Tiedmann's thoughts, "I am not going to pay the debts. Not the largest one anyway. It was imposed on me through a crooked mining scheme of which I was the innocent victim. I am going to remain dead." And with a hearty handshake he joined the New York passing throng.

Mr. C said he was a retired planter from a remote part of the British Empire. He was an over-bearing type of man who, while claiming to be an Englishman, had a very sinister foreign look. However, he had money and was superficially affable with most people. Mr. X was a clerk in a long-established retail shop — a Uriah Heap sort of person.[8] Led on by Mr. C's apparent bonhomie when he made purchases in the store, he decided to call upon him socially at Mr. C's next house party. Mr. X was there, making himself somewhat conspicuous.

Whether it was the sight of Mr. X in proximity to his daughter or the effect of one more glass than he could conveniently compass, beefy Mr. C suddenly seized Mr. X by the collar and trousers-seat and violently threw him out of doors.

This *contre-temps* had faded into the background of social memory when Mr. C came into the foreground again when he was overwhelmed with extraordinary public scandal of the feminine sort; he soon departed for distant regions.

D & E were a Prince and Princess from the Continent — of what precise part, none exactly knew, but their names were pleasingly aristocratic, albeit rather embarrassingly unpronounceable. Socialite doors flew open — at least most of them did — business houses readily extended unlimited credit. And then, red faces. D & E soon appeared in their true characters: that of common impostors who thought that they could readily impose on unsophisticated colonials.

CHAPTER 16

At Bay at Midnight

Although my husband had received a thorough legal education in Victoria with additions in San Francisco when he
returned there for awhile to study law with Mr. Pearkes, an Ontario
lawyer then practising in San Francisco, he, from pleasure, continued a keen student of law in leisure hours long after his call to the
B.C. Bar in 1874.

By 1884 he was an experienced practising lawyer who took a
keen interest in the welfare of the Bar of which he was elected a first
Bencher after the incorporation of the Bar society. He was also, by
natural bent, a deep black letter lawyer, as the ancient expression
put it. This I know from his constant study of old law books in his
extensive law library which closely followed him into every home
we made.

Still, that alone would never have taken him to the Bench. Then,
as now, politics were the main factor. He sometimes said, with a
smile, that he had made himself, through political activities, such a

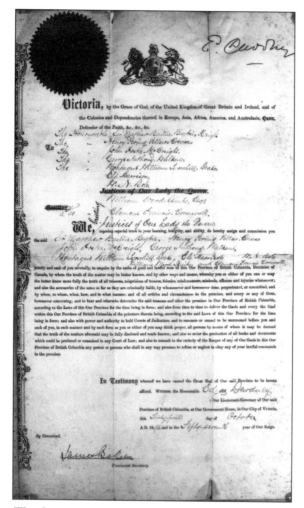

The document appointing Eli Harrison and others
Judges in the province of B.C. Courtesy of L. Wilson.

nuisance to certain politicians that, to be safely rid of him for good, they had insisted that Ottawa appoint him to the Bench for life, although he had only entered his thirty-third year.

The first of the huge thick parchment commissions under the Great Seal of Canada, with the signature of the King's representative at Ottawa prominently written on the top, making him a judge, was for the widespread mainland districts of Cariboo and Lillooet.

This was somewhat awkward, however, for residential reasons. At the time of my marriage my husband owned an acreage at the top of Fort Street, Victoria, known for its numerous and handsome oaks, which we called "Oakwood."

There was a cottage there but a tenant was occupying it at the time. As soon as it was vacant, we moved in and decided that, for the present, he would travel on the judicial circuit while maintaining the home at Victoria.

We owned the place for upwards of half a century, and at a later period it was at such a congested corner of three streets — Fort, Yates and Harrison (named after my husband) — that the passage up Fort Street was popularly known in town as The Dardanelles. But at the time of which I write there was no house within sight; it was an almost uninhabited district.

I had three small children and a Chinese cook who went home to town after dinner. I had no nursemaid at that time. When my husband left he gave me a small, pearl-handed pistol, and although it was almost second-nature for the people of that time to take chances in lonely places, he expressed his anxiety at leaving.

On this occasion there had been unusually severe weather, and snow in heavy drifts (some of six feet) lay about the house. It was midnight. I was sitting by the fire, writing. Suddenly my attention was caught by the turning of the handle of the outside door. Quickly taking the little pistol from the black velvet pocket I had made for it beside my bed, I went to the door and listened.

The handle slowly turned again. I called out "Who's there?" There was no answer.

Presenting the pistol to the door, I said as firmly and strongly as I could: "If you don't go away, I'll shoot straight through this door!" The only response was a thud, as if a man had jumped from the verandah to the ground. I returned to the sitting room and sat down to listen. To brace my nerves, I poked the fire as vigorously as possible. For about half an hour all was silent, and I was thinking about retiring when I heard a noise like the prying of a window in the kitchen. I went in, in the dark, and shot through the window pane; all was silent again.

A few minutes after returning to the sitting room I heard the sound of a ladder being placed at the window of the dining room which was some height above the garden, due to the slope of the ground on that side.

I returned to the dark kitchen, and putting up the sash that was splintered by my last shot, I called out as loudly as I could: "You are determined to get into this house and I am determined to shoot you. These shots will bring the police." Though I knew there was small chance of that, this distance from town. With that there was a scrambling from the ladder and to my great relief, I heard a man run off in the snow.

In the morning I found plain marks in the snow of the various attempts to enter. Before the next nightfall, I asked my sister Annette, who was then in her 'teens, to stay with me until my husband's return.

A short time after this, while I was driving with the children, the house was robbed. All the jewellery I owned, except what I was wearing, was stolen, including some family heirlooms from England which I prized greatly. I bitterly regretted having trusted them merely to a locked drawer and the rest to a box, cleverly — I thought — hidden under a mattress which was over a box mattress. No better hiding place, in the house at least, would have availed as the robbers so thoroughly ransacked the rooms that nothing could have escaped them.

The burglars were never apprehended and none of the valuables were ever recovered, with one exception. A detective discovered a cat's-eye opal ring set in 18kt. gold of rather unusual design. It was the least valuable thing, and being rather disgusted and heart-sick I told the authorities that the detective might keep it for himself, if he wished.

CHAPTER 17

Interesting Callers

Life in the bungalow was far from being all loneliness and danger. We had many interesting callers, some of whose names are well known in B.C. history.

There was Amor de Cosmos,[1] dynamic politician, noted for his twenty-six-hour speech in the B.C. Assembly; he was editor and owner of *The Standard.*[2] His name was really William Alexander Smith but, while in California, he had had it changed by an Act of the State Legislature, to Amor de Cosmos, which he interpreted: Love of the World. He was a large, tall, striking looking man with an abundant head of jet black hair, worn long, and his heavy beard was just as black. Some said they must be dyed.

Bishop and Mrs. Hills:[3] both charming and he like one of the prophets of old. Then there was Sir John A. Macdonald[4] for a brief visit with my husband. Bitter was my regret when, on returning from a walk, I saw his visiting card on the salver. That I had been at home! But my husband talked with him.

Eli Harrison, Sr. (1824–1907) in his Grand Master's
regalia, c. 1878. Courtesy of L. Wilson.

Sir Matthew Baillie Begbie:[5] tall and very pleasant; white hair, white moustache, white beard and black eyebrows. He used to sing in St. John's choir and his rich deep voice could easily be distinguished.

Mr. Justice Gray came most frequently, as he lived not far from us on a corner somewhat below the crest of the hill (on the corner of Moss and Fort Streets); he and his amiable wife were fond of strolling among our oaks.

Chief Justice McColl[6] and Chief Justice Theodore Davie[7] (as they later became) — prominent in law and politics came often — being quite close friends with my husband.

I might mention here that Eli I had taken up Freemasonry with enthusiasm and became Grand Master in 1878, in 1880 and in 1881. Dr. Robie L. Reid,[8] the Grand Historian, recently wrote me that my father-in-law and Dr. Powell were the "only two men who have been honoured in B.C. by election as Grand Master for three successive terms."

On April 22, 1878 Eli I had dedicated and laid the foundation stone of the Masonic Temple, Victoria, and it was consecrated by him on October 23, 1878.

My father-in-law was, as I mentioned in the covered wagon days, inclined to mysticism, and this led him into what is called, I believe, "speculative Masonry." He received the degrees of the Ancient & Accepted Scottish Rite from four to thirty-two and was then appointed Special Representative or Deputy for the highest thirty-three degree for the Province, serving for six years.

My husband also advanced in the work and was a thirty-second degree. At the time of his passing he had represented the Grand Lodge of England in B.C. for forty-four years. He compiled and annotated the Masonic Code for B.C.

This interest in Masonry, especially in its mystic side, led to a close friendship with the remarkable American Freemason General Pike.[9] (I understand that a magnificent temple of the Scottish Rite is dedicated to him in Washington, D.C.)

It was a period when large heavy beards gave many men a patriarchal appearance, and, it must be admitted, that beards made some men, young and old, look very handsome.

General Pike fairly towered in our small house, being well over six feet, and he was awesomely huge as he sat at the dining table, for he was broad as well as tall.

General Pike wore a full beard and long hair; he had very clear, bright, penetrating yet benevolent eyes. He had been a general in the Confederate States' army and, in his delightful Southern inflection, told us many interesting anecdotes. But it was plain that his all absorbing interest was in mystical Freemasonry and certainly I have never met a man whose noble character was more strongly impressed in features and manner.

I have an interesting letter from him in his own distinctive handwriting written on thirty-three degree letterhead to a member of the family. We had a great many social cards and letters written by people who played important roles in the history of the West; some of the writers are now almost legendary. Specimens of these letters, cards and official documents were acquired from me by the late Mr. John Hosie, Provincial Librarian and Archivist, June 30, 1933, and affixed in a manuscript book of 100 pages, 17" x 21," for preservation in the Archives, Parliament Buildings, Victoria, B.C.

One day, as I was clipping roses on the trellis work on the verandah of the little house, I was startled by a man's voice behind me. Turning, I saw a tall, handsome stranger. No, he was not a stranger. It was Gilbert Malcolm Sproat[10] to whom I had been introduced some weeks previously. I had been told at that time that Mr. Sproat had won a $1,000 prize for the best essay on "The British Opium Policy in India and China" awarded to him by the Viceroy of India and the Governors of Bombay and Madras, 1875. He also was correspondent on the North Pacific seaboard for the London *Times* (1875-1877 and later).

As I spoke to him, Mr. Sproat had but recently completed his duties as Dominion and Provincial Commissioner to adjust the Indian land question (1876-1880) and had called to see my husband for a legal opinion in connection with his report.

My husband was not at home, but, as a lady at the moment came up the drive for afternoon tea, I invited Mr. Sproat, too. We had a delightful afternoon, for Mr. Sproat was a most interesting person and had even then been delving into curious nooks and corners of B.C.

Sproat Lake, near Alberni, Vancouver Island, has long borne his name. On its shores are to be found mysterious petroglyphs cut by some ancient race (as there are near Nanaimo and at some other places).

Mr. Sproat had had a romantic career. Born in England, after education at Hutton Hall, Dumfries and King's College, London, he decided to adventure in Mexico. There he married Katharine, a daughter of Henry Wigham, Master of the Mint, Mexico.

Coming north to B.C., he was on a committee in 1858 studying the welfare of British merchant seaman. During the years 1860-1865 he was a government agent on the West Coast of Vancouver Island and held a like office and that of Gold Commissioner in Kootenay, 1885-1890.

He was an adaptable writer: turning from long government reports, he was equally at home with his "Select Odes of Horace in English Lyrics" or with "Scenes and Studies in Savage Life," a highly prized B.C. pioneer work. Mr. Sproat also wrote regularly for the New York papers.

Mr. Sproat for many years lived near Sproat Lake and in other wild places. One of my family, my son Victor, came to have an intimate knowledge of his affairs and in later years was given by Mr. Sproat a copy of Captain Walbran's classic "B.C. Place Names," all annotated throughout in Mr. Sproat's handwriting and containing many old clippings relating to the subject of the book. "It's like *Coke upon Littleton*," enthusiastically exclaimed a lawyer, to have Sproat upon Walbran. For no two greater authorities on early B.C., ever lived.

When Mr. Sproat finally passed away, spending his last illness in Mrs. Wilson-Brown's old house (I knew her well and she coached me in school subjects), another pioneer told me she was so amazed at the size of Mr. Sproat's chest as he lay there, that she slipped a tape around it — the measure ran to forty-eight inches!

⁓

As the reader may be interested in an eye witness account of the Interior of B.C. at about the time Mr. Sproat was a Gold Commissioner there, I will give my husband's memoirs for a chapter or two.

Before doing so, perhaps I should mention that pioneers are usually pictured as heavily armed and otherwise fortified. In the more than twenty-five years of constant travelling for thousands of miles in the interior of B.C. and on his circuit on Vancouver Island, as barrister and judge, what did my husband ever have with him? A revolver and Johnny Walker? No! A copy of Cicero's *Orations* or other work; Vergil's *Aeneid* or *Telemaque par Fenelon,* in the original, were indispensable items in his valise, together with long bars of genuine imported Castile soap (of course unscented) which he cut up as needed. The classics were always with him through the years and were read in spare moments. He also wrote out translations in his fine legal hand, of which I still have many pages.

CHAPTER 18

A Trip Through the
Wild Interior

*(abridged and adapted from the
unpublished memoirs of my husband)*

When I was a young barrister I travelled some distance in the interior of the mainland of B.C., and a number of times, from the middle to the end of 1870, and many other times in later years.

On the earlier trips I went by paddle wheel steamer to Yale and there met a Mr. McIntosh[1] who was to be my companion on the ride. Well mounted, we made an early start.

We soon passed near to Hill's Bar[2] where the outlaw Ned Mc-Gowan[3] took refuge after his flight from the Vigilantes[4] following the murder of John King of the *San Francisco Bulletin*.[5]

As we rode on I noticed far above our heads on the sides of the canyon, lines of red which indicated that we were riding over what would be beneath water in the rainy season. Climbing the steep road up the mountain sides, we passed, in places, over wooden cribbing or planking hanging above the boiling current. In clefts of the cliffs, Indians were perched on platforms projecting over the river,

Cariboo Wagon Road in the Fraser Canyon. BC Archives, H-00290.

fishing for salmon which go up the river from the sea in immense numbers to spawn. Now and then we saw miners working rockers and sluices — they were Indian and Chinese. Earlier in the 1850s they had been white men from California.

The first day we made Boston Bar, twenty-five miles out of Yale. It was on the bars of the river along here that much gold had been mined by the white Argonauts. The names were suggestive of the mixed crowd of adventurers, such as Sailor's Bar, Cornish Bar, New York Bar, Union Bar, Emory's Bar, Kanaka Bar, American Bar, Murderer's Bar, China Bar, Dutch Bar, Mormon Bar and so on. All these names had been informally bestowed by the wild rovers who camped there in the heyday of this sort of mining.

Not far from Lytton we bought melons grown in the remarkable dry belt of B.C. It is some 200 miles wide and commenced as soon as we got out of the Canyons of the Fraser River. In that dry belt the climate and scenery is entirely different. No great evergreen forests but dry plains, though very fertile when irrigated, and rolling uplands.

However, we saw a few pine trees. Bunch grass,[6] sage, wormwood and a species of cactus abound. Beyond was the Selkirk or Gold Range of mountains.

When we came to the meeting of the Thompson and Fraser Rivers we knew we were at Lytton,[7] named in 1858 after Sir Edward Bulwer-Lytton (later Lord Lytton),[8] the famous novelist and student of the occult, then a Colonial Secretary. He had handled Governor Douglas' request to Downing Street for the formation of the separate mainland colony of B.C., separate, that is, from the colony of Vancouver's Island.

We found many Indians at Lytton, all of them appearing to belong to the Church of England. I was much attracted by the Rev. J.B. Good,[9] and his remarkable command of Indian dialect; he had even translated the Church services into it. There were two churches, one for whites and the other for Indians in their village nearby. I thought it would be interesting to attend service in the

43 Miles from Yale. BC Archives A-03875.

Indian church. It was all-Indian and very impressive, though I could only surmise what they were singing and saying.

After changing horses at Lytton, we rode on along the left bank of the Thompson and crossed at Spence's Bridge,[10] once called Cook's Ferry. The weather was extremely hot; tethering our horses, I took a plunge in the Thompson. On mounting again I was sharply reminded that cactus grows in that region as some had got into my clothing.

At Ashcroft we called on Mr. Cornwall (later Lieutenant-Governor and a Senator) and accepted his hearty invitation to stay overnight at his large ranch. He casually remarked that one of the hands had fed our horses on grain or corn three years' old, as there was no sale for it in the immediate neighbourhood and it would be unprofitable to send it down to the coast. After an enjoyable stay with our most interesting and agreeable host, we had not time to

Freight Wagon at Grand Bluff in the Fraser Canyon.
BC Archives, A-00350.

proceed to Pavilion Lake which is said to have "the bluest water on the continent."

Instead we rode on Savona's ferry, crossed Kamloops Lake and entered that town. "Look out your horse doesn't bolt," warned my companion. "Why?" I asked. "Because there is a camel hereabouts." It was a survivor of the stupid and naturally ill-fated attempt to import and use camels as pack animals; the sharp stones of course cut up their spongy feet and it was impossible to shoe them. Not only that, but the presence of the camels was a nightmare to the pack horses and pack mules, which, upon meeting a camel, would promptly bolt over the river bank, plunge down the mountain side and destroy themselves and cargo.

At Kamloops I was given an unbroken horse; I demurred at first, not liking to deprive the owner of a valuable animal, but I accepted when I learned that the price of such horses was only $5.00. My companion offered to ride the horse, and, being an expert rider, was never thrown though the wild horse did his best, time and time and again, until the end of the trip. My mild pony looked quite smart, having had his mane roached, i.e. cut off, and his ears and tail cropped.

We rode through the Nicola valley. Although the streams were low and, in places, had dry beds, we saw any number of fine large salmon in the creeks, they having made their way up the Fraser, through the canyons; up the Thompson; up the Nicola and up streams flowing into Nicola River, to the head waters of those streams, there to spawn and die where they had been born.

The country had the same endless dry look, when, having reached a stream near the Cascades,[11] the whole aspect suddenly changed to the delightful green scenery so dear to the coast dweller. We rode along the banks of this stream, my companion singing a joyous song which he said was a favourite of the Forty-Niners,[12] until we got well into the Cascade Range.

While crossing, my companion broke into song again at the sight of a stampeding herd of wild cattle along the opposite shore. But a coyote slunk out of our way. Looking back, I saw that the coyote had turned around also and was gazing curiously at us. Coyotes can give a good run to foxhounds, I found out on a later occasion, when riding with the Cornwall pack of foxhounds.

As evening fell and we neared the summit, we started a number of grouse, which were called, locally, fool hens. And such they seemed to be, for we killed four for dinner, simply by throwing sticks at them. We could have killed many more, but four sufficed. They simply sat on the boughs of trees, without attempting to fly away. At the summit, the snow of yesteryear was still lying on the ground and this was September.

When morning broke we were forced to remark on the magnificent view, as used as we had become to scenes of grandeur. We made an early start on the return trip, going by way of Fort Hope.[13] It was very steep, nothing better for foothold than large, bare and often slippery boulders and cascades jumping from rock to rock on their way to form the Coquihalla stream which empties into the Fraser near Hope.

Fort Hope is another old Hudson Bay post founded in 1847, about sixteen miles this side of Yale but on the left bank of the Fraser.

Though the level country about it is small in area, it is very fertile. The Coquihalla flows through it and there is a variety of trees. In the front is the Fraser and, at the rear, the Cascades, which, with their numerous beautiful waterfalls, tower high above the valley. In a favourable location in Hope, an Order of Anglican sisters long maintained an excellent boarding academy for girls.[14] The Duke and Duchess of Cornwall and York,[15] later King George V and Queen Mary, visited the school in 1901.

Hope was the end of river navigation and when that became impossible because of the winter, the inhabitants, before the roads were made, travelled to the coast, when necessary, over the frozen Fraser river as a highway, dragging along canoes for use wherever the ice was thawed.

At Hope I boarded the river steamer for home. My bucking wild horse had by this time, in the skilful hands of my companion, become thoroughly docile and walked over the gang plank without a vestige of his former stubborn and fiery disposition.

~~~

At the end of the 1870's, I again travelled into the interior, going further to the Cariboo country, acting as Crown Prosecutor at the Assizes.

Political feeling ran high in B.C.,[16] and there was no friendly feeling between the Provincial Government and the Express Company subsidized by the Dominion Government to run stages from Yale to Cariboo carrying the Royal mail and passengers.

The Provincial Government requested me not to travel by the Express stage, but to hire for my use a buggy and two horses in Victoria and to charge it to them. Furthermore, I was to use a code in telegraphing since there were people about who could read the ticking of the telegraph if the message were not in cipher.

It was not so difficult to get the horses and carriage to the mainland of B.C. for starting, but I did not like the rule of the road on the narrow highways in the mountainous part of the vast country, which was: that the light vehicle must keep to the outer side of the narrow road, next to the perilous edge, from which could be seen the roaring river far below.

As I drove along, I met with gangs of road menders clearing away fresh slides that blocked the road now and then. Fortunately their custom at least was that when I came in sight with my buggy, they would move to the outer side with their steel barrows and tools while I drove by on the inner, safer side.

I had not gone far past one of these gangs, when I saw a wagon train approaching, drawn by oxen. It consisted of two very heavily loaded wagons, one fastened behind the other and drawn by sixteen oxen.

Little as I desired to do so, I drove by the outer edge hanging over the swirling river. It seemed to me, as I held my breath, that the oxen had abnormally long horns and that the margin between us was negligible, while on the other side I felt as if at any moment the wheels of my carriage would just slip beyond the edge.

Some of these wagon trains loaded with heavy merchandise were even longer, being made up of great wagons drawn by sixteen or twenty-three oxen, horses or mules. Sometimes I met with covered wagons, solitary horsemen or parties of riders, and once a cavalry man in picturesque uniform.

At Jackass Mountain[17] I reached a place where the roadway consisted of simple planks over-hanging the river. A train of heavy wagons somewhat ahead of me was being accompanied by its owner who had, for one reason or another, got out at this point to walk beside the leading wagon. Suddenly, for no known reason, one of the horses gave him a push with its nose and he fell through a small space left between the ends of the planks and the rock of the mountainside. With a wild cry he rolled down the steep bank into the river.

His companion halted the wagons and hurried to the outer edge of the planking but they could only stand there helplessly watching until he was finally engulfed and carried away by the surging waters. None so firmly caught in the grip of the Fraser has ever been seen again.

Further on, I was alarmed to find a sharp turn round a steep, rocky bluff jutting out into the river, and in front of me I could see only the resistless river. It looked as if, had the road been built any further on, it must have been carried away by the mighty force of the torrent.

The Judge, appointed and paid by the Dominion Government to preside in Provincial Courts, travelled ahead of me in a special stage driven by one of the Express Company's best drivers. When I caught up with him by reaching the same stopping place at night, he would say to me in all seriousness. "Well, I feel so relieved you've turned up; I thought you'd never reach here."

An ox team pulling wagons on the Cariboo Road at Clinton. The Clinton Hotel was one of the oldest. BC Archives, A-00346.

One of the cases on the calendar at the Kamloops Assizes was that of an Indian charged with murder. As I drove into the town, I noticed a native chewing tobacco as he negligently sat on a fence surrounding the jail. I asked the Government Agent what he was doing there and he replied: "Oh, that's the accused Indian who is to be tried for killing another Indian."[18] I remarked that he should not be allowed about in that loose sort of way. "Oh, that's alright," continued the Government Agent, "he won't run away. I've sent him down to the river lots of times to bring buckets of water for use about the jail. He understands that he must not run away."

This Indian had, sometime before, left Kamloops[19] in the company of an Indian acquaintance and had come back without him. Another Indian whom he had gone off with on a previous occasion also had never returned nor been seen again. When charged with murdering the one whom he had last been with, he voluntarily stated that he had killed him. The Judge, however, and I think quite properly, would not take this statement of his as a sufficient plea of guilty.

After the sessions of the Court had closed. I drove from Kamloops back to the main Cariboo Road, calling at Cache Creek[20] and from there crossed the old Brigade Trail.[21] This, before the wagon road,[22] ran for hundreds of miles through the country to carry goods and furs of the Hudson's Bay Company between their widely scattered posts established for trading with the Indians.

I then reached Clinton about 3000 feet above sea level. Nearby is the habitat of the Big Horn mountain sheep and a species of deer called the Mule Deer which has very large ears.[23] Only the most hardy vegetables grow near Clinton[24] because of the altitude. Yet when it was freezing at Clinton I have seen a child eating a piece of a water melon which had been grown at Lillooet[25] only forty-seven miles away.

A few miles from Clinton and only a few yards from the wagon road, is one of the most awesome sights in British Columbia so far discovered. It is called The Chasm.[26] It is a long box canyon, the three perpendicular walls of which are layer after layer of painted rock; the great height, the strange colouring, and the remarkable rock formations, create a curious effect on the mind. One might fancy it the hall of fabulous giants. At a great depth below the wagon road is a lake and marsh land which, at the height from which you look, presents a pretty landscape of lake and seemingly green meadows in a miniature kingdom. This chasm opens into the Bonaparte valley.

The road ever ascends until at 83 Mile Hill the panorama is of the most marvelous and extensive range. I believe the height above sea level is near to, if not more than 4,000 feet. Then one descends to Lac la Hache,[27] a region much like Kamloops. About thirty-five miles further I came to the stables of the main supply of horses for the stage line, and where used-up stage horses are rested.

Freight wagon with 10 pairs of horses on the Cariboo Road (1880).
BC Archives A-09603. Courtesy of Kamloops Museum, #1007.

After I had passed through the San José Valley I reached 150 Mile House[28] at an altitude of about 3,300 ft., so-called as it is 150 miles from Lillooet by the Harrison-Lillooet road.[29]

Climbing again I crossed Carpenter's mountain and made a steep descent to Soda Creek[30] on the Fraser, 1,450 ft. above sea level. Across the river I entered the Chilcotin country and its wide grazing lands. Passing Alexandria,[31] I went by the Australian,[32] the Bohanon and Kersley ranches[33] and crossed the bridge at Quesnel-mouth[34] — a small town at the Quesnel River. The altitude was about 400 feet lower than Clinton and the climate much milder in consequence. I then entered a wet, woody country with dense vegetation.

Having passed the Cottonwood River and reached Lightning Creek,[35] which years ago yielded so much gold, I had now entered the mining country of the Cariboo. This name came from the

View of the Great Chasm, c. 1865. BC Archives, G-00790.

French word for reindeer, they resorting to this region. I also saw the Arctic hare and the Ptarmigan.

Stanley[36] was once a very flourishing place on Lightning Creek, but I found it practically deserted. Next I came to Williams Creek[37] and along there, at one time, were the towns of Richfield, Cameron Town and Barkerville. Barkerville is 4,200 feet above sea level.

I found nothing left of Cameron Town. At Richfield the only buildings were the Court House, the log house in which the Stipendiary Magistrate used to live in former times and another building. The rest have been buried by tailings — the debris washed away from the mines.

Barkerville surprised me, for I hardly expected to find the ground floors of buildings along the same street at different heights — no two on a level. The sidewalks are also different in height as to the ground floors of the buildings they are in front of, and I went up and down steps to reach the different levels of the same sidewalk. To get to opposite sides of the street, I had to go up and down steps to get to and from bridges crossing the street. This is due to the tailings accumulating, and people from time to time raising their buildings to be above the tailings, and each one raises his building as high as suits his fancy or his purse.

Noticing what appeared to be a barber's pole sticking out of the ground, I remarked it to a resident, who replied "so it is."

"But where is the barber's shop?" I asked.

"Oh, the barber's shop is buried beneath the tailings and so is the rest of the pole."

While I was there, a law suit arose as to who owned a building, or rather what remained of it. The building had been a two-storey one, one storey used by the volunteer fire company and the other by the amateur dramatic club and the Philharmonic Society. As time went on, the tailings buried the lower storey, so the two-storey building had, in effect, become one-storey, and the question arose as to which of these associations owned this now one-storey building.

The rich gold mines of the Cariboo, though at a high elevation, lie in a basin, the sides of which are the Bald Mountains,[38] so-called because there is not a jagged peak among them, and the moment I got to their summit I was surprised to find myself on rolling plains over which one could have galloped on horse back.

These mountains are covered with heather and, I was told, in the season for flowers they are covered with a most beautifully variegated coloured carpet of flowers. The view was not quite as grand as I expected, due to the fact that the valleys could not be seen; it was just a great sea of apparently endless mountains.

As I knew that Barkerville was dependent for its supply of vegetables on the outside world, I had brought with me, for eighty miles or so, a large sack of onions, the only vegetables I could get, and they went in a few minutes after my arrival, as presents to different people.

The Sternwheeler Enterprise *and the Colonial Hotel at Soda Creek, c. 1868. BC Archives, A-03908.*

100 Mile House, the Cariboo (1868). BC Archives, A-03896.

When I arrived on this trip, although the flow of gold had decreased, the Cariboo was still prosperous and Barkerville had two banks, an opera house, a very good hospital, a neat Church of England, an excellent library and a restaurant which served meals in the famous style of Mons. Driard of the "Colonial" and "Driard"[39] fame of Victoria. The people remaining had not felt the pinch of hard times and were bright, intelligent, well informed, courteous, generous and very hospitable.

It was no mere politician's compliment when one of the Cabinet Ministers of the then Government at Ottawa said that a Dominion cabinet could at any time be found in the Cariboo from among the miners, not a few of whom, he thought, were well qualified to govern the whole Dominion.

Near to the close of the Assizes, the Judge, who was very anxious to get back to Victoria as soon as possible, insisted on my joining him, for, while he could do from sixty to eighty miles a day — having relays of horses at every express stable — I could only average about twenty-five. I was therefore only too glad to accept the invitation and I left my team to follow and drove on with him to Lytton, the last place on the circuit.

I had to put in several days at Lytton after the Court closed its sitting, waiting for the arrival of my team. There were not two dozen white people there. It was constantly blowing, with sand flying about. The hotel was a long, ramshackle, dismal building. The landlord and his wife were French, who had in some way got stranded there. They sang together, in French, songs of La Belle France, which instead of cheering them up added to the melancholy of their exile.

So next morning I told the hotelkeeper that he must really find something to interest me; that I didn't see how I could stand it out till my team came. Laconically he said "Come with me," picking up a couple of shovels and a pick. "I will show you one very curious thing." Following him I came to a flat or bench on the other side of the Thompson River, covered with shifting sand.

150 Mile House in winter in the 1880s. BC Archives, E-09983.

He commenced digging and soon uncovered a skull and then some stone arrow heads. This incited me to dig, too, and I soon dug up a number of skulls, several skeletons and bone implements, a bone comb, some flint arrow heads; a skeleton evidently of a woman with a copper band covered in verdigris, on one of her wrist bones. Then I stopped to speak to mine host. No answer. Looking over the plain and across the bridge I saw that he had gone back to the hotel.

Having something of interest in view now, I filled up the rest of my time by going over there each day and excavating, while waiting for my team and its driver. I found pieces of mineral paint and other interesting relics. I found that the Indians had no knowledge of how the remains came to be there. All they would ever say was, "They are that of some strange people of a long, long time ago."

I determined to some day return to excavate there, but when I did so two years later on my way to Lillooet, I found to my surprise that the Smithsonian Institute, so my informant said, had dug up and taken away several wagon loads of relics since my first visit, and I concluded it was not worth my while to try after they had got through.

It was on that same trip to Lillooet, however, with a Chinese interpreter, that I learned of the very strange ancient Oriental disks, the account of which I will give elsewhere. My team soon reached Lytton and with the same driver I made a relatively quick descent to Yale where I took the boat home.

CHAPTER 19

Edging the Precipices

S uch is the gist of my husband's unpublished memoirs of his experiences in the interior prior to the railways. Now I will give my version of travel there about the same period.

When my husband enthusiastically suggested that I accompany him on one of his many trips into the Cariboo after he had become a Judge,[1] I was at first somewhat startled. That vast, mountainous region of grand vistas, precipitous plateaus and hairbreadth highways was a mysterious, forbidding empire. I knew that there were many small but important centres, with at least some of the amenities of life, but I also knew that travel between them required nerve and no small amount of natural upholstery with which I was not supplied, as the narrow winding roads were both sheer and awfully rugged.

To a Victorian, it was pretty much like suggesting a trip to Tibet, of which the original edition of the good Abbé Huc's fascinating book had given me a wholesome caution about venturing into a sea of endless high mountains.

Artist's rendering of the Cariboo Road in the Fraser Canyon.

However, several years of close attention to domestic life, without a real change, made me on second thought welcome adventure even of the most robust sort. So, leaving the children in the care of obliging mother, dear sister Annette and a governess, I accompanied my husband on one of his judicial circuits all the way to Barkerville.

We took steamer from Vancouver Island to New Westminster and from there by river boat to Yale. At Yale the government placed at our disposal a private stage. It was high-swung and hard to enter. The seats were of leather and many robes, fur rugs and cushions were piled in. This looked like easy riding, but as soon as the stage got under way I realized that the springs were of leather only.

It was November and although we had plenty of warm wraps, we began to feel the cold. We frequently changed horses and drivers, sometimes using four or six horses, though we had started with only two.

Some distance from Yale, we were staying at a wayside inn, enjoying a wonderful steak, when the stillness of the night was broken by a dreadful howling. At first the inn keeper and driver thought it came from a coyote, but the more we listened the more certain we became that there was something human in the sound. Several men took guns and lanterns and went out to investigate. In a few minutes they brought in a much bedraggled and half-crazed Indian. He had escaped from jail about a fortnight before. His morale was low and he was about starved. The men fed him well, but the next day the constables took him back to prison.

We drove all next day and night, not changing horses until three o'clock next morning at an inn. The long hard days and nights of driving, with broken rest at some of the more primitive inns, had by no means accustomed me to this manner of travel and at the last stop I had to be carried out of the stage to the inn. I was really too tired to sleep. While lying awake I heard a strange noise coming from the loft. No one surely could be sleeping up there, I thought. The only other guest in the otherwise empty inn was the Hon. Mr. Justice Walkem[2] who had joined us at the last change of horses. (His brother, Joseph Boomer Walkem, was a prominent K.C. (King's Counsel)[3] in Kingston, Ontario, Another brother was Dr. Walkem, also prominent in pioneer B.C.).

It was evident that the noise had been heard by others, for there soon came a cautious tap at the door, and the voice of Judge

B.C. Express Company's Stage Coach on the Cariboo Road.
BC Archives, A-03067.

Walkem called to my husband in a stage whisper. After he had succeeded in attracting my husband's attention, he said in low excited tones that he felt sure that certain escaped murderers, whom he named, were hiding in the loft.

Judge Walkem had been a Premier of B.C., and was far from being a man given to idle fancies, so my husband was duly impressed. He dressed quickly, took his pistol and joined Judge Walkem, who was also armed. I slipped on a fur coat and awaited results. The two jurists then awakened the landlord, who felt that the reward which was out for the fugitives was well within his grasp. The three armed men cautiously crept up the rough steps leading to the attic. Mine host went forward most carefully while the two jurists took up a judicious position near the foot of the stairs, bravely grasping their weapons.

Loud guffaws from the attic caused us all to exchange inquiring glances. The explanation was soon forthcoming. Putting his head through the aperture, the landlord, while trying to regain his composure and respectful manner, called out that one of his female dogs had taken a fancy to go up there to have her pups. My husband who was rather fond of jokes and comical situations especially connected with animals, laughed very heartily. But Judge Walkem seemed offended and abruptly left the party.

We resumed our journey at noon the next day. The road in places seemed even steeper than the breath-taking ones we had already traversed, and our driver stopped to cut tree trunks to attach to the stage for additional brakes. The weather was quite frosty but no snow had yet fallen. On one of the mountains we had to spiral, going down to rise up higher each time. At the foot of one mountain was a lake and a horseman skirted its shores; he looked no larger than a toy soldier.

The night following that one we stopped at a place called the Australian's. It was dark when we entered the inn. A dozen men sat at a long table, facing great plates of the fattest pork I had ever seen, garnished with huge boiled potatoes. On side dishes were thick slices of bread, piled high. A large black cauldron of coffee stood at the head of the table, smelling as if it had been boiling steadily for at least three days.

Being quite hungry, I took all this in as I passed through to the room provided for me. It was a neat bedroom but very small. I sat down on the little rocking chair and requested a glass of water but could not drink it when it came as it was rainwater with worms in the bottom. I asked for tea, but they had none. Instead, a steaming cup of the coffee was brought in. While I was debating with myself whether to chance drinking it or not, I heard a tapping at the window.

There was a black bear's full face with his paw up as if he were trying to push open the window. I called out loudly, then ducked under the bed in preference to going among so many rough-looking men. My husband soon came in. We both looked through the window but no sign of bruin. We went into the dining room to tell the news and were astounded to see the huge bear calmly standing at the table, begging for food like a dog.

The innkeeper told us that the bear came for all meals in the dining room, seemed always in the best of humour, was patient, had good manners and, above all — a special virtue in his eyes — never bothered their chickens.

As that inn only had pork, bread, rainwater and atrocious coffee, we drove on immediately, despite the attractiveness of bruin, thirty miles to the next stop.

Flurries of snow now made driving more difficult. The driver who had taken his seat on the box after the change of horses, was reluctant to try the canyon before Barkerville. I should say that while one sometimes drives on the bottom of canyons — as in California — getting along canyons on this trip meant skirting the very edge of vast declivities. The one before Barkerville had, in addition, a mountain steeply towering above the narrow road which had, with great difficulty, been cut into the mountain's side. Hence there was no escape either up or down, but certain death for any mis-step, either way.

It was midnight and the driver to comfort himself took a companion on the box. To further ease the passage they both began to whistle. This had the reverse effect on the Judge who, at last, ordered them to stop. I learned later that neither the driver nor his friend had driven the canyon in the dark.

Just at the entrance of the canyon was a small wayside refreshment cabin. While we were taking tea, the driver's companion overheard the proprietor saying that he wouldn't dream of driving the canyon at night. It certainly wasn't safe. This from a person experienced in those parts so discouraged the man that he refused to go and left the driver to try it alone.

My husband was anxious to reach Barkerville, hold Court and return before the predicted heavy snows set in. So we drove on. It was a narrower road than usual; in fact no room for another vehi-

Stage Coach edging a precipice on the Lytton Road
(with passengers walking). BC Archives, I-57564.

cle to pass, except at a very few and far-between spots. But as it was always said that no one ever travelled through there at midnight, we at least felt safe in that respect.

All of a sudden, as we were going upgrade, and it was rather slippery because of the light snow that had just fallen, we heard piercing shrieks ahead of us, and, as they continued, the driver stopped.

"Perhaps the road has given way, Your Honour, and someone has been put there to warn us," he said.

The two men with one lantern walked ahead, leaving me in the dark stage, the six horses unattended. True, they had tied the horses to the stage, but I did not relish the situation. Meanwhile the shrieks continued.

When my husband and the driver reached the voice, it proved to be that of a highly excited man whose eyes were staring from his head. He shouted to the foremost man approaching with the lantern: "Are you man or devil?"

He had a team of horses backed against the sheer mountain side and, when he had somewhat recovered his wits, he said that in all his forty years of residence in Barkerville and vicinity, and much travel through that country, it was the first time he had heard of anyone on that road at such a time of night. (Forty years was something of an exaggeration, as the famous road from Yale to Barkerville had been built by the Royal Engineers from England between 1862 and 1865).

He had to back his team all the way to Barkerville, which he said was distant some mile and a half, a good deal of it steep. Even among some of the most expert drivers in the world (as these Cariboo drivers were), this was, in itself, something of a feat.

When we reached Barkerville it was bright moonlight; a white blanket of deep snow lay everywhere, with giant icicles two and three feet long, glistening on all the eaves — a beautiful sight. The noise of our six horse stage driving in at that hour seemed to awaken the whole community. Lights quickly appeared in all directions and men and women were peering out at us. Two or three of the residents at once proffered us a night's lodging and gave the Judge a royal welcome. The women, although it was nearly 2 a.m., insisted on making us a dinner — the best roast beef, bacon, butter, bread, eggs and coffee we had had since leaving Vancouver Island.

CHAPTER 20

Departure Bay

The doors of the horse-drawn cab slammed; the three jumpety boys and their graceful sister were all eyes while the baby girl blissfully had hers shut tight. "Gowey," the Chinese house boy, hopped to the box seat; the old red-nosed public cabby flicked with his whip the impatient horses, although they needed no incentive to get off the noisy wharf, out of the way of rolling tar barrels and barrows loaded with passengers' boxes from the little steamer that has just tied up from Victoria.

We drove through the small, straggling town of Nanaimo[1] whose first train[2] to Victoria had safely reached there but recently. The long established boat service from the capital seemed preferable to us.

After several miles through the country, we reached the clear waters of Departure Bay and turned into the grounds of a fine house. This was to be our home for several years. My husband had recently been appointed Judge of the Court of this county,[3] extending up Vancouver Island north of Victoria. We had decided to try and live in the county, while the children were small anyway. My husband had completed full plans for a house on an acre he had on a hill overlooking Nanaimo, but the work would not be finished for a long time.

We therefore arranged for the lovely Dunsmuir house[4] within a stone's throw of Departure Bay. It had been built by James Dunsmuir,[5] later Premier of B.C. (1900-1902), and then Lieutenant-Governor of the Province (1906-1909).

The house had ten rooms, large, light and finely decorated. A separate back stairs led from the kitchen up to the maid's room. The grounds were attractively laid out in several acres, with the usual stabling and outhouses, etc. From several of the large windows, through the treed grounds, one had a fine view of the bay in which many ships often rode at anchor.

Some writers of good repute, of late, have been again examining the old Chinese doctrine of *Feng-sui*. It will be recalled that this theory, briefly, is that houses have atmosphere, good, bad and indifferent. This house had one of the best "atmospheres" one could wish. Even though the house was somewhat isolated, one could hardly feel anything but cheerful and optimistic in it.

I have never been attracted by psychic phenomena, real or fancied. It may, therefore, be assumed that I have never been predisposed to be carried away by "wishful thinking" or genuine manifestation. I give the following accurately, however it may be interpreted.

Delighted with this lovely house, I was seated by the cleared dining table one night, puzzling my head over a Latin translation. (All through my married life, my husband, strange as it may seem, was ever eager to study Latin with me and correct my work or help me in my struggle over some idiom or obscure Latin grammar). Preoccupied and in the best mood, I felt I had the right answer and was wondering what the Judge would say when he returned from some late task at his chambers in the Court house.

The Dunsmuir House "within a stone's throw of Departure Bay."
The photo includes Laura and James Dunsmuir & their daughter "Birdie."
B.C. Archives, H-03007.

Then a strong feeling came over me to glance up, and there I saw the hall door partly open. A face was looking at me. Not any face I knew. A good child's face.

I stared some moments then went to the door, looked up and down the hall, saw nothing, and quickly slipped upstairs to the nursery: door shut; all sound asleep within. I then went down again to play some favourite pieces on the piano in the music room. After awhile, I looked around again expecting that the door might have opened. It was shut, but the face was there, floating as it were, with the child's sweet expression. I never saw it again.

Some days later I told the incident to a friend, who said that a very young child had fallen down the servant's stairs and had been found dead at the bottom.[6] That happened long before we came to the house, but it was the first I had heard of it.

There was no one else in the house; the doors were locked. Faithful Gowey lived at some distance in his quarters in the garden.

Anticipating a possible question: no, I had not been reading Cicero's well known story of ghosts, but was puzzling over some much more elementary Latin work.

~

Gowey was superstitious, and firmly believed in psychic phenomena.

When we had no garden man, Gowey[7] attended to our part-Arabian carriage horse, Bess. This was an exceptionally clever horse and her very horse sense made Gowey hate to have anything to do with her, as he said with a look that amused me, that she had a "devilo inside."

While he used to prepare her meal of oats, by wetting them in the kitchen, Bess, in the paddock or in the stable, would whinny, and he used to exclaim almost in terror: "You hear that, Missa Hallison, how she know I make food?" Before I could answer, he supplied his own with complete conviction: "Devilo tell him!" shaking his head.

He always double-barred his door at night — with large, heavy bars — on account of this nervous, high strung horse.

CHAPTER 21

Bess

"Well, my dear, I may be quite wrong, but I do hold the opinion that riding horses soon become much more responsive and intelligent than those attached to carts, carriages or even to dog carts!"

"Perhaps you are right," I said. "We have no riding ponies here at present; the cleverest horse I know draws a phaeton[1] and has never been ridden. But do see our red ramblers," I added, as the tea party broke up. We moved beyond the latticed verandah to the roses.

"I must be going now, my dear," said emphatic Mrs. O[2] in a few moments. We had re-entered the house. She was the first to step into the hall and recoil with a little scream. There stood Bess with the long hall behind her! She put out her soft nose to me and slightly whinnied. The ladies turned pale. What couldn't a heavy horse like that do in a house?

I picked some pieces of cube sugar from the tea table, and with endearing words and the sugar, backed her step by step out the way she had come.

Bess, I explained to my friends was quite a pet. She used to get out of her paddock, step up on the back verandah, walk to the kitchen window and help herself to the pies Gowey had put out to cool. She was also very fond of jam and was particularly keen during preserving time, to obtain the first skimming.

On this particular day, the party had made us forget to give her some tit-bit, and she herself had discovered no pie. Regardless of her weight, she thought she would come right into the house to see whyfor. After that, Gowey was as careful to keep the outside doors shut as he was to bar his own quarters, for, needless to say, Bess's incursion into the house was regarded with absurd superstition.

I often drove Bess myself and one day, when coming home over the road lined with tall timber, she probably saved my life. She suddenly stopped dead and wouldn't budge an inch. I rarely used the whip, as the mere rattle of the whip in its socket was quite sufficient to make her go forward.

On this occasion, it was of no avail. So I used the whip several times; Bess only reared. I took out the cube of sugar I often carried in case I wished to catch her when in the paddock, as it was hard to secure her in the usual way, and Gowey or the garden man wasted much time in trying.

Just as I was going to get out to lead her with sugar, a huge tree fell across the road, so close that she could have touched it in a step or two. Bess reared terribly, but I had a good grip on the reins and finally quieted her.

I don't know what Gowey or Mrs. O would have thought of that. I never tried to put his pidgin English to the strain. It would only have worried him. Not, of course, that I had escaped, but how she had known.

Perhaps, if she had gone steadily forward, she would have driven the phaeton beyond the tree by the time it had fallen. It all happened in a split second, and as I measured with my eye the heavy crushing power of the long arms of the evergreen on either side (so much devastating strength), I figured that her second-sight, or whatever it was, saved my life.

CHAPTER 22

The Eastern Thakur

"Oh, Missa Hallison, come quick, come quick! See that man at the door!" Gowey was breathless from running upstairs.

"What's his name; what's he want, Gowey?"

"I no-no. Maybe he fool 'em Gowey. You heap savy," he said ingratiatingly, as if he feared I would insist on his returning to the door.

It was beyond the hour for a social call,[1] and as the Judge wasn't home yet, I decided to go rather than bother poor Gowey.

Well might he look surprised; for there stood a tall Oriental in Eastern clothes. We now have many Sikhs in B.C. (Singh is often part of their names, it being, I understand, a clan name indicating Lion). Then, they were a rarity, but I am not sure that he was a Sikh. Certainly he did not give me the sometimes arrogant stare which East Indians often now direct at B.C. white women.

His look was mild, benevolent and self effacing, yet of assured strength that caused me no anxiety. After a few polite remarks on his part I gathered that he was a passenger on Captain Salmon's steamer which periodically put into Departure Bay from San Francisco, and like other passengers had been rowed ashore to see the sights.

Whether the immigration regulations of that day allowed such short shore visits I do not know, but I did see some travellers from Captain Salmon's ship visiting the shore once in awhile. In any case, there was the East Indian, however he got ashore. He had the manner and dress of one of assured position. He asked when my husband would return. I told him any minute.

After he had admired the view and politely looked around, I invited him to wait in the library, but thanking me, he asked if he might sit in a camp chair on the porch. He had not sat there long, when my husband drove up. They went into the library together and talked a long time. In those days, ladies, especially wives, were not often told things.

My husband said that they talked on many subjects to while away the time before he returned to the boat. He was a Thakur or East Indian chief and surprised my husband by the wide range he had of various cultural subjects.

One point I think rather impressed my husband, more than another, and that was that he gave my husband a curious shaped jointed pipe and some sweet smelling resinous material which he suggested should be mixed with his tobacco.[2] But as he left he produced its exact duplicate from somewhere about his person, and began smoking it. As the pipe was long, its ready appearance was something of a surprise.

A dour Scottish acquaintance regarded the pipe and especially the resinous mixture with some suspicion; his theory was that the supposed Thakur was trying to introduce my husband to the use of some form of drug. But it was harmless enough and the unusual aroma lasted for years.

Gowey was equally astonished by the appearance of an Admiral of the Imperial Russian Navy who came to dinner some time later.

Mr. Justice J.F. McCreight, first premier of British Columbia.
BC Archives, A-01449.

He somewhat resembled the Thakur, with a long, full black beard, finely cut straight nose and noticeable eyes. Now and then men-of-war of the Russian navy were in Departure Bay, but the Admiral had come from his ship which was at Esquimalt. Other naval officers, British and Russian, called occasionally.

The Russian Admiral I have mentioned proved to be a most interesting guest and it was with much reluctance that we saw him go. My husband drove back with him to Nanaimo as he was holding a session of Court that night.[3]

When they had gone, I sat up until early morning, never dreaming that desperately anxious eyes were watching my windows for the light to go out. When my husband returned he was surprised that the lights were still on and that I had not retired.

After return from Court next day he told me that a naval deserter had been arrested who, in answer to close questioning, said that he had been hiding in a garden waiting several hours for the lights to go out in a house by the sea, as he planned to enter and get a suit of clothes there. If I had turned out the lights and gone to bed early!

Mr. Justice J.F. McCreight,[4] a tall, thin man not very impressive, called quite a few times. He had been prominent in a lodge of Freemasons in Nanaimo. He retired from the Bench and spent the remainder of his days in France. Although he had made some progress in Freemasonry he became an ardent Roman Catholic.

Mr. Justice H. Pering Pellew Crease[5] (later knighted), of the noted B.C. legal family of that name, called when on circuit. On the first occasion I had, unfortunately, spoken well of Gowey's cooking. At dessert time, Gowey brought in his masterpiece: a deep apple pie. These are made with a large cup in the centre to draw the juice. Portions of the attractively browned, deep flaky pastry were soon covered with thick whipped cream as only one's own cow in the country can provide. I thought the visiting Judge received his portion with some anticipation. But after the first taste, his expression changed in the most singular way.

By then I had tasted my serving. It was acrid with salt! Gowey — who used sugar generously — had mistaken salt for sugar. Our guest took it in good part; both jurists indulged in more than a judicial laugh. Gowey quickly substituted jellies and more whipped cream he had prepared for the evening. Later I found him almost in tears. He was really a good cook and this absurd mischance greatly humiliated him.

CHAPTER 23

Riding the Unfinished
Trans-Continental

When we came to Departure Bay the Esquimalt and Nanaimo Railway had just been finished. This line ran from Nanaimo to Victoria, about seventy miles. Several quite high trestles and a tunnel of fair length had to be traversed.

The railway to Esquimalt was completed March 29, 1888,[1] and was subsequently added to and later acquired by the C.P.R. We had been guests at the ceremonies of completion. My husband, however, as a barrister[2] on circuit in the Cariboo, had a more intimate view of parts of the transcontinental C.P.R.,[3] while it was building.

This railway was started by the Dominion government which spent millions on the survey work alone, between the years 1871 and 1878. In 1878 Sir John A. Macdonald, Prime Minister of Canada, had work started in B.C., through the Fraser Canyons, Yale to Kamloops. The old wagon road had been kept open for the continuous stream of stages and awkward wagon trains, each more than one hundred feet long. This necessity added much to the extreme difficulty of the task. There was heavy loss of life, due mainly to rock blasts and drownings. By 1883 the line had traversed the canyons. On November 7, 1885 the last spike completing the whole system was driven. In June 1886 regular transcontinental trains were operating.

As my husband was there while Mr. Onderdonk,[4] who had the contract for construction in the Cariboo, was working, and he sometimes rode on the hand cars used for inspecting the partly completed line, he wrote out for me his personal experiences of those historic railway days.

With some abridgement, they follow in this chapter and the next:

In 1883 while the Onderdonk contract with the Dominion Government for building the railway through the canyons was in full blast, I had occasion to go into the Nicola country to defend the interests of a man who was accused of killing an Indian.

The rails were laid to Port Moody and I thought I could go up by train from the coast to where the cantilever bridge now crosses the river in place of a basket on a wire cable.

It was February and bitterly cold, although I wore clothing warm enough for Victoria. At Port Moody (Vancouver) I found there was nothing definite about the coming of a train. Stating my object in the trip, I persuaded a railway official to put at my disposal a hand car. These are worked by hand by men on each side of a bar who work it up and down like a see-saw. Five men were given to me to pump it, and I was assured that if we started before daylight, we would reach Yale the same night to catch the stage which would leave Yale the next day.

The rails were frosty. It was very cold and in places we got the full force of the winter's wind blowing against us down the river. We could hardly move the car and had to take it off the rail and rest awhile behind an embankment away from the wind. Instead of reaching Yale that night, we only reached Harrison River. A Chinese had a restaurant there. After dinner I suggested that we proceed, tying a lantern on the hand car, but the men refused. It was so cold that I had the Chinaman put bedding on the dining table, and I slept on the table while the men sat around the stove, taking turns filling up the stove until daylight.

Next day we proceeded but slowly as there were gangs of workmen busy on the track, and the man in charge of the hand car would run over and talk to them before going on. We reached Emory's Bar[5] near Yale at dusk. The telegraph operator hailed our car and said: "Thank God, you've turned up with that hand car. You must push on to the big tunnel above Yale as quickly as you can. A number of men have been killed there by a rock slide."

There were still gruesome signs of the tragedy when we reached the slide. A repair gang, with the aid of our men, soon had the track clear. "How much do I owe you?" I asked the boss of the hand car crew when we reached Yale. "Not a cent, sir. You paid for all our meals and treated us well. I am truly sorry you missed the stage. As far as I am concerned, the trip has turned out alright as I have just had a wire to take the car into the big tunnel to-night."

"What about the men?" I asked.

"Oh, they're all right. They've had a free ride up and can easily get a job here."

The stage had gone. I looked up a man with a sleigh and two horses who said he would drive me that night so that I could catch the stage the next morning before it left Boston Bar. He urged me to put on more clothing and filled the sleigh with straw. I was ready to start; the price had been agreed upon.

"What are you waiting for?" I asked.

"Well, it's like this, Sir, I won't go unless you also agree to stop half way, so I can warm up and have supper. You'll have to pay for all I eat."

"Eat all you want," I replied, with a depressed look at his hungry appearance. I lay down on the bottom of the sleigh and was soon in a deep sleep.

I was being shaken awake. I looked around; there was nothing

In the 1880s the CPR was competing for freight with the
Cariboo Road. VPL 3263.

but a rough cabin. "Here is where I eat," the sleigh driver said as he turned to roughly awakening the owner.

My driver worked at high pressure and soon had the owner supplying a sumptuous table. He started with an oyster stew and went on until he had run up the bill to five dollars and a twenty-five cent cigar, then sat puffing by the stove.

"We'd better be getting on," I said at last.

"Look here, Sir," he suddenly exclaimed as if a bright idea had struck him. "I can fix things up better than catching that stage." "How?" I asked.

"I'll manage it so you won't catch the stage and you can sue them for damages!"

"That won't do at all. I must catch it."

Reluctantly he dragged himself into the sleigh and we were off. We shot into Boston bar in a short while. The stage horses were just being put into the shafts. I quickly entered the stage. It was bitterly cold. In some places the road was bare of snow but covered with ice. The driver would then push down the brake, hold it down with his foot and drive the horses down hill as fast as they could go, the stage swaying about so much that any moment I thought it would leave the road and roll over the cliff.

"You are not half protected from the cold," I was told at Lytton. "Get off your boots, put on three or four pair of sox and get 'Arctics'."

When I had done that, it was not easy to move and I was still cold. I had also become rather nervous about the stage slipping and rolling about.

"You must get off and put the rough lock on the wheels," I said at last.

"Then you'll have to hold the horses," he countered.

"No I won't."

"What am I to do then?" he asked.

"Fasten your brake down, tie the reins to it and I'll get out till you've put the rough lock on." This he did. Passing Spence's Bridge, we drove on the Nicola River which was frozen hard.

I spent several days and nights on the enquiry as to my client's supposed connection with the murder, with results satisfactory to him. My client then returned with me in the sleigh. Just as we started there was an eerie sighing in the air. The snow began to thaw and icicles to drip. It was the Chinook.[6] Almost instantly, where we had before driven on solid ice, there was slushy ice water to the knees of our horses. About three miles from Spence's Bridge the snow was so far gone that we had to get out of the sleigh and walk.

When I arrived at Spence's Bridge, I could not hire a vehicle of any kind, as the drivers were afraid of boulders falling, loosened by the sudden thaw. Finally I located Mr. Onderdonk, brother of the contractor of the railway, and he let me have his buggy as far as Lytton. I was to have it driven back to him and to pay for all damages, if any.

At Lytton I got an express wagon and went as far as Skuse's Flat where they had a wire and basket to pass one over the river. When I arrived a gale was blowing and the basket was violently swaying to and fro. I decided not to try it. I planned to get an Indian or a Chinaman to carry planks and place them over cracks in the ice of the river, but learned that the train would not pass for three days.

The inn keeper wouldn't hire out his horses, so I gave my bag to an Indian. "Come along," I said. He grunted and we started off together on foot, I intending to go to an Indian camp and get an Indian to carry the valise on one horse and I ride another. But before I could carry out my purpose, I met a teamster with a heavy freight wagon. He asked me when the train would be along. I told him I had heard that it would not be for three days.

He was disgusted as he had been waiting for several days and no train. I got him to take me in his empty wagon to Kanaka Bar.

When we arrived, there was not even an Indian pony, so I said, "You'd better take me on to Jackass Mountain."

"Well, I'll do it on one condition," he answered reluctantly. "And that is: if you give me your word that when we get there you won't ask me to take you further!"

"All right." He drove me to Jackass Mountain and left me there. I could find only one Indian pony. I left my valise to be forwarded whenever the man could do so, and started off on the pony. When I had reached a long way down the mountain, I met with a cattleman I knew and asked him where the train was.

"I don't know. I left Yale very early this morning on horse back. It left at the same time but I've beaten it so far."

A little further down the mountain, I heard the train whistle on the other side of the river. It was now dark as pitch; the snow was deep and soft. Suddenly I saw a light near the road. When I reached the house I heard a row within. I entered and saw many Indians in the crowd. All had become silent. I asked the bar keeper to get me an Indian who would accompany me to Boston Bar and who would take my horse back to Jackass Mountain next day.

"Certainly," he answered.

"I also want a plug of tobacco."

"All right, here you are."

"Now I want you to cut up the plug into several pieces," I said. He did so, and seemed to be glad to get rid of me.

I rode on, the Indian on foot piloting me in the dark. Occasionally the Indian would slip in the snow and give a very dissatisfied grunt. I was ready for that with a piece of the plug; whenever he got up, I would give him one, and in this way I kept up his morale.

I spent the night at Boston Bar and sent the pony back by the Indian to Jackass Mountain in the morning. I had felt quite certain to get a conveyance at Boston Bar to take me to Yale. But the proprietor would not rent me one, being afraid that the horses might be injured by falling stones or slides in the sudden thaw brought by the Chinook wind.

Going to an express stable I asked the man in charge to take me to Yale. He refused, saying they were stage horses and he would lose his job if he used them for any other purpose.

I told him the purpose of my trip; this aroused his interest. "I'll take you across the suspension bridge and put you down at Ten Mule Flat."

I demurred for fear of his losing his job but he insisted. He left me standing on the railway track wondering what to do next.

There were some shacks about, apparently all deserted. A man came out of one, looked hard at me, and said: "Are you hungry?"

"Yes," I replied.

"Come in here." I went into his shack and he cooked some ham and eggs and made me some coffee. After the meal, I was wondering if he would be offended if I offered pay. I thought I had better. He was quite astonished at my offer and refused. He had given me this meal thinking he was helping out a broken tramp, as appearances were not in my favour.

I stood by the track, preparing to signal the train, when the Superintendent of Police came up in a sleigh. He was surprised to see me there and drove me to Yale in his sleigh. At least he tried to, for thanks to the Chinook, the road was without snow most of the way. We often had to get out and walk.

Having come up from Port Moody on a hand car I tried to return that way, but the railway men scuttled the idea. The Superintendent of the line came up and agreed, but added, "Why not go on the early morning train?" This I did. He gave me a pass, and in this way, riding in the caboose, I reached Port Moody, having my meal, on the suggestion of the Superintendent, in the dining car used by the trail hands.

The track was not yet ballasted properly and three times the cars got off the tracks. It took us eighteen hours to get from Yale to Port Moody. The regular boat to Victoria had gone when we arrived!

CHAPTER 24

Early Water Rights

(further material from the unpublished memoirs of my husband)

I subsequently took in Lillooet as part of my circuit as Judge of the Cariboo-Lillooet districts. Lillooet, or Cayoosh, is on the west bank of the Fraser. Back of it lies the steep Cayoosh Creek canyon and beyond, Seton Lake. In 1858 a trail had been opened through Harrison, Lillooet, Anderson and Seton Lakes[1] to avoid the Fraser Canyon.

Before the wagon road was built, supplies went by mule train up the old Fur Brigade Trail from Yale to Boston Bar, and from there over Jackass Mountain to Lytton and Lillooet. When I travelled there the place was reached by trail from Lytton or by coming south from Clinton over immense Pavilion Mountain.[2] To get there I found that the road zig-zagged up from the old Harrison-Lillooet Road to a splendid road to the top of Pavilion Mountain.

I was surprised to find there, at an altitude of between 4,000 and 5,000 feet above sea level, a large rolling plateau. There were a number of farms on it, all irrigated. There was constant strife between the farmers as to the use of water. The questions coming before me caused me many an hour of anxious thought as well as hard exploration over these lands, climbing and sliding down the sides of the mountain till I got to understand the situation.

Fortunately I was then able to bring to an end their useless litigation and hard swearing before me.

(I here insert a letter to my husband from the Justices of the Supreme Court at the capital, by the hand of the Hon. Mr. Justice J.H. Gray, addressed to Judge Harrison at Clinton)

SUPREME COURT
BRITISH COLUMBIA

Victoria August 1, 1886

My Dear Harrison,

I send you the report of the celebrated Judgement in California on the question of Riparian rights. Thornton, who concurred in its conclusions, told me himself he considered it as sound as if it came from Westminster Hall. At any rate, I am sure it contains all the old law on the subject and will prove to us a most valuable compendium should any future case arise in this Province. I fancy the only difference between our own conclusions in the Martell case and that judgement, will be found in the application of our Local Statutes. I have not had time to examine it at all and speak more from what I heard of it in San Francisco.

Now as I wish it for all our Judges, not myself alone, I think if you have time it would be of great advantage to cut it up in columns and paste it in contiguous pages, in an ordinary portable sized copy or form book, leaving a margin, to note upon — a good margin. And I wish you would put your own observations, indicating the differences resulting from the application of our local statutes. Foolscap cut about the size of the ordinary law reports would be most convenient to carry — so that the Judge could take it with him whenever he learns that a case relative to Riparian rights is likely to arise on the Circuit which he takes.

It may give a little trouble, but I think you have a most happy faculty in book arrangement as well as a logical power of analysis. I attempt the latter a little sometimes but always break down at the former. So you will be doing us all a Public good if you will take hold. Write me when you have time how you like it.

After driving across this plateau, the road zig-zagged down the mountain side to Lillooet. As I descended to the Fraser towards Lillooet I saw three benches or steppes. One could easily imagine that at some time, when at the height of the highest steppe, the Fraser River must have run through a gap through the mountains at Lillooet and thence down to the present Harrison River. From a distance, the mountain sides at each side of this gap look as perpendicular as if cut out by the hand of man through the solid rock.

I left Clinton (about 3,000 feet above sea level), drove through the Cut-off Valley, climbed to some 4,500 feet above sea level, then descended Pavilion Mountain. I drove along the left bank of the river, ever descending until I reached Lillooet, only some 840 feet above sea level.

On the way there, there was a ditch and flume eight or nine miles long, built by the miners to carry water to mine a flat just opposite Lillooet. Passing Fountain,[3] where excellent grapes are grown, I arrived at the ferry to cross the Fraser. I drove onto the large boat on which were other horses and vehicles, then following a wire cable,[4] the ferry moved across the river by the force of the current.

Lillooet always struck me as an unusual looking place because the houses, almost without exception, had been built of adobe, that is, blocks of sun-dried clay, shaped like bricks but much larger. In the summer, it was easy to fancy oneself in old Southern California or Mexico. At the Court House, built in 1860, the chimney made of this adobe, was still intact and but little affected even where exposed to the weather.

The climate there is delightful. Miners mining for gold,[5] work in the open at the beginning of December. Beans, tomatoes, peanuts, melons, grapes and other fruits flourished and ripened on the trees, bushes and vines. On making a Circuit through the country, I found that the farmers and cattle men were all making a good liv-

Mule train in the Cariboo (1860–1880). BC Archives, E-05563.

ing, but the mines in the Cariboo had fallen off in their yield of gold and the population had consequently become less. It would not pay to work the poorer class of diggings as the cost of transportation and living was too high. To work the deep ground required more capital than could be raised in the country.

But the hopes of all were centred on successfully controlling the waters of Harvey Creek[6] and reaching bed rock there. There was every prospect of success as the work was in the hands of the best and most experienced miners. Each day was being looked forward to, as it might bring the news of a great wash-up of gold.

To reach Harvey Creek, it was necessary to travel over mountain trails on foot or on horseback. A party of four of us set out to make the rounds of the various claims in the country between Barkerville and the forks of the Quesnel. We came to the claim of which so much was expected, called the "Cosmopolitan."

They did their best to get me to stay over, asserting that everything was in perfect running order; thousands of dollars of gold was in sight; the wash up would come any day now. Nearby I met a miner who was shepherding his claim, in other words, holding onto it, without any real development. He was extremely hard up; all his hopes were centred on a successful clean up in the promising claim next door.

We did not wait for the promised development but went on to the Forks.[7] Here was quite a village, with houses, stores, men, women and children, but all Chinese, except the Government Agent, his wife and their two sons. The white miners had abandoned the place long since.

Pushing on over the trails we passed a caribou within a few feet of us. It stood staring at each one of us, until we four had ridden past. This caribou, although it was a fine, large, noble-looking animal, lacked the traditional horns and was no doubt a female.

At last we arrived back at Barkerville. We leaped from our horses and the first thing we asked was, "How about the Cosmopolitan?" There had been a mishap at the workings — only a temporary setback, they said. But later it proved that all the work and money spent on the Cosmopolitan at Harvey Creek had been expended in vain. The poor miner who had been holding on, expecting that his neighbour's success would give his own claim a high value, was so disappointed that he committed suicide.

CHAPTER 25

The Finding of the Strange Disk

"**M**y Lord" (for my husband had been presiding at the Assizes and also as a Supreme Court Judge with full powers), "may I now give you the full particulars you desired of the ancient disk I told you about in Lillooet on your last Circuit?" In solemn tones and carefully chosen words, Ah Quan, the Chinese Court Interpreter, leaned forward in a rather tense manner.

"Most certainly, Ah Quan; I have been looking forward to this and am all attention." Court had closed for the weekend and there were no outstanding incidental matters.

Ah Quan had travelled far since the last meeting and this was the first opportunity for an extended talk. "My cousin of the Chew Kung Tong" (Chinese Freemasons) "was near Hazelton[1] prospecting for gold. You know there is not much to be done there now. He decided to explore in new territory. You know the Indian medicine men about there have long declared a very — er, extensive taboo over the whole territory? It is really a vast unknown land, Judge

Hallison, but you know this better than I, Sir, anything I might say further would be —" Ah Quan made a slight effort and "adscititious" came out complete. Ah Quan had painstakingly acquired many exact English words but some of them seemed to have come from Dr. Johnson's Dictionary.[2]

The Judge was too interested to even faintly smile. He merely lit another self-rolled cigarette and nodded. He had long heard of the queer Indian village in the remote highlands far beyond Barkerville, beyond Hazelton even. It was called Kispiox:[3] The-Village-Of-The-People-Who-Hid. Situated on the dark, full-bodied Skeena River, it was noted for its singular and rather sinister looking totem poles. He also recalled that a vast region back and beyond had long been strictly verboten to all Indians, not by the whiteman but by the stern orders of the dour, black-eyed medicine men.

Just why it was a forbidden area, no whiteman seemed to know. There was a "Forbidden Plateau"[4] on Vancouver Island, altitude about 7,000 feet above sea level but, in comparison, it was a small area. This was limitless wilderness. Speculation was to the effect that it must be fabulously rich in gold and the witch doctors wanted to keep the area for themselves, but none of them showed signs of secret wealth.

Ah Quan continued, "Although the Indians warned my cousin that he must not go into that land, he, with a few friends, decided to do so. They wandered some time and saw nothing unusual; just the same rugged grandeur and colossal work of nature we know so well elsewhere in the interior. Then, one day, after long aimless wandering, my cousins came to a branch of the Skeena or of the Peace River;[5] they could not, of course, be sure. Camped there, they washed gravel in the hope of finding large gold nuggets, which, as you know, can sometimes be easily found. A bit beyond the high water mark of the stream — for it was then little more than a stream — they noted the basin caused by the fall of an exceptionally large tree. Making a fire in the space left by the main roots in the fall, they dug a bit to clear the spot. Then it was that they hit something hard."

"A stone, of course," commented the Judge a trifle impatiently.

"No, your Honour, not exactly. It was the cover of a stone jar."

"A stone jar?"

"Yes, first its lid, covered with hieroglyphics and then the full jar, equally marked in the same way."

"Was it empty?"

"No Sir, it was full. Full, not of gold nuggets as some might hope, but of ancient disks — sixty-four of them. Ancient Chinese it seemed to be, so ancient that none of my cousins could even identify the ideographs, although some of the design was suggestive. While much discussion of this discovery was in progress, an Indian appeared. As we know, there are many tribes of Indians in the Province, and in the interior some markedly differ from those by sea level. But here was an Indian more different than any my cousins had seen. Not of course as a whiteman, but different just the same. One of my cousins held up a disk. 'You sabbe?' he asked, trying several dialects. At last the stranger seemed to understand, either the dialect or the movement that accompanied it."

"What then?" asked my husband, hoping to speed up the interpreter.

"Something very remarkable, Sir. This strange Indian said: 'You and me — blood brothers. You and me had the same ancient ones. They come from over there — way far — big canoe.' And he stretched to his limit towards my flowery land. But my cousins did not believe. Who believes all the Indian say? They are a people of fancy, who with fancy, people the wilds. But sometimes it is not fancy — it is truth they say but in a different way. One of my cousins I think, smile. He like gold, not fancy. Then the Indian no like. 'Our fathers bring this and this along, blood brothers,' and as sure proof to my cousins, he brought forth from a blanket pack some of the bright religious vessels of Northern Buddhism.[6] My cousins are not Buddhists but one of them know something of that. He saw the bell and dorje,[7] censers for incense and similar things. They might have come from Lhasa or from Peking.

"They were not the gold my cousins were looking for — but all were so surprised and intent they did not see the shadow, until my cousin Pong look up. A medicine man was looking at him with the bad eye. Very bad. He said nothing to my cousins, but he grunted to the Indian — made signs — and with much fear he covers up those things, and not look at my cousins any more — but see just the eyes of that witch doctor. Him very scare," Quan concluded in pidgin English.

"Most remarkable, Quan. Most remarkable; though not very surprising to me. But what happened to your cousins then?"

"Nothing happened, Sir. They were alone as before — that is all. 'When we get to Barkerville, they will not believe,' said one of my cousins. 'But we have these,' said Pong, as he poured the disks back and forth from the rare stone jar.

"In the course of the season, my cousins got back to their tong in Victoria. The disks were soon all distributed among our people; no one could read them or be sure how old they were, but they were held to be precious.

"Permit me the honour of giving you one, Judge Hallison; no one else of your race has its like from that ancient stone jar." Ah Quan would not hear of refusal.

He had previously, on an occasion, shown the signs of Chinese Freemasonry, and as my husband readily understood them, he felt he was giving the disk into no alien hand. Some of the companion disks had been sent to China. Others had been secretly shown among Chinatown "cousins" and as virtues were ascribed by some to the possession of the disks, they were actually copied by local Chinese jewelers, so that the modern imitations confused the investigation into their age somewhat, for more often than not, a copy and not an original got into the hands of the researcher, the originals being kept very privately about the person or in private rooms.

However the disk of which I now have clear photographs, did come from the ancient stone jar in the remote place described and with the Indian comment. This was certified as true by the Court Interpreter who had long been known as a highly trustworthy man. The photographs show a metal band around the disk. This was

The disk (both sides) with ancient Chinese lettering.
Courtesy of L. Wilson.

added to strengthen the disk, as it was aged and had a crack running through the centre, which is clearly to be discerned in the picture.

Questions to China brought the answer that such disks had not been made for a very long time; these particular ones had probably been made prior to the Christian era, although they might have been of about the time of Atisha[8] in Tibet.

Several white experts have given their opinions, writing from the leading institutions on the continent. The translations, as independently given, pretty generally agree, in the essentials. But if it is possible to identify the actual issue of the disk, it has not yet been done, and therefore doubt as to its age remains. All agree that it must be several centuries old at the least. How long it has been in British Columbia is another question and so is one relating to how and when it came.

Taking the Indian's story at its face value, the disks might have been brought over from the Orient anywhere from before the Christian era up to about A.D. 1500 or 1600. It is possible, of course, that all the experts are incorrect in some important particular as to the wording on the disk. But that is not probable; the translations as given by distinguished Orientalists are as follows.

CHAPTER 26

Translations of the Disk?

T he first translation was given as follows:

On one side: The eight diagrams from the *Book of Changes*[1] with the names in ancient Chinese characters.

On the other side: "The Heaven is round while the earth is square." Then follows six musical rules and nine mathematical formulas in between, with the following as an order rather than an invocation: "Wherever the God of Charms goes, all evil spirits shall disappear."

The translator added the comment: "This is a charm of the Taoists.[2] The inscriptions on the medallion are of *very ancient* Chinese and Persian origin."

Taoism is the name given to the philosophy of Lao-tze.[3] Lao-tze was a great sage, saint and philosopher who preceded Confucius.[4] Like the teaching attributed to other Oriental sages, some of his scriptures are said to be understandable only through having a key volume.

There have long been Chinese schools of the mysticism of Lao-tze, their ascetic monks being known for their reticence. In Japan, priest-mystics of this sect are known as Yamaboosis, or "hermit brothers," as sometimes translated. They are also said to be skilled at healing and making charms and amulets. A work[5] in the last quarter of the last century gave striking instances of their supposed powers when dealing with certain individuals.

The second translator said that the disk contained an Emperor's order to his subjects to keep the law of six rules and nine chapters. This, the translator thought, referred to a fundamental belief of Kwas philosophy.

The third translator wrote that one side of the disk bore the eight lucky symbols, known as the PA QUA, with the Chinese equivalents. On the obverse was a long inscription reading thus: "Tai Shang's charm says: Heaven is round and earth is square." Then are references to the Six Rules and the Nine Regulations. And there is this saying: "Wherever the spirit of this charm shall visit, all devils shall be exterminated. Let this immediate command be carried out with all dispatch."

A fourth translator says that one side gives eight Trigrams but that "the arrangements as a whole is not orthodox."

Turning it over, he rendered the inscriptions thus:

"The *Mighty Spell* says: 'Heaven is round, Earth is square; the Six Notes and the Nine Sections tally.' Wherever good spirits come, ten thousand evil spirits will depart as speedily as Lu Ling (acting under) imperial orders." He observed also that the *Mighty Spell* is probably a Taoist book or document of some sort. The above quotation from it is based on the most general and fundamental concept in Chinese philosophy, namely, *yang* and *yin*, the two principles from whose interaction the phenomenal universe has arisen. The literal meaning of the word *yang* is "clear"; of the word *yin*, "obscure"; and the two together constitute a "pair of opposites." He remarked that the inevitable characteristic is that neither member of the pair can be understood independently of the other. Typical pairs of opposites are: light and dark; hard and soft; high and low; good and bad etc., and by extension, day and night, male and female; heaven and earth; round and square; North and South, etc. In each of these pairs, the first member is characterized as *yang;* the second as *yin,* which, in turn, may be symbolized by the trigrams

————————
————————   and   ———— ————   respectively."
————————   ———— ————

Obviously such a system of terminology may be expanded indefinitely and applied to any aspect of phenomenal existence.

A fifth student of these subjects commented:

"This disk is certainly a Chinese talisman and might have been brought over to B.C. by Buddhist priests or it is more likely still to be pre-Buddhistic as it is a Taoist charm. Lao-tze lived in the later period of the Chou Dynasty.[6] It would be interesting to know whether these and other relics found in British Columbia of Chinese origin belonged to that period or whether they were brought over at a later date by Buddhists.

"The symbology of numbers has a great deal of meaning in China and one finds 3 and 9 constantly recurring in Chinese buildings, etc. The number 8 (PA in Chinese) is often recurring in numbers of temples. Eight is a symbol of entrance into a new state of 'regeneration.' Note, there were 64 (8^2) discs in the stone jar found by the Chinese. Also, one side of the disc shows 8 diagrams from the *Book of Changes.*

"The other side seems to be a formula built up on the numbers 3 and 9. The language 'Heaven is round' etc. is typically Taoist.

"With regard to the numbers 3 and 9: 3 is the number of perfection — The Higher Triad[7] — and 9 (3^2) is the attainment of perfection — Initiation.

"I am reminded in these numbers of the Temple of Heaven[8] in Peking which is supposed to have been built in the Ming dynasty[9] (14th century). The temple itself is built with three cone-shaped circular roofs, with mosaic blue pottery tiles topped by a golden ball. The temple stands on a white marble circular base with three tiers of stairs leading up to it. Three plus three, or three roofs plus three terraces.

"South of the Temple of Heaven is the famous circular marble altar (used by the Manchus[10] for sacrifices to Heaven), 210 feet across and open to the sky. Built in an ascending marble stair in three tiers or terraces of nine steps each tier. The stairs are placed to face the four corners of the Earth thus dividing or cutting the circle into four divisions like a cross.

"Compare this with the Chinese talisman: six rules and nine formulas or 'Heaven is round and Earth is square.' This, clearly, would symbolize Spirit and Matter. 'Heaven' is symbolized in the blue temple with the number three repeated, and the 'Earth', the altar with its three tiers crossed by the four flights of stairs of nine steps."

Then, I have heard that the "Heaven of Mind" is a Chinese expression when referring to Universal ideation on the mundane plane and *"Tien-Sin"* when referring to the abstract, subjective, ideal heaven.

But I think the reader will agree that a satisfactory translation has not yet been given; nor has the when, how and why been answered. My guess is that there will yet be discovered in British Columbia many more interesting relics of a long unknown past, and even if it be decided that the first discoverer was not Hoei-shin, a Buddhist monk of 499 AD.

The legend of Hoei-shin's visit to B.C. and other parts of Western America, under the name of Fusang, has gained some credit in recent years. So much so that the Vancouver artist John Delisle Parker[11] painted a rather striking canvas of his junk, the "Tai Shan," anchored off Nootka on the West Coast of Vancouver Island, on his supposed visit to spread Buddhism, ca. 499 AD in Western America.

CHAPTER 27

All the Families Were Not Large

I t is generally supposed that all the pioneers had large families; this was not so in our case.

When I returned to Teignmouth for short visits, I found that the elder of my two brothers had been making headway in engineering. He had some success with ships in B.C. at the turn of the century. For instance, there was the *H.M.S. Amphion*. In 1902 this was the flagship of the Royal Navy at Esquimalt and it was the pride of the station. The warship was bringing Lord and Lady Dufferin, when in a dense fog it ran on the rocks near Plumper Pass and was quite badly damaged. My brother Bagster[1] received the contract for steel plating, and I see by an item in my book that he had put all of 78,640 lbs. of new steel plating into the ship.

This brother married the niece[2] of a B.C. financier, Mr. Flummerfelt, on a visit to her uncle from Ontario. They purchased two acres on the Gorge Road and engaged Mr. Soule, an early architect, to build them a large house there. The ceilings were twelve feet high; such was the style then. There was ample stabling for the swift

Annette Seabrook, at age twenty-eight, sister of Eunice Harrison.
Courtesy of L. Wilson.

horses he kept and quarters for the Chinese house and garden
boys. Later, he and his wife and their family of two moved to the
States, where he had success with a number of practical inventions.

My younger brother Ivan[3] went to the Klondike,[4] and found
gold; he then purchased a ranch on Galiano Island. He married
the widow of a curate, the daughter of an Anglican clergyman.
Their daughter has, in turn, become an Anglican missionary and
has a religious caravan on the far reaches of the Peace River.

I had one sister, Annette, who we all conceded was the beauty of our family of four. She had golden hair, gray-blue eyes, rather classical features and a voice of unusual and pleasing inflection — a characteristic recalled by strangers and mentioned to me by those who did not know I was related, long after her premature death. In height she was not more than five foot-two, with a trim figure and feet that took a size two and one-half shoe.

Mother took her to Boston, New York and Chicago to study art and music for two years, which she did with some success; her pastorals in oil and portraits were exhibited. A local paper called her, without flattery, the Rosa Bonheur[5] of B.C. But soon after returning from New York she seemed more interested in acting the Gibson Girl[6] to the life.

I never see one of the Harrison Fisher[7] driving girl pictures without recalling my sister. Her smart handling of Jacob and the jaunty high-swung dog cart typified her. Everything about the equipage had to be just so. One of the bothers of mother's patient garden man was the shine of the brass fittings (she had discarded the nickel) and the state he had to keep his clothes in on those days when he sat back-to-back to her, in order to get down to fetch parcels on shopping excursions.

My sister drove with a swish that met the approval of the registered and well trained carriage dog that invariably accompanied the shining equipage at the correct distance.

On June 27, 1899 my sister left Teignmouth to marry Charles A. Godson in the same church I had visited for a like purpose many years before. Mr. Godson was of a well-known Toronto family; out West, he batched for awhile with the late Peter Secord Lampman (subsequently His Honour Judge Lampman)[8] in Victoria, then went to Vancouver. In Vancouver, Mr. Godson became a prominent business man, owning theatres and concerns.

My sister died in 1916 and her husband in 1926. They left one child, a daughter, who married a Vancouver lawyer.

CHAPTER 28

The Case of
the Crooked House

The three horse-drawn trucks had reached the crest of the hill alright and the six men doggedly spent half the Indian summer day walking back and forth, perspiring, as they unloaded time and again.

At last the twelve rooms of the newly finished house on the high land back of Nanaimo were sufficiently stuffed with furniture, plus an overflow into two rooms in the basement. I had been rather disconcerted trying to locate the front door, and at last was unable to find a suitable entry at all.

Although prepared to be well pleased and not at first daunted by the tacky varnish everywhere, I met with depressing things: a roof lower than plan, some walls crooked, new plaster cracked, and stains and marks on every side. No traps to some pipes and around them rude gaps. No boiler, no drains, no cesspits, no outbuildings — as if they were never in the building contract.

While we were still trying to feel pleased, Jim Chong (Gowey had gone to China on a trip) lit fires and nearly smoked us out. Nor could most of the smokey chimneys be remedied. Then we also discovered that the roof was upheld by a crooked brace and that an iron rod practically held the house together. In short, the house was so far from specifications that the many divergencies could not be remedied. It was plain that not only our discomfort would continue, but that the drainage situation would prove dangerous.

Even more than a half century ago, a house should have been nearer its contract specifications, and certainly the house at Departure Bay had been well built. I pointed all these things out to the builder, as he walked with me from room to room on inspection. He maintained a dour silence.

When we finally arrived upstairs in the large school room[1] whose admittedly good plate glass windows gave a fine view of Nanaimo and its harbour, but which, at the moment let in an ominous whiff of sewage, I concluded with a reference to the smell.

"I ha' smelled wurst in Glesga' and ha' been thro mony a' mair crook'd dour way. A' wheel," he added, as he glanced at the uninhabited neighbourhood, "tis a bra' place to practise the bag pipes."

I see in my record book of that day that there was a realty boom in Nanaimo at the time, and by some mutual compromise we were able to be quit of the place. So after three weeks, we packed up again and left, glad to be back at Departure Bay.

Clive Phillips-Wolley[2] (later knighted) offered us a place of his at one time, but we finally decided to go to Victoria. This was my first meeting with Captain Phillips-Wolley, but my husband already knew him. He became quite a figure on the island, and has, I believe, won a permanent place in Canadian letters.

Captain Phillips-Wolley had been called to the Bar by the Middle Temple, London, but inheriting large properties in England, he led a rather retired life until he decided to go overseas. After arriving in B.C. he became an inspector of mining districts in 1896, and for awhile owned and published the *Nelson Miner.*

He was decidedly "ultra" — an extreme Imperialist whose restless pen was ever working for the cause and the Navy League of which he was president. At the time of the Russo-Japanese War,[3] he (like my husband) was an ardent supporter of Russia and prophesied that trouble would come from encouraging and sympathising with Japan. Sir Clive's political ideas generally were not acceptable to Western Canadians, but in this particular, at least, he proved a true prophet.

After some further time at Departure Bay, we went to Victoria. Looking for a place convenient to Corrig College, the Collegiate School and Angela College, we found a large house and acreage with the usual outbuildings, not far from where the late Senator William John Macdonald had his home, "Armadale" (later an apartment house).

The place was flanked by a fine row of tall poplars (later a concrete sidewalk), a thick holly hedge twelve feet high, yielding an abundance of red berries, single holly trees equally rich, ash, laburnum and hawthorn.

The spacious grounds included roomy tennis courts, and its then suburban location is shown by the Judge having gone into a tennis court one day near the glass conservatory and impulsively shooting a raccoon out of a tree. The property has long been citified and the grounds were, years ago, cut up out of all recognition. We lived at the place while our house on Harrison Street was building.

CHAPTER 29

The New Parliament Buildings[1]
and the New Court House

B arges moving past the mouth of Departure Bay filled with huge granite blocks, told of the construction of the new Parliament buildings at Victoria. A new Court House was building at Nanaimo at about the same time.

Mr. Francis Mawson Rattenbury[2] who designed the former also had the latter in hand. As Judge of the County, my husband (who sometimes also held Court in Victoria) was several times consulted by Mr. Rattenbury as to the accommodation needed, etc. My husband dabbled a bit in architecture and, when a youth, might have followed that profession in San Francisco. It seems quite a jump to law, although Blackstone[3] was at first an advanced student of architecture. Mr. Rattenbury was glad to find that the Judge had a natural interest in the subject.

The Nanaimo Court House, of handsome stone, became one of the finest on the coast. In 1897 when it was finished, it included, besides a spacious Court room, a Barrister's robing room, a law

Rattenbury's Nanaimo Court House, 1896.
Courtesy of Nanaimo Museum.

library, a witnesses' waiting room, a room for Crown Counsel and a room for the Judge's private chambers.

Mr. Rattenbury, after exhibiting in the Royal Academy in England in 1891, had come to Canada and settled at Vancouver in 1892. He designed the new Parliament buildings in Victoria, in 1893.

The very formal ceremonies at the opening of the new buildings were held in 1898. It was a splendid occasion of glittering uniforms, stylish dresses, bands, choirs and immense crowds.

Strange to say no photograph seemed to exist of the scene within the chamber. While going through my many files I was happy to

Opening of B.C. Legislature in the new Rattenbury building, 1898.
BC Archives, A-02645.

find one.[4] No one, I suppose, can be sure how such photographs will turn out; this picture is only a little blurry as to some faces among the spectators. Otherwise it is remarkably clear.

Lieutenant-Governor McInnes[5] is seated as the King's representative. My husband, wearing legal wig and the judicial robe, clearly appears nearby and I have the adjoining position. Aside from Bishop Hills I cannot recognize the other people since many face the other way. My husband and I, like the Lieutenant-Governor and a few others, are facing those on the floor of the House. Among the latter, one notes here and there a legal gown and barrister's wig, for at this date the legal wig is still being worn in B.C. Courts.

This large picture that was evidently given us at that time, I sent to the Archives, Parliament Buildings, Victoria, along with other material. But I had a copy made for the Judge Harrison biographical collection and it is quite clear also.

In addition to regular judicial duties as County Court Judge, my husband was a Local Judge of the Supreme Court with full powers as such within his judicial district. A clipping before me from a daily of the period is headed: "AN IMPOSING CEREMONY: Judges Bole[6] and Harrison Sworn in as Local Supreme Court Judges, Yesterday. Justice McCreight Administers the Oath of Office to Two Well Known Men." In the course of 51 lines of description, it remarks: "Before October 1889, the power of swearing in officers under the Federal Government was vested in two Supreme Court Judges only — the Chief Justice, and Mr. Justice Crease.[7] But since that time the Commission has been extended to all judges of the Court. The two gentlemen upon whom the honor was conferred yesterday are both so well known that a sketch of their careers would be almost superfluous."

My husband also re-drew and adapted English Acts for use in B.C. and drew some himself. In this connection, he received the following letter from the Attorney General of B.C.:

ATTORNEY-GENERAL'S OFFICE,
January 25, 1896

To Hon. Judge Harrison

. . . You will observe reference to your name in the report itself as having contributed valuable assistance in drafting several acts. You will perceive your work in its entirety in the Interpretation Act, Affidavits, Agents, Agriculture, Alien, Apprentices, Arbitration, Creditors' Trust Deeds and the Acts relating to Associations; these are printed just as you drafted them. The remaining statutes drawn by you were the Bill of Sale, Bail, Bond, Cattle Farming, Cattle Ranges, and Sheriff's Acts.

Lord Herschell[8] had some correspondence with my husband in connection with the uniformity of laws in the English-speaking parts of the British empire. He gave his opinion, as requested on several occasions, and received thanks. (Some of the material on this subject is on page 45 and 46 of the MS book mentioned).

The late Chief Justice Archer Martin,[9] who, before his recent death, had been some forty years on the Bench in B.C., and whose decisions are known and appreciated far and wide, wrote the following letter to my husband. I give it *in extenso* as an illustration of the historical foresight of Mr. Justice Martin, as, since it was written in 1902, the importance of preserving such material as he refers to is now fully recognized:

THE SUPREME COURT OF
BRITISH COLUMBIA
LAW COURTS
VICTORIA B.C.

3rd January 1902

My dear Judge —

When I was in Nanaimo the other day I noticed in the bureau in the corner of the Judges' Room among a pile of old papers and gazettes &c. (apparently destined for the waste paper basket) two old pamphlets relating to the Crown lands of Vancouver Island which I ventured to take for the purpose of glancing through them, as I take an historic interest in the affairs of this Western country, as you may have gathered from my book on the Hudson's Bay Company. It occurs to me that perhaps they belong to you, and if so I shall of course return them to you; but if you have no particular use for them I should be glad to purchase them from you at any reasonable figure, because I have a very large collection of works relating to British Columbia and "all is fish that comes to my net" in the way of adding to it even though now such matters are of no general importance or interest.

Hoping you are enjoying good health and wishing you the Compliments of the Season.

Believe me,
Very faithfully yours
Archer Martin

I might add that on a number of occasions my husband was named with Chief Justice Sir Matthew Baillie Begbie, among other Judges, a "Justice of Our Lady the Queen" in the Commissions of Judges on the Assizes, and he held trials under such Commissions.

The significance of that will be especially appreciated by lawyers (*vide* "Vancouver's First Assize" 1892, *The Advocate*, Vancouver, B.C., December 1943, p. 189 et seq.)

CHAPTER 30

Camps

The quiet of the afternoon was interrupted by the swish of phaeton wheels over our front drive, with the up-rush spray of small stones to the fender, as the brake was suddenly applied.

And then Bagster called out, "Hello Eunice! Have you a free afternoon? Then get your hat and cloak and come with me!" There was no resisting my brother in that infectious mood.

But where was he driving? I asked, after we had gone beyond the city limits. Soon I recognised Cordova Bay — more distant then, it seemed, and certainly fringed by more forest.

We were quickly down steps to the broad beach of fine sand. "Do you see that camp?" he asked. I looked at a long line of tents — about a dozen, each with a crossed British and Canadian flag at the top, and a two plank sidewalk in front of the line.

"Whose tents are those?" I asked in astonishment.

"Yours and mine," he answered. "Here," as he deftly guided me along the new boardwalk, "is the dining tent; next is the cooking-

The Harrison family "at camp" in 1898. Eunice is 2nd from the left;
Eli is 5th from the left. Courtesy of L. Wilson.

tent and beside that is a tent for the China house boy. Here's your husband's, and so on."

Bagster showed me over it all, while the odour of new canvas, new floors and side boards of the tents, pleasingly blended with that of the warm inland coast waters and the high evergreens that almost touched the backs of the tents.

"But — but, what is the meaning of all this?"

"Just that we're all going to spend several weeks' camping by the evergreens of Cordova Bay beach," answered Bagster. To stop my laughing protests, Bagster turned on the latest model of Edison.[1] It was 1898.

So began exhilarating camping days.

I have several snapshots of that early camp with its line of tents. The China boy, with his white coat, apron and long queue stands proudly beside the cook tent, only too pleased to have a part in the white man's eccentricity.

Bagster stands nonchalantly in front of one tent, in the dress of a successful business man of 1898 just in from town before changing. The judge, now arrived from the Nanaimo Circuit, stands rather heavily by a log, and wears a tall, hard black hat, something like a bowler.[2] A pepper and salt Norfolk jacket[3] of 1898-cut is the only concession to the beach. The others look as if they had stepped out of *Harper's Bazaar.*[4]

It was an old Victoria custom, until about the start of the first Great War, for a great summer exodus of residents to beach camps in the long vacation. Some of the beaches were practically under canvas for the summer months, so numerous were the parties of campers.

At night, countless fires made from the abundant drift wood lying on every hand, gave off a rather savage lighting effect, and the smoke from the various sorts of sun-dried woods — which had long been tossed smooth and white by inland seas — often had a pleasing fragrance. Amateur musicians were not only within and in front of tents but they took to rafts, canoes, row boats and yachts. That was when the beaches had become more crowded and public. Otherwise it would be limited to two or three parties far away on a mile stretch of sand.

The camps were nearly all given rather fantastic and often facetious names: "The Three Black Crows" or something à la Chinook, i.e.: IKUMUKUM.

They ranged in size from one or two tents to really large and elaborate affairs on the foreshore of one's own property or adjacent to that of one's friend's, as in the case of Bagster.

Sometimes the tents were accessory to a beach cottage set somewhat back from the shore line. Everyone we knew had some such summer place, with log cabins in the wooded country for Fall shooting. My older sons regularly took to fishing tackle, shot guns and rifles, when they temporarily put aside law studies for a fortnight every Fall. Often they strewed the concrete floor of my basement with dozens of pheasants, and grouse, several deer and count-less quail — with plenty over for presents to legal and other friends.

Once there was a large timber wolf which soon became the won-der of passers-by in the window of a down-town taxidermist, who had asked permission to display it for a few days.

"Quick, mother! Whig has cut a vein!"[5] He had been handling a new, very sharp small game axe. Hurried flight to the first aid mate-rial; fast bandaging by none too expert hands. I got my son Claude on to the down E & N train for Victoria, which fortunately had not left yet. Of course there were no motor cars then.

On that occasion, we were camping beside Shawnigan Lake, some of the elders staying at the old Strathcona Hotel, then in its hey-day as a fashionable summer resort. This accident cast gloom over the opening of camp, for he was our favourite out-doorsman and the life of such a party. The cut required stitching and the mark of it, I believe, is on his wrist to-day. A close call.

I don't know whether I was more anxious about the Fall hunting or the summer camps. Both could become dangerous. Knowing the good they did, I forced myself to become philosophical. No use crossing bridges. As a matter of fact there were no further outing accidents in our family.

On one occasion in the pre-motor days, I went on a visit to Bag-ster's and Todd's camp,[6] several log cabins picturesquely set amidst the pines beside Sooke Lake. The road at that time was particular-ly steep. The coachmaker was busy all the previous day on Bagster's vehicle; besides mysterious things, to my sight, he added special thicknesses of leather attached to the brakes. Once under way in the large coach drawn by four horses, Bagster's full tilt down the steep Sooke hills was something to remember even by one who had been in the Cariboo.

We held camps in various places, including at Bowkers, Cordova, Allbay, and by Oyster Bay and Blainey's Crossing. The boys had shooting lodges at Sahtlam, Sooke and Leech Rivers.

At one hunting place, the stream ran through a veritable Bret

Harte land,[7] plus the rich, heavily furred evergreens such as only B.C. can provide. Walking by the stream, we noted a strange foot mark, but no stranger was known, or likely to be, about.

Early next morning, a man was just glimpsed slowly wending his way, but certainly not furtively, up stream. Followed, he turned into a shack beyond the first wooded knoll.

A knock on the door brought him out.

"What are you doing here?" Whig asked.

"Just a little panning in thar stream, stranger. It keeps me alive, along of a bit o' fishing and hunting; not too bad for over seventy-five." He evidently did not realize he was trespassing. Eighty cents per day from very fine grains of gold painstakingly sifted every day was trouble enough without wondering who might own the wilderness. Probably it was Crown Land anyway.

The old prospector was allowed to stay and given some provisions for winter — he proved an excellent caretaker and good old fellow.

Then came word from a district hospital. A prompt call there was welcomed by the physician: "Glad you came; you seem to be the only friend he has. No relatives that we can discover. There is nothing the matter with him that we can find. He came to us to get rid of a frog which he said he had inadvertently taken internally while drinking from a stream."

"We gave him a thorough going over. But he is not convinced that the frog has gone. In fact, the notion seems to be growing into a delusion. We are uncertain how to proceed."

Whig made a suggestion. A few days later the physician put the old man under an operation. As he came out of a whiff of ether, the nurse showed him a small, green frog.

"Here he is. We got him out at last. You're all right now," she said. The patient went away happy.

On Whig's suggestion, a bit of play acting; a pretence at a minor operation, and the frog was "out" sure enough, for it had never been "in" the old prospector.

CHAPTER 31

Broken Hulks
and Broken Lives

"Here she comes!" I excitedly exclaimed from a launch going up the Gorge[1] when I saw the incoming *Dora Sieward.*[2] She was mine. Well, not quite all mine. I had a one-third interest in her.

As the trim schooner from the icy Northern seas glided on to join the long row of other sealers moored in the inner harbour (their tall spars for many a year a Victoria harbour landmark), I was delighted with her even before I was told that she had brought in more skins than the combined total of Captain Grant's *Ainoko,*[3] *Penelope* and *Beatrice.* In fact, only the *Vera* and the *Arietis* had done better in a fleet of thirty-six sail.

Captain Grant[4] was a Captain Cuttle-ish sort of man, only more authoritative as became a landowner. His large home near Point Ellice bridge is one of the oldest in Victoria. On its lawns were once laid out several drowned bodies from the sunken street car that plunged to its doom through the broken bridge nearby.

I never stopped to think that maybe I shouldn't even have imper-

sonal shares in such a business, that is a business perhaps not quite
in harmony with the spirit of animal humane societies. But whether
one regarded sealing as a humane sort of work or not, the fact is
that a great many old-timers depended on it for their livelihood.
When the sealers came back from their rough, wild voyages, having
survived arctic wind and waves, and announced a good catch, it
meant relief to hundreds: to sea captains and men, to ship chandlers, their families, not to mention the ship owners and the public
in general. The old papers featured these headlines:

> FAIR PROFITS FOR SEALERS. ALTHOUGH COAST
> AVERAGE LESS THAN LAST YEAR'S, EXPENSES WILL
> BE CLEARED. WHITE HUNTERS MOST SUCCESSFUL
> — OWNERS WILL SHIP TO LONDON ON SPECULA-
> TION.

A spring catch ran from 10,472 to 15,896 skins and none were
offered to local buyers. Then later came this cheering news:

> HIGH PRICES FOR SEAL SKINS. Season's catch sold in
> London at highest Figure on Record. Sealers Jubilant
> over results as 1902 was an Off Year.

To facilitate the business handling of ships, my father with six
other ship owners formed a holding company, The Victoria Sealing
Company, Limited,[5] in 1900. The name of its agent printed in the
company's articles is Francis Brooke Gregory, a general legal practitioner, and Colonel of the famous 5th Regiment of Coast Artil-
lery; later a Justice of the Supreme Court.

Captain Grant was one of the incorporators. Business was good;
the fleet was intact and in excellent shape. Then came an international treaty for the preservation and protection of fur seals. It
closed down all operations, for years to come. As compensation to
the sealers, the Canadian government received $450,000 for the
loss of the sealing business; later this was increased to over one
million.

A Commissioner from Quebec, who had been secretary to the
Board of Arbitration to determine disputed matters on account

The Dora Sieward *under full sail. BC Archives, D-03209.*

between Ontario and Quebec in 1893, was appointed: Louis Arthur Audette.

Sittings were held at various places in B.C. According to the report[6] (Comm. Vol. 3, p. 3) the Commissioner said: "Had it not been for the tenacity of The Victoria Sealing Company remaining in existence, Canada would not have been in as good position to make this treaty with the United States. . . . As a result of their operations they certainly kept Canada in the business" (Comm. vol. 3, p. 8). He made other admissions of the sort (Comm. vol. 1, p. 309; vol. 4, p. 922).

Mr. Found, Deputy Minister of Fisheries, wrote a memorandum for the guidance of the Commission, in which he said: "Morally, there is no question but that the Victoria Sealing Company should receive compensation, and that such compensation should be as

Men working on the sealing schooner Saucy Lass.
BC Archives, B-00619.

generous as possible compatible with conditions." And he suggested that it be the $200,000 advance payment which the U.S.
had already made under the treaty.

Despite that, Commissioner Audette reported back to Parliament that in his opinion the Victoria Sealing Company should
receive nothing!

According to papers in my possession, the late Premier Brewster[7]
of B.C. and Sir Wilfrid Laurier were indignant. My husband, with
some of the Directors, made a special trip to Ottawa to show that
Parliament should not be prejudiced against the Company's claims
by Commissioner Audette's advisory report.

Sir Wilfrid Laurier wrote July 14, 1917: " I certainly will support the proposition that you are entitled to compensation, as I suggested to you verbally."

Again, later, he wrote: ". . . If I were in your place, I would try again next session. Each new effort will bring you nearer to success."

These efforts continued for years and dragged along like the supposed Chancery case of "Jarndyce v. Jarndyce,"[8] with like tragic results. Fine sealing schooners rotted at their moorings — only a very few were sold at a low price for scows and the like.

Going one day down to the beach at a summer place, I saw one of the sealing ships lying on its side, stuck in the mud, and photographed it.

Many lives — old tired lives — were broken by the failure of compensation to come, although now and then the prospect of justice at last glittered in view, only to ever prove a mirage. Broken hulks, broken lives. I personally lost upwards of $12,000,[9] including my own interest as well as that which became mine through the estates of decedents.

Yet in the papers before me, Sir Wilfrid Laurier had written: "You have justice on your side, and I feel confident that you ought to win and will." (See also his criticism of the Audette report, House of Commons debates 6299 & 6300, on the floor of the House, September 18, 1917.)

CHAPTER 32

"You Can't Take It With You"

M any remarkable characters and individualists have come to
Vancouver Island from time to time, and have stayed a while,
returned, and come North again — perhaps a number of times.

Of all of them in Victoria's long history, I don't suppose any were
more remarkable than Miss T from Boston. She was a thin maiden
lady of rather patrician features and quite light hair. She had inher-
ited very extensive properties and was said to be worth several hundred thousand dollars, if not a million or more. There was no
doubt that she had it, but she lived modestly indeed, in one room
and bath at a private, select *pension*. She was somewhat older than
either of us and had known my husband and me in the earliest
days. At the turn of the century she was coming North to summer a
while.

We were sorry to soon discover that Miss T's chief interest lay in
a small rather misshapen poodle dog called Chickolit. This dog
had an extensive wardrobe and its clothes were quite often

changed in the course of a day. I am bound to say that even the most ardent dog lover would have some difficulty in admitting this lazy, over-petted creature into his circle. After seeing it and its actions, that is.

If spoiled children are a trial, spoiled canines are worse. At least the manager of the *pension* thought so, to judge from the silent agony depicted on his face when the dog's antics unpleasantly forced its existence on his notice.

One day a messenger came to the house with an urgent message for me. I tore it open. No one was dead, but Miss T seemed near to it, for I was urgently begged to call upon her without delay. Arriving at the *pension,* I found her nearing complete collapse. Someone had died, but no one human, no one even a dog, in the ordinary sense. It was Chickolit, the manager's *bête noir.*

I was about the nearest friend Miss T had in the district; she copiously wept on my breast and I did my best to comfort her. The proprietor, at any rate, was comforted by my appearance, for he had begun to tremble for fear Miss T would fall into some uncontrollable fit that was beyond his power to cope with.

Miss T's grief lasted a long time. It would have touched anyone's heart had it been over some fine, devoted dog, but I confess that as much as I sympathized with anyone in sorrow, the thought of that horrid, spoiled, stupid poodle froze my sympathy. She did not suspect, so far as I know, that some annoyed neighbour well might have been pressed beyond the enduring point and had stooped to poison. For days Miss T kept to her room and then, when she did come forth, it was in deep mourning. She wore mourning for the rest of her life for this dog and on occasions tied crepe to the cushions in memory (the creature spent most of its day on a silk cushion). None of her friends could induce Miss T to abandon mourning.

She owned buildings — in which were stores, places of amusement, etc. — and large vacant lots. She paid a heavy taxation, and that on the lots was above all reason. The value having been fixed for taxation purposes during a boom, what she had to pay was pretty fantastic. Strange to say, although she complained bitterly about the absurd taxation, when some purchaser ready, willing and able was found who would pay a good price, she would wilfully refuse, although the offer would have relieved her and given her a good sum.

In this way she capriciously lost many chances and, in the end, many a piece went to the city for the tax arrears, which accumulated. It was, therefore, a most aggravating thing for anyone to try and help her in a business way.

This went on for years, since she would, every other year or so, travel up and down the coast, staying at this and that hotel.

Came the day when my husband and I stood beside her open coffin in a southern state burial parlour. She looked as she had ever done. As much as we were sincerely sorry to see her thus, the idea behind that since-famous phrase, "You can't take it with you," came to me. For she had rarely been happy herself or conferred it on others. More than one simple-hearted young woman, who had served her every whim through the years, as companion, at meagre pay — possibly led on through the hard discipline by broad hints of a substantial legacy — found her labour and life spent in vain.

Miss T did not die poor. On the contrary, she left several hundred thousand dollars. Her will, if she ever made one, was never found, so far as is known. Very remote connections, who had not put up with her trying peculiarities for years, and who had, in fact, scarce known of her existence, came in for handsome shares in the general distribution.

Going to the hotel where she had been staying, I found much the same situation as in the far earlier days of Chickolit's death. The manager had wanted her to leave, for, while she paid her bills, the bell boys came to resent an exacting daily service unrewarded by the usual tips. Moreover, the manager said, as tactfully as he could, she seemed to lack an appropriate wardrobe and would wear odd-coloured stockings, etc. And that didn't help a hotel of his grade. He couldn't seem to understand that she was really rich. But we were more surprised by another discovery.

Almost by chance we went with an attorney to a remote part of a hill overlooking the harbour. There in a rare lovely spot, so unobtainable in that city, was a fine stucco house: hardwood floors and every room vacant. At least that is what we thought.

Mounting a further pair of stairs, we found one more door off the highest hall. We had been told the house was empty, but turning the handle we discovered it was a fully furnished bedroom: a four poster bed and an abundance of clean linen and clothes.

This property had long stood in her name, as legal owner, yet had remained unoccupied for a long time — there were no neighbouring houses within sight. But once in a rare while she must have spent a day or night there. She had lived at the local hotel for years; had lived at hotels in other cities for years. She had had close business advisers, yet none knew of the house. No physician, no friend, no companion had had an inkling of it. We learned of its existence through a careful search of the county tax records when we drove into town to learn what could be found after her death.

Why she had lived and died in this unsatisfactory if not somewhat surreptitious way, none seemed to know. Had she had secret love affairs? None that we ever heard of or could discover after her death. Naturally, since there was a large estate and no will, her past was investigated by many.

But if you happen to know "all about" Queen Elizabeth, you would understand — so said her local physician, with a slow, cynical and rather unpleasant smile. He said he had recently been reading a new book on England's "Virgin Queen."

"You have the answer to the riddle of her personality, there. Miss T immediately occurred to me when I read the book. She was just the same," he said.

After driving to another and distant city, perhaps 1,500 miles away where Miss T had also lived, I stood in a woman doctor's office. "Yes, I was her physician for a long time and she came to me

whenever she lived in this city. I know nothing of her business matters. In fact I know nothing at all, except one thing. Miss T was a
member of —— (here she gave the name of a rather sinister secret
society). She went rather deep in it, but refused to go beyond a certain point as she said the instructions had become, definitely, the
black art."

CHAPTER 33

Early School Days

We never took up permanent residence in the Cariboo and Lillooet, or in Nanaimo county, where my husband was Judge — because of the children's schooling and future careers. Perhaps it would have been to our own personal advantage to have stayed for good in that marvelous land of the Cariboo or at Departure Bay, but we felt it our duty to go to Victoria where there were so many opportunities — and, of course, the capital was the metropolis then.

The four boys attended the private boarding academies, the Collegiate School[1] and Corrig College.[2] The former was under the auspices of the Church of England. At least at the time of which I speak, the Lord Bishop of Columbia was "the visitor." It had long been in existence; in fact my husband had himself attended it when he was a boy.

When my boys attended the school, the head was Mr. John William Laing, M.A., Oxon. He had been the head master of Mayo

Eunice Coote neé Harrison, eldest daughter
of the author. Courtesy of L. Wilson.

College, Ajmere, India, 1878-84; in India he had been the guardian of H.H. Maharaj Rana of Ih'allawar, Rajputana, India. In 1896 he had explored the central portion of Vancouver Island, hitherto a sealed book. This adventurous streak no doubt came from his having been President of Oxford University Athletic Club, and he won for Oxford in track events against Cambridge. But the effects of the climate of India had been hard on him and he did not reach advanced old age.

Under his guidance the Collegiate School continued the old English school tradition of *Tom Brown's School Days*. The school had many worthy junior masters, either from Oxford or Cambridge. They invariably taught in their academic gowns. The thrashing canes were also very much in evidence in all forms. The school had an excellent cadet corps under the instruction of Staff-Sergeant

Clarke.[3] School sports, plays and break-ups (school holidays) were among the social events in Victoria, and the school colours of dark and light blue were much in evidence.

The four boys also attended Corrig College (at one time called Victoria College). This had also been long established in Victoria and traced its history back to 1860. The College at the time our boys attended, was headed by the late Dr. J.W. Church,[4] Cantab. He conducted it in new buildings at Beacon Hill in 1890. They were formally opened by The Hon. Hugh Nelson, then Lieutenant-Governor of B.C., attended by the Premier, The Hon. John Robson, and the Speaker of the Legislature, The Hon. D.W. Higgins.[5]

The city in a booklet entitled *Victoria Illustrated* (1891) gives considerable space to the history and standing of this college. It finally closed its doors in 1916 and Dr. Church passed away the following year. The classrooms were demolished in 1934. Many hundreds, if not several thousands, of pupils came to the Collegiate School and Corrig College, during their hey-day, from almost every quarter of the world; all parts of B.C., Alaska, Washington, California, Japan, India and England were well represented. The printed lists occasionally published by the institutions showed that ex-boys had done well in almost every part of the British Empire and the U.S.A. Scholastic standards were high and deportment, as understood by English gentlefolk, was an important factor. The academic courses afforded the equivalent of a modern university education.

Our two daughters Eunice and Bernice attended Angela College[6] (its building now an apartment house), and the youngest was also a boarder at All Hallows, Yale, taking up residence there shortly after King George V and Queen Mary (the Duke and Duchess of Cornwall) visited the academy.

After Angela College, my mother took Eunice, the eldest girl, to Ontario where she married John Colborn Coote of London, Toronto and Vancouver. The youngest girl, after graduation, married Lieutenant-Colonel Forsythe of the Gordon Highlanders, commanding officer of a military camp in the First Great War.

CHAPTER 34

Social Victoria

Social life, of course, mainly centred on the King's Representative (the Lieutenant-Governor) and the Chatelaine at
Government House, Rockland Avenue, Victoria. The first mansion
was called Carey Castle, but it was destroyed by fire.

People who desired to take part in social life would leave their
social cards at Government House and write their names and
addresses in the large visitor's book kept on a table at the left-hand
as one entered the front door. If, however, when you called, the
Governor and Chatelaine were "at home," you would personally
see them and write down your name in the book on your way out.

Thereafter, those on the book would receive invitations to various affairs held at Government House, such as garden fêtes, balls
and receptions to meet such personages as the Governor-General
when in Victoria on tour from Ottawa or England.

At the very formal openings of the Provincial Legislature (one
chamber in B.C.) some were invited to seats "on the floor" of the

House, gaining admission by numbered card, the smaller numbers, in my day anyway, seating the holder nearer the Speaker.

On New Year's day the Lieutenant-Governor alone received visitors from 3 to 6 p.m., and so did many others including the officers of the Royal Navy and the garrison at Esquimalt. The men in the family usually wore — as some did Sundays on going to church — frock coat, striped trousers, silk hat and gloves, one glove on and one carried in the left hand, when making calls New Year's day.

But the ladies stayed home and received guests during the same hours, men making the calls on them. It was the custom to have the visitors served in the drawing room with light refreshment, in other words, wines, tea, coffee, sandwiches and cake.

Visiting cards were engraved or printed in script (a few in Old English script) with the days one would be "at home" noted thereon. Mine bore the words "Last Two Thursdays," as those were the receiving days in that part of town. On receiving days, only ladies called, and the Chinese house boy served in the drawing room, tiny sandwiches, cakes, "lady fingers" and tea.

In the earlier days, the balls given by the Freemasons and the Royal Navy at Esquimalt rivalled in brilliance those held at Government House. Some of these social customs have fallen into desuetude.

Weddings at that time were staged in the grand manner; society editors and reporters "wooed the muse" and hard pressed the adjectives. It was also the custom, not only to acknowledge the receipt of wedding presents personally and privately, but the society editor had a reporter note down each present and the giver's name, with the most meticulous care. Thus, those who gave wedding presents in effect received two acknowledgements, one publicly. My record books are full of such clippings. As a specimen, I might quote from one.

The time was around the late Nineties and the place a church, though not the cathedral. However, "the Lord Bishop" officiated as the paper, at the outset, is careful to inform the reader. The bride had six bridesmaids and a train-bearer.

It takes almost a dozen lines to describe the wedding dress. By the sixth paragraph, the reader gets to the bride's home where, "owing to excellent arrangements and three large marquees on the lawn, there was no crowding."

Then follows a paragraph after which the reporter lets himself go romantic with the following: "Seldom has a jollier wedding party assembled to witness a happy bridal. Soft strains of music were heard during the afternoon from Mr.——'s orchestra, and a constant ripple of laughter and merry voices were mingled with the harmony of violin, flute and harp."

Two more paragraphs are devoted to describing dresses and then: "The gifts were — even in this time of lavish gift-giving — exceptionally beautiful, a room being filled with lovely and valuable things for plenishing the home of the young couple. . . . " There follows a formidable list indeed which takes over 250 lines of small type, not purposely selected, but the usual small type then used throughout the paper.

The presents ranged in value from cheques of unstated amounts (except one from England which the reporter notes was "for piano"), to cushions, handkerchiefs and sachet. "Servants and Friends of the couple in England" sent out a pair of silver candlesticks. The list of givers includes about every name famed in the history of the colony and many of those who later took equally prominent parts. As the sub-head of the article says, a bit choppily: "The Scene of Happy Event Attracting Society Audience."

Included among the bridegroom's many jewelled presents to the bride is a "bicycle." As is customary, of course, those invited examined the gifts but I do not recall the bicycle sufficiently to be able to say that the reporter should have added: "built for two." But the "Gay Nineties" were in Victoria.

Among some gifts which might be thought a bit curious now are several sets of Shakespeare, one of them described as "a half dozen volumes of Shakespeare's Plays." The cumulative effect of it all is

*Artist's rendering of the Driard Hotel (at left) and the Victoria
Theatre (at right). Courtesy of L. Wilson.*

rather overpowering. The papers seemed to delight in supplying
such publicity, and while some families rather incited this sort of
thing by first casually slipping green-backs into the under-paid
reporter's hand, yet, in many cases, the people most concerned
rather feared too much exuberance in the write-ups, for then, as
now, and no doubt world without end, there is ever that step "from
the sublime . . . "

No one will know to whose wedding I refer when quoting from
this gem of early social reporting, but, in any case, I should add in
all sincerity, that the bride and groom were fine, modest, charming
people and the wedding was a truly delightful — yes, a gorgeous
affair. The bride's father was not only "a leading citizen"; he was an
exceptionally fine man in every way and a gentleman in all senses
of the word.

Then there were the amateur theatricals. I don't suppose there was ever a community of people without charades, private theatricals, and amateur public performances. Old Victoria certainly was keen about them. Many were put on in the ancient Victoria Theatre, part of the famed Driard Hotel block, which was later taken over by David Spencer, Ltd. after one of their disastrous fires.

A moving spirit in private theatricals at one period was witty, charming and pretty Mrs. Harry Helmcken. Her husband was H. Dallas Helmcken, K.C., the second son of the Hon. J. Sebastian Helmcken who married a daughter of the first Governor Sir James Douglas, as I have mentioned. Harry Helmcken's law firm Drake, Jackson and Helmcken, was for long a leading one on the coast. Among the happiest memories of one of my sons are those connected with five happy years association with that law firm, including frequent success in important litigation and public affairs. The latter included removal of the large and historical Songhees village from the entrance of Victoria's inner harbour, whose aroma had met me so forcibly when I first approached Victoria, as I have said.

Mrs. Harry Helmcken's two attractive daughters by a previous marriage, took leading roles in Gilbert and Sullivan light operas, *The Mikado, Pinafore,* and a musical play called *San Toy.* One of my daughters had minor parts, and I well recall the stern disapprobation which my husband showed for one of the costumes when she brought it home from rehearsal. Tears flowed, but the play, or rather her part in it, went on. It is hardly necessary to add that the costume would now be regarded as dully decent.

Included in the usual difficulties which beset all amateur productions, there was actually the threat of legal action over the use of certain copyright songs, in one instance. It was not a light opera with which Mrs. Helmcken and her daughters were associated, but another much like a Gilbert and Sullivan farce. One of the leading roles was taken by Miss Worlock, a daughter of the pioneer banker of the firm of Messrs. Green & Worlock. Before the fourth performance it was publicly known that legal proceedings had not only been threatened but an application for an injunction to stop the play was pending in the Supreme Court.

A full house greeted the fourth performance, and although all must have known of the dire legal threat hanging over the play, many were startled when in the palace scene where the Chinese Emperor and his court were assembled, their attention was caught by the stamp of heavy official steps down the central aisle to the stage. Mr. Siddall, the grave and stern deputy from the Sheriff's office, whose duties included serving injunctions, stepped authoritatively on the stage, closely followed by an assistant baillie.

At the tense climax Mr. Siddall burst into: "THE CHINESE FATE":

> *Stop, stop, every fiddle*
> *I'm here in the middle,*
> *I'm Deputy Siddall,*
> > *Ha, ha.*

The girls of the chorus, dressed as Chinese maidens, ran in, singing:

> *He is Deputy Siddall,*
> > *Ha, ha.*
> *My professional function,*
> *To serve this injunction,*
> *Without a compunction,*
> > *Ho, ho.*
> *Come along, come along,*
> *If you sing that sweet song,*
> *It is wrong, it is wrong,*
> > *Don't you know?*
> *And even that wail,*
> *Will nothing avail,*
> *Come with me to jail,*
> > *Ha, ha.*
> *Chorus —*

Go with him to jail,
            Ha, ha.
Yes, yes; 'tis my trade,
    It's the Jameson raid,
    And don't be afraid,
            He, he
Chorus —
No, we're not afraid,
            He, he.
We'll out-sing and talk 'em
And walkem to Walkem,
And thus we will baulk him,
            Ugh, ugh.
Chorus —
And thus we have baulked,
            Ugh, ugh.

Mr. Powell, a young man of a prominent family, fond of amateur acting and singing, had cleverly disguised himself as Mr. Siddall and, supported by Lieutenant Hood of the Royal Navy, brought down the house with their imitation.

However, the last verse alluded to the Hon. Mr. Justice Walkem (whom I mentioned as once being with us in the Cariboo) and he was to hear the injunction. The comic take-off, with its allusion to "walkem" was in contempt of His Lordship and Court, or perilously near to it. But the play was only scheduled for another performance and the legal efforts were abortive.

Victoria's amusements were far from being all indoors. There were several cricket pitches, besides those belonging to the Collegiate School and Corrig College. Baseball, of course, was quite unknown at those institutions, although girls played a game much like it, popularly known as "rounders."

Judge Eli Harrison in his later years. Courtesy of L. Wilson.

White flannels, blazers, caps with shields and badges, blue and striped coats — and, of course, broad Oxonian accents were all very much in evidence in the summer. Soccer or "association" and rugby football in winter. Also, some ice hockey in the winter, and field hockey in summer. Lacrosse was also a favourite, but was banned at the private schools after some serious accidents.

Before the long vacations, when with the closed Courts of Justice many went out of town to country places, there was one great early summer event: the regatta on the Gorge. The Gorge is an arm of the sea extending inland for several miles from Victoria's inner harbour to a slough. Fairly wide at the mouth, it is about the width of the Thames for much of the way. At one point the shores are quite close and there is a little bridge. At low tide the torrent under it is so strong that boats and canoes cannot possibly get by (though many have tried) and have to be pulled along from a cat-walk at the side under the bridge. There was a sinister rock a bit in front of the bridge, completely covered at high tides, on which many a daring diver came to grief. Along one section of the Gorge there were once lovely gardens extending to the water's edge with private boat houses like those on the Thames at places, for it was one of the fashionable residential districts of Victoria at that time.

The regatta held on the Gorge, in or about and somewhat below the bridge, was a great outdoor event in the lives of many Victorians for generations. Along the whole course were decorated barges, boats and in fact craft of every sort. The colours of the various schools, such as light and dark blue pennants for the Collegiate, and correct English boating costumes were much in evidence. The James Bay Athletic Association (J.B.A.A.) sculling club also took a prominent part and had their club and boat house first near the causeway in the inner harbour before it was removed to near the Gorge bridge. Many of the most ambitious and progressive young men of the town belonged to the athletic club.

Vast crowds turned out to view the various sorts of boat races. Probably the most spectacular event was the Indian war canoe race.

For months the Indians of B.C. prepared for the then annual event. Almost every tribe of B.C. Indian was represented, some coming great distances such as the once war-like Haidas from the Queen Charlotte Island. There were also Indians from Northern British Columbia, the Kootenays, the Chilcotin, the Okanagan, Shushwap, Nootka and the Cowichan. Their long canoes raced forward as if propelled by some elemental force, of which the strange heads painted on their prows might be symbolic. No doubt their unique cut had something to do with their speed, but it was, in the final analysis, a test of sheer muscle by the twenty or so paddlers in each canoe, assisted, perhaps, by their low throaty grunts. There was a sort of comic relief in the canoe race by squaws. It was a pity when the fine, stirring example of really authentic Indian craftmanship and athletic prowess passed with the regatta.

CHAPTER 35

The Peculiar People

Scream after scream cut the midnight air. Heart-rending, terrible. Then silence. Half an hour later, another scream — stifled, muffled.

I was on the second floor of the old St. Alice Hotel, Harrison Hot Springs,[1] B.C. As there was no commotion anywhere, not even the opening or closing of a door or window, I decided to postpone enquiry until the morning. A fitful night's rest came to an end when "Hot-oughter, Hot-oughter" was sung by a Chinese house boy as he shuffled along the halls, proffering a large jug of hot water at every door, evidently the customary way of supplying it.

We had arrived that night on the Transcontinental;[2] had stopped at a little station and had been driven by a sad rig along a long, dusty road flanked by sombre forests. Ahead of us lay an old fashioned, weather-beaten structure of three or so storeys, with a series of wide, outside stairways which joined the broad verandahs of each floor until the ground was reached. The quaint old place has long since been destroyed by fire.

After breakfast, we sought the hot springs. They advertised themselves by an odour of rotten eggs. Finding several hand pumps, we readily brought up sulphur smelling water, boiling hot. Hot, warm or cold, it was disgusting and was made no better by fancy glass mugs bearing an indelible picture of the St. Alice Hotel, the forest, lake and a boat. One of the souvenir glass mugs is before me at the moment.

As we were not there for invalidism, we were soon boating on the extensive lake. It was larger than Shawnigan Lake[3] on Vancouver Island and surrounded by a much more primitive wilderness of forest. After a short row, we came to a beautiful, high waterfall, roaring icy white foam and clear green waters down to the lake. Landing as close as we could, we quaffed many a glass of marvellously cold, clear water. Striking out in another direction we saw a deserted cabin on a small treed island. About to examine it, we were driven off by a very fierce Eskimo husky dog which appeared to be the sole inhabitant. When we returned to the hotel, we were ready for a hearty lunch and determined not to spoil it by the addition of "dish water" from the hot springs. The waterfall water some of us thought much better for health.

At lunch, the screams of the previous night returned to my mind. I touched the bell and called the manager.

He listened to my statement with a sad expression. Then in a low voice: "You will notice, madam, at the table by the last window as you leave the dining room, a lady and youth about fifteen. They are mother and son. He has hip and bone trouble and wears a leg iron. He screams almost every night. It cannot be helped. We hope, madam, that you will make allowances and overlook the unpleasant sound now that you know the cause."

We were, of course, full of sympathy for the nice looking boy and his kind, patient mother. Later, I met her and her son on one of the verandahs. She took me aside and explained his unhappy plight. For years he had had hip trouble; his leg was in an iron by day and had to be stretched — no matter how great the pain, on a rack with heavy weight at night. He had in this way suffered terribly for some years and the long strain had so depleted his nervous energy that he was at the St. Alice to obtain what rest, and recruit what strength, he could from the hot springs.

He was still there, with his brave, good-natured smile, when our stay came to an end. Many a time I wondered how he could survive pain that forced such agonized cries from his unwilling lips. "It is expensive, too," his mother said, "and interferes with his education. We have one of the best doctors in B.C." I recognized the physician's name. A high-priced specialist, now dead, whom people came to consult from as far off as San Francisco. I had had some experience of his undoubted skill.

Whenever Harrison Hot Springs was mentioned in later years, a picture of that boy and his mother came into my mind. I wondered sometimes what had become of him. Then one day I accidentally met his mother in the city. She recognized me at once and came up.

"I am sorry your stay at the lake must have been spoiled by those terrible cries. My son is perfectly well now. After much more suffering, I took him to an osteopath or chiropractor. He told me there were misplaced bones and that the treatment for which we were paying so dearly was quite unnecessary, in fact worse than useless."

"Do you mean to tell me," I exclaimed, "that those years of agonizing, cruel suffering were quite unnecessary?"

"Absolutely. A few adjustments by the bone practitioner completely cured the trouble. The medical specialist's treatment was wrongly based and simply piled agony upon agony, causing more harm than good, in fact doing only harm."

This was astonishing. I knew the M.D. was an A-1 surgeon. But here was a specialist of another sort.

Poor boy, poor mother. Both suffered expensive tortures for nothing.

⌇

It was near Harrison Hot Springs that I first heard the strange tale of the seven- or eight-foot hairy giants[4] that are supposed to live in the mountainous wilderness in the hinterland. Indians claim to have seen them. They are said to be an ancient race that has lived in seclusion there, from some very remote period. Many Indians claim either to have seen them or their gigantic footprints.

Travellers in Asia tell a somewhat similar story of the lower reaches of the Himalayas where one explorer says he stumbled upon a wild dance held by grim, furry giants whom explorers have dubbed the "abominable snow men."[5]

It has occurred to me that perhaps the observer had unwittingly run into some species of witch dance, during which the circling figures act queer creatures to the life, having first donned complete disguises — that he may have mistaken disguised natives for hairy giants.

At least that mistake could easily have been made in B.C. at one time. Anyone suddenly coming out of a forest and sighting certain dances in which the natives impersonate gods and devils, in complete, monstrous disguise, would swear he saw the most extraordinary creatures dancing about, not human at all. And the Indians, in most weird make-up, of which museums have specimens and photographs, with carefully sustained character during the long "dance" would give no inkling of being what they really were: simply natives dressed up as gods or demons. That might be a natural explanation of the strange stories of the "abominable snow men."

The natural explanation of the huge hairy men of some of the mountainous wilds of B.C. is that natives mistook some exceptionally large specimens of grizzlies for gigantic men completely covered with fur. Now and then this type of bear does attain gigantic size and at times they stand upright and walk a bit like men. Against that easy explanation is that the huge footprints are positively not of bears, they say, and it must be admitted that Indians ought to know footprints. The legend persists to this day, despite the fact that a magazine article a year or two ago, giving some pretty good testimony, met with much criticism.

Recently I have been dipping into an exhaustive scientific report of B.C. Indian legends painstakingly made on the spot, a few years ago, by, I think, scientists sent out from the Smithsonian Institute. It had aroused my interest to try my hand at drawing some extraordinary legend from an old Indian living nearby, whom I have known many years.

So I called in at the eagle nest where "Jeannie" sat working on a half-woven basket. She was smoking a clay pipe upside down and looking much as she did well nigh sixty years ago, when I saw her with her baskets in mother's garden.

She was glad to see me, the more so as a smart raven had awkwardly hopped from one branch to a closer one of a nearby tree as I approached. And that was, to Jeannie, a good omen.

After personal greetings and an exchange of family news, I diverted her to the subject of Indian legends. Soon I would have been quite overwhelmed with the lore of pure naturalism — the bird and animal myths or superstitions — attributing to the birds and animals almost human intelligence and speech. I got her off that, after an effort, and said: "Yes, Jeannie I know all that. What I want to know is something *very* strange. Something different."

She cocked her eye at me in a whimsical way: "Since white man come, there is none. Him and the newspapers, they know all." She said it in her pretty good, but very slow English. Perhaps there was a trace of irony in her last remark.

"But you know me, Jeannie," I urged. "I am not the kind of white person to laugh. Tell me something very, very strange and very true — not just a story for papooses." She would not have taken that last from any other white.

Jeannie re-filled her pipe with some tobacco I brought forward at this point, having come, of course, with various gifts.

Reassured, she said, "Well, I think it very strange about those Peculiar People," as she lit her pipe with a small coal which she took from a brazier with a pair of tongs.

"Peculiar People?" I queried.

"Yes. That is what the Indian call 'im. They were given no other name by the Indian. They came before the King George men."

Native woman kneeling to weave basket. RBCM, PN6844.

"You mean Spaniards," I said.

"No, no," she commented with disgust. "Not Spaniard; not Frenchie; not Boston-men; not any of them sort at all."

"These Peculiar People had strange power. You know those rocks at —— " and she named various places along the coast of Vancouver Island and elsewhere. "Well, they did magic with those stones and at those places."[6]

"What do you mean by magic?"

But she could not make it very clear. "They did not die like we Indians die. No, they were quite different, the Peculiar People, that is what we called them."

"Oh," I said, "you mean spirits of dead people?"

"No, no!" she answered. "Not spirits at all. They were men, I have said. But not the white man kind. They had much strange, strong power. The Indians were afraid of them. They did not mix with the Indian. They lived by themselves. We did not trouble them. We feared to. They did not trouble us. Sometimes they helped us in trouble. But they did not mix. But we saw them quite often. Yes, it is true."

"That was long ago, Jeannie?"

"Yes, very long ago. Mother's mother tell me when I was a girl. *She* saw them; her people saw them when they come by canoe at —— You know the place? Those Peculiar People had gone before or just before the white man came."

"Died, I suppose," I hazarded.

She grunted in some disgust. "They not die. They go far back, Wake-si-ah," and she waved her hand to indicate the far distance. (Could it be to the taboo land back of the village of Kispiox, "the village of the people who hid?" I wondered.)

"That is all I can tell you. I think it is much. Some day the white man who knows all and laughs at Indians, will know that it is true. The Indians feared the Peculiar People but they not hurt Indians. They had power. Yes, with the rocks and the waterfalls. They were real people, the Peculiar People. It is not too far back," she added as I rose to go to look about the place. "Some day the white man will know it is true. The Indian not lie about the Peculiar People."

That is all old Jeannie could tell. On that trip anyway. Enough is enough. The Indian is not garrulous and it is hard to get him to talk. Hard to get him to trust you, because they have long disliked the white man's laugh about their many curious stories. When the Indian does talk, it is not very much at any one time. I knew Jeannie would tell me no more that trip.

Certainly the routine ritual of the Ojibway in the various degrees of the Midiwiwin[7] secret society, as that of other Indian secret societies (of which several are known to still exist in B.C.), used stones.

Quoting the gist of a scientist's letter who says he has visited the place four times, I find he tells of the discovery of a vast initiation ground laid out by the meeting of rivers.

The first group of boulders represents a snake nine feet long facing a tortoise five feet long. They lie on flat, granite glacial rock. No flaking or chipping, but the heads of each are extremely realistic. Surrounding them is a circle, probably a snake or several snakes about 300 feet in length. Four miles further on, in evident relation, is another snake thirty-two feet long curving up from the river into the woods behind, the head pointing as though guarding the trail.

Another granite outcrop about forty acres in area, is nearly a mile from the first set. It covers about eight and one-half acres and is apparently the ceremonial site itself, laid out in interesting courts connected with rows of boulders. A fourth set of stones seems to be a map of the country. There are pointers giving direction to a series of lakes, with a rough cross indicating the points of the compass.

Obviously, there is still much to be discovered about this pre-Indian people with their secret powers.

CHAPTER 36

"Sealing Wax ... of Cabbages and Kings"[1]

I don't have to look into the large old minute book of 1891, with its five hundred pages sagging there on the shelf. I know that my husband was kept busy as a Judge on the county circuit of Vancouver Island; on the Court of Revision in some districts (first commission dated in 1885); on the seasonal Assizes; as local Judge of the Supreme Court with full powers; and in drafting, adapting and revising statutes, besides making suggestions to London as to the uniformity of laws in British colonies.

In addition to that, he was named Commissioner[2] on various Royal Commissions of Inquiry. This method of factual investigation has long been a favourite one in Canada, both in the Dominion and in the Provincial spheres of action. The Commissioner appointed is nearly always a Judge; the government also appoints its Counsel, and of course provides a secretary. Sessions may run on for weeks or months and may be held in various towns. The report turned in is usually pretty formidable in style and length, while the cost is always high and sometimes shocking.

As neither the executive nor the legislature pays the least attention in most cases to these long reports from Commissions — as it appears to the general public — there has been quite a bit of complaint and satire on the holding of so many Royal Commissions on apparently unnecessary subjects.

These Commissions in B.C. are under a statute called The Public Inquiries Act.[3] So when my husband was appointed a Commissioner to inquire into the Public Inquiries Act itself, it must have seemed to many of the lay folk that such an investigation was the final Gilbert and Sullivan[4] touch to the whole procedure.

However, since those days, while some criticism continues, it is now becoming widely recognized that the findings of the various Commissions contain invaluable material not obtainable by present research, and all the findings of Commissions through the long years have been indexed for ready access to rare material often of essential use to-day. Whatever some of the lay folk may have thought of the method, those on the Commissions gave their work the most conscientious and meticulous care.

Among the Royal Commissions held by my husband at about this period were the following: to enquire into charges against a police magistrate[5] and the general conduct of his office, December 15, 1894; to enquire into the conduct of officials at the provincial jail,[6] January 15, 1898; to enquire into the management of the fire and water departments of the City of New Westminster as to the Great Fire[7] which practically destroyed that former capital of the mainland colony (named by Queen Victoria), on the night of September 10 and morning of September 11, 1898; to inquire into the grievances of the settlers on the lands granted to the E. & N. Railway,[8] October 12, 1900; to inquire into the conduct of the Provincial jail at New Westminster,[9] July 24, 1901.

Certain other unusual events associated with my husband's work held my interest deeply. One was the coming to the Island of T.R.H. the Duke and Duchess of Cornwall and York[10] in 1901, who, it was known, would become King and Queen. (H.M. King George V and Queen Mary). As usual, on all Royal tours, the whole population showed the greatest enthusiasm and many fine decorations, parades and decorated boats welcomed them to the island. Along with other Judges and their wives, my husband and I were duly presented to the future King and Queen.

Then there was the engrossing topic of designing and building a new house[11] on the property at the crest of Fort Street hill. My husband had sold some of the land, retaining five large lots which made one acre. Part of the adjoining land I see is marked with the initials H.P.B. on an old map, but I couldn't say at this time what they stood for. A long strip fronting along there, running between Fort, Yates and Pandora Avenue, and a small piece actually on Pandora Avenue, was given to the city for streets and the city then gave the street the name of Harrison.

What so many liked about our acre was that it was laid out by nature: hillocks of solid rock (not conglomerate) beside the long front fences, covered with thick, "cushy" green moss, through which great oaks grew. In the centre of the drives, another solid moss-covered rock island with three large oaks, one covered with ivy. There were also large white and purple lilac bushes. In the next round, one large oak, a lawn and a small rock covered with periwinkle. The main lawn contained very large oaks with widespread arms. Towards the Harrison Street fence were more oaks, lawns and a large Oriental plum tree that was covered with a mass of small white flowers in spring.

The drives in the grounds were never *built* to my knowledge. They were just naturally there. Of course the garden men, through the years, from time to time gravelled and tamped them down to keep the surface in good condition, adding sharp up-standing rock fragments along the margins.

Cutting the lawns also kept them busy. But aside from such attentions, the whole was as nature had set it up. The branches of the oak trees were so thick in the leafy season that the front grounds seemed to be completely covered by a canopy of oak foliage. I do not believe that one could look up at any point of the heavens with-

The grounds of the Harrisons' Victoria house, "Oakwood."
Courtesy of L. Wilson.

"Oakwood," the Harrisons' Maclure-designed home. Courtesy of L. Wilson.

out seeing an oak leaf or a sheaf of them above one's head, unless one got on to the roof of the house.

For years the sight-seeing trams,[12] tally-ho's[13] and motor busses, going up "The Dardanelles,"[14] as narrow Fort Street by our fence was dubbed, called out "Oakwood" to the attention of tourists. Fifty years later, after the acre had passed into other hands, a number of the trees were cut down and the property split up. But several clear photographs I have show the wealth of ever-spreading oak branches and leaves when we had it. There was no more fitting name than "Oakwood." But that was after the sun "had moved North" each year, for, alas, later in the year, the fantastic shapes of the oaks came to the foreground, though I have heard some say they liked them bare.

Worse than the stripped trees, was the immense work that followed for the Chinaman who with his Chinese baskets or wheelbarrow, spent days on end taking up the leaves and burning them in the back gardens. Sometimes the tent caterpillars cut the early leaves to ugly brown lace work on parts of trees, but that was rare. On the whole, however, I could not recommend to anyone the use of oak trees in front grounds; evergreens are far better and far less trouble. Still having the oaks by "gift of God" as the lawyers say, we grew fond of them in our fifty years and noted their slow but steady increase in girth — some became quite immense.

We were much more fortunate this time in an architect and builder. In fact, the late Mr. Samuel Maclure[15] took the matter in hand, with the late Mr. Mesher[16] acting as contractor. Mr. Maclure was a leading architect and an artiste to his finger tips. He was tall, dark, slender and wore a semi-Vandyke beard; he had a quiet, cultured voice and a distinguished appearance.

A Maclure house was a hallmark of the best homes in Victoria. Not that I should say ours was among his best plans; our limitation on expenses rather hampered him, but the twelve-room house (plus two in the basement) was so far set back from the heavily treed front that we wanted the money put into solidity of construction rather than in exacting refinement of design.

Mrs. Harrison's fourth son, Herschel, and his bride on the steps of "Oakwood." Courtesy of L. Wilson.

For one thing, we achieved a basement unequalled in old Victoria. Heavy concrete throughout and concrete plastered over the high and wide side stone work. A high light basement of many windows and electric light at night, extra heavy beams and posts, white-washed a strong bright white throughout, except for the two rooms which had cream-painted wood walls over the concrete.

Several large heavy blocks of brick work for chimneys, with automatic drop ashes from the first and second floors. The coal and wood bins were wooden partitions laid on the concrete and thickly white-washed white. It was a white, light, dry, cheery basement.

Not one piece of wood that went into the building of the house had a knothole. That was personally seen to by my father, who, having plenty of time on his hands, watched construction most carefully. Once he stopped work on the front staircase and had the contractor take the work out and put in a stairs with an easier tread.

In fact, selected wood throughout was used; in consequence, about thirty-five years later, the same basement and house, with minor interior alteration, became a large, select block of suites with self-contained entrances. Many houses built at the same time had by then decayed or been pulled down, because of the foundations. Appraised in writing by architects in 1928, it was stated that our house was in A-1 condition and would cost $25,000 to build at 1928 prices.

I mention this, since from the long-range viewpoint, it seems to prove that extra attention to a basement, pays. But, on the other hand, if one has a long-range viewpoint, why build for too many years ahead? In face of Victoria city taxation[17] the question, from my experience, seems unanswerable. For, who can build a house, however well designed, that will not be outmoded well within thirty years? City people are ever moving out into lower taxation zones nearer the forests, pressed on by excessive taxation from the centre, and that alone encourages radical changes in design.

There were seven rooms upstairs with bath and also separate wash hand basins etc. My eldest daughter, Eunice,[18] had married and lived in the East when the house was finished and as the remaining family of seven members gradually dwindled with the graduation in law of the elder boys who moved North to open their own law offices, the bedrooms were turned to other uses: an extra sitting room (one was 15 by 21 feet, another 11½ by 14½ feet), a sewing room, and an upstairs library that housed two thousand books.

We had built in the upstairs sitting room a rather curious old fireplace that had been in the earlier house; I was told it was one of the first brought out to the colony from England. Downstairs there were three rooms, each 17 by 21 feet — drawing room, sitting room and dining room. The last two could be thrown together by pressing the sliding doors. And this was done on such occasions as Christmas and New Years when the dining table usually sat twelve or more.

The American president and political philosopher Thomas Jefferson,[19] who, along with many other skills, was an expert though amateur architect, designed a number of houses in Virginia and it is stated that anyone can recognize a Jefferson-designed house by the fact that the staircase going to the second floor cannot be seen from the front door.

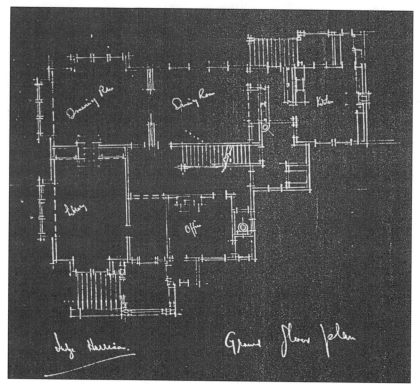

Maclure's ground floor plans for "Oakwood."

It so happened that we also avoided what Jefferson so detested. First, one entered a glassed-in porch conservatory. Two doors lay ahead. The small one opened into a small vestibule which led to a door to my husband's law library and den. The large door opened beside the small door, and it led into a large vestibule, off which was the drawing room door. At the end of the vestibule hung heavy *portières* and only when they were drawn did the stairs at the end of the main hall come in view.

In my brother Bagster's home on the Gorge he had had speaking tubes put in the various rooms; that was something of a novelty and I do not think it worked too well. We used a system of electric bells with a number dial in the kitchen. We could contact the China houseboy from the library, from drawing room, from sitting room, the front doors or from upstairs. In the dining room, the bell came up from under the flooring and could be touched by pressing a spot on the carpet near the seat by the head of the table.

When the telephones came into more general use, we added one upstairs to the one on the ground floor. We had one of the earliest numbers, 889, and continued up to Garden 5829 near the start of the recently concluded war.

There were no stationary tubs at first, the house laundry being done Mondays by a laundry Chinaman in a special laundry shed adjacent to the basement. There he boiled and washed clothes and sent out the starched items to the laundry.

On Mondays there was often commotion in the kitchen that could be heard in the dining room through the "butler's pantry" despite three swing doors. For on those days sometimes three were in the kitchen: the cook, the garden man and the washman, and at their luncheons they seemed to be discussing politics in several Chinese dialects. Once we had a Japanese cook, his Japanese arrogance ill-concealed from the garden man. And when one of the boys came home from school in his cadet school uniform with a bugle, the Jap, on being asked something about Japan, said: "Please let me blow that. I will show you how we do in the Japanese army."

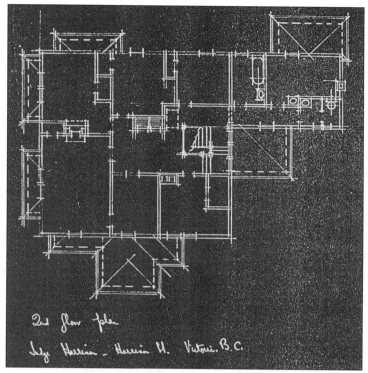

Maclure's original 2nd-floor plans for "Oakwood."
Courtesy of L. Wilson

As there were several mouth pieces, he was allowed to. Then the Jap let fall his real nature. "Some day Japan will fight here and everywhere and win."

At another time I had a most modest well-behaved pretty Japanese maid, quick and efficient. One day when running to catch the street car, she received a stunning blow from one of the cars of the four lines that passed our place. After several weeks at the hospital and no permanent harm, we got her ample compensation from the Company without trouble. At another time we had a little old Japanese that attended to the furnace very primly and decently. After a year or so he was killed one day while riding his bicycle on a slippy road.

But for the rest of the house boys, they were all Chinese and in almost endless succession, some staying two years or so, others but two minutes. Garden men as a rule stayed longer. Pong for about ten years. Once or twice there was a Hindoo wood packer or garden man for lunch, but he refused to eat with the Chinese and, asking for pure boiling water and a few other simple things, uncoiled his turban and made his own lunch in the garden.

Heating was by hot air at first. But after several years my husband had a pet idea of putting in a hot water plant and eighteen radiators. It made the house very warm in winter. The furnace was stoked by a side pump, but it was not automatic. One of the Chinese started it in the morning, stoked it once or twice in the day time, then banked the fire after dinner. It was an effective system, but was more in the pay of the coal merchants than in ours. Aside from the initial cost of conversion to this system, over $2,000,[20] the coal bills were excessive. It was not worth the investment in my opinion.

One could drive in through the front grounds, circle the drive and so around to the back of the house. There were also on the side street, large and small back gates for deliveries. Also, a rose garden in a corner by another tall old oak. Then a space for a marquee or summer tents which we always put up in season. Pear trees. Behind a hedge, Pong's garden of greens. Then some more, smaller oaks. In the far corner a wire enclosure about fifty by twenty feet. At first, quail were kept there by one of the boys.[21] Later it was used as a pen for his Irish setter, Tess; later again by Flip, her son, a crossbred black water spaniel, with very curly black hair, and who was handsome and clever. Then when Tess died, Flip had two Persian cats for company. Later a Great Dane pup, Bellachey, who lived to old age.

I happened to be looking out of my bedroom window one night while the City Hall clock, distant one mile, was striking twelve. My attention was caught by a black object which disappeared over the six foot, v-point board fence. I suspected it might be Flip and said so the next morning. Someone then carefully examined the far off six foot high wire enclosure; no sign that Flip had been out, which he well knew was wrong.

Several days later an older son, studying late in town for a Bar exam, said that as he was about a block from the house, he saw Flip from a side street hurrying for the house as the clock began to strike twelve.

We set a watch and found that this dog would scramble over his six foot wire enclosure, cross the back gardens, go up a ladder which carelessly lay against the v-point board fence and from thence jump down, cross the front grounds and then to town. After spending a couple of hours, he would run for home when the city clock started striking twelve. It was a clever idea, but we did not encourage it.

This dog once cut his foot badly; the veterinary put in some cat gut stitches, but the moment his back was turned, Flip tore them out. When he had torn them out a second time, we let nature take its course and the foot healed without trouble.

This dog had to be kept in an enclosure, for, while a mixture of mild good hunting strains, he was quite combative, taking particular exception to grocers, butchers and postmen.

"Bellachey," however, although rather fearsome in appearance, was the mildest, best natured and best mannered dog I have known. Jet black, with a white star on his chest, he loved to go to town with some of the family. He went through stores and shops and used elevators, showing polite, restrained interest in everything. He was admired by many and it was soon understood that, although a full bodied Great Dane, he was decorum itself, and never dreamed of biting. At night his bark was heavy and ominous. A very useful dog and good companion.

CHAPTER 37

Going South

"It's nice," I said to the children, "that the orchestra is playing 'God Save the King'; they must know that there are a number of Canadians on board."

I glanced out of the porthole of the salon as the ship gained headway for the South through the Straits of Juan de Fuca, and, in so doing, happened to catch the eye of a passenger nearby. She commented: "It's not God save the Queen. It's 'America, Land of the Noble Free.' We have moved away from Queen Victoria's colony." This brought home to me that I knew very little about the United States. Our schools did not teach American history and very little of its geography. This was the case even though, from the Dallas Road bluffs in Victoria, one can see the grand, snowy range of the Olympic Mountains in the United States (but named by a British naval officer), the magnificent background of the moving seascape. It enthralled Kipling[1] who wrote that it reminded him of the Himalayas. On a clear day, one can see the town of Port Angeles, Washington, some twenty miles across the straits. But the

States might as well be in Tibet for all we on Vancouver Island know what is going on there.

It was rather different with my husband. Although always a warm admirer of British Colonial administration and its fine recognition of Colonial Bench and Bar, and although he had personally annotated A. Todd's classic *Parliamentary Government of the British Colonies*[2] (of which a U.S. edition appeared in 1880), my husband also greatly admired American Constitutional law. Along with the Prince of Orange's sword[3] in the covered wagon, Eli I brought with him a fine, annotated edition of the U.S. Constitution. My husband prized it highly, as he did Montesquieu's *Spirit of the Laws* and Daniel Webster's collected addresses.

Whenever my husband visited San Francisco in Freemasonry or as a Bishop's delegate to the Episcopal Church conference there, he was at home with their judges and lawyers. (Much like B.C., California took the English Common Law as of April 13, 1850.) He knew Chief Justice Hastings well and also met him in B.C. Chief Justice Hastings used his own money to found the law school of his name in San Francisco.

I pondered all this after the lady's comment.

My two youngest children,[4] a girl just in her 'teens and a much younger boy, were on a few months' trip to Southern California.

The Judge went weekly his judicial circuit, returning week-ends. The older children[5] were grown and had entered or were just entering the legal professions. Wong was an excellent cook and the garden man a good one. There was no reason why I should not be away for a short trip when the late Dr. O.M. Jones said I ought to go South to relieve muscular rheumatism, so bad in the wet weather.

After three days at sea, we entered the Golden Gate on the *S.S. Queen*.[6] The population was over 300,000, an amazing change from when I had passed through in the Sixties and when my husband had come up in 1858.

It was a time — even in 1906 — when it was "not the thing" for ladies to travel alone, although two children helped. But even at that, one was expected to stay at a "family" hotel. We drove first to the Lick House,[7] but the foyer seemed too "masculine." We then tried the old Palace Hotel.[8] After resting a bit, we set out to see a friend of the family. Passing through a constant din of thick cross currents of traffic, noting horse-drawn street cars, we made our way on a cable car, rather fascinated by its queer, noisy, incessant bell and the strange clutching gears and brakes.

Finally we arrived at St. Ignatius College where I met my husband's old friend the Reverend Father Woods.[9] Father Woods, formerly an Anglican, the son of Archdeacon Henry Woods, had become a Jesuit priest. This did not affect my husband's friendship for him, although many Protestants inwardly deplored the change in him. Father Woods showed us through the College, but stopped at one place and, with a smile, said that we could not enter, but he took my son into the dormitories.

When we returned to the Palace Hotel again, there was just time after dinner, to catch the *S.S. State of California*[10] for the trip farther South.

This steamer we came to know and like better than any on the U.S. coast, although, at one time and another, we sailed on its coastal contemporaries: the *Umatilla, Senator, President, Governor, Santa Rosa, Indianapolis* and *Avalon*.[11]

Perhaps the captain of the *State of California* had much to do with the preference. He was a large fair man, with kindly, rather protruding blue eyes; he had a fatherly manner and, as he always showed us so many helpful attentions, I came to believe that this originated in a friendly tip from Father Woods, as I later learned that the captain was of his church.

We were proceeding on to Santa Barbara but it was much too stormy and there was not much of a harbour there. Accordingly, the ship went on to San Pedro and from there we ran into Los Angeles, thus entering that city for the first time at midnight. It then had about half the population of San Francisco.

From there we went back to Santa Barbara. After staying awhile at the wide spreading Potter Hotel, later burned down, we took a bungalow on the corner of Pedregosa and Emerson Avenue. We explored the quaint, old adobe missions, with their sandalled and robed monks as in the Middle Ages. Father Ludger Glauber was then Superior; he died in San Francisco in 1907. The children and I studied French and Latin with Professor Spoorman and his wife, who were Germans, and with Father Lavy who lived at the end of Eucalyptus Lane, Montecito Valley.

A newspaper, *The Independent,* now no longer published I believe, interested us greatly. With its black headlines and always carrying, somehow, the dampish feeling of wet printer's ink, it was unique in appearance and editorship. It was a special delight to the children, savouring as it did of the rival editors in *Pickwick*[12] and of those in *American Notes*[13] and Macready's *Diaries* (Toynbee edition). What a lot of fun has gone out of journalism with the establishment of our present sedate school!

We then moved to San Diego and stayed there awhile. We looked over Mrs. Katherine A. Tingley's[14] headquarters, academy and printing press, located on Point Loma — several hundred acres, with much waterfront. The place was as bare as a desert, except for sage brush, when she acquired it, and they planted palms, eucalyptus pepper and the like — altogether many thousands of trees and shrubs.

At the time we were there, tents were supplementing the buildings, and some of these, of unique design, had not been fully completed. She also had a Greek open air theatre, the first in America, it has been said. The academy struck us as being conducted on severely impersonal lines.

We attended the Fisher Opera House (or Isis Theatre as it was later known) in the city of San Diego itself, when Mrs. Tingley presented a large orchestra composed of pupils in a public recital: Mozart, Chopin, Beethoven and the other classics exclusively. Of course this was long before Balboa Park with its open air organ, just as it was before the days of Hollywood.

A few days later, we drove in a horse-drawn stage across the Mexican boundary to Tijuana, Mexico. The rainy season was on and the water in some places came well over the floor to the vehicle; we had to hold up our feet for quite awhile. As there appeared to us to be nothing else to see, we attended a bull fight, but when the horses spilt blood from ugly wounds, the disgusting nature of it all repelled us and we went out before even one bull was finished. I felt confirmed in my opinion that we were not squeamish, when I read the heading the *Colonist* used a few weeks later in referring to an episode in the life of Queen Victoria: "Queen Victoria's Trying Ordeal. Her Majesty witnesses horse literally torn to pieces in bull fight."

It was now time for us to return North. We went part of the way on the *State of California* again, but for the rest took the *Santa Rosa*, which we did not like at all. There was a middle-aged couple on board who made repeated efforts to develop our acquaintance. "Now when you get to San Francisco, stay at this hotel," she said, giving a name. "It's a real family and ladies' hotel."

As the old Palace of that time seemed very masculine to us, we sought this other hotel. It was hard to find. One or two of whom we inquired rather stared at us, I thought. Then I asked a policeman and he readily directed us. It was a devious way. We did not like the feel of the place. As I was discussing the location of rooms with the clerk, who wanted to give us separate rooms on different floors, I saw several young women with highly painted cheeks adjusting their negligees by the hotel desk.

I suddenly felt that once in, it might be hard to get out of that hotel, so I determined to pretend an engagement with friends and said after that we would return later. All eyes were turned our way in a peculiar appraising look; without waiting for an answer, we hurried out as quickly as possible. We at last reached Market Street and I then identified at a drug store the name of the hotel recommended by Father Woods: the St. Nicholas.[15] We went there and certainly found it a ladies' and family hotel.

The next day we went to Oakland, Alameda and Berkeley where I recalled that my husband had a sister and brother-in-law whom I had never met. He was a professor in the medical school of the

University of California. After a brief visit with them, the professor suggested that my sister-in-law, daughter and I go one way to the ferry, and he, with my small son, would follow shortly in his run-about motor car.

This we did. When they did not arrive at the ferry, I began to feel a bit worried, especially as horse-drawn vehicles were everywhere and while motor cars were fairly numerous, they were rather novel. At last they arrived. They had had an accident. As the professor was making a left hand turn into a main artery, he had run into the side of a moving street car. It was a close shave. Just touch and go. And they had to foot it to the ferry, the car having been too badly damaged.

After dinner in San Francisco again, we went into a sidewalk amusement place. It appeared to be the exact model of a passenger coach on a train, with real light, bell, etc. We entered and after the bell rang, the car began to shudder and sway as if moving. Then, motion pictures (of which we had already seen examples in Victoria) were shown on a screen at the end of the car, the scenes being of railway travel. This heightened the effect of travel on a train. However motion pictures were not general.

Roller skating was the popular diversion at the moment. There was a very fine large rink, like a horse-show building, and we attended as spectators. It was the centre of San Francisco's better type of amusement. The huge new place was packed with a youthful crowd of several hundreds. Bands played and with the roars of skates, laughter and repartee, it was like some grand carnival; professional skating "turns" stimulated the amateurs until finally a star performer and his youthful daughter climaxed the show with a whirlwind number. As the happy laughing crowds poured out of the place, one could hear appointments made for to-morrow night at this great new place of amusement.

But they never kept them.

We retired to the fifth floor of the St. Nicholas quite late on the night of April 17, 1906.

CHAPTER 38

A Strange Awakening

M y bed was shaking. As I awoke I heard a loud rattling sound, very like hail stones striking with force against a window. We realized instantly what it was.

The floors, walls, ceilings, all the furniture, the two large chandeliers shook violently. Plaster was falling from many parts of the ceiling. We got up and hurried to the window to look out, but we reached it with difficulty because of the swaying. Once at the sill we held on as tightly as we could. What we saw down in the street below held our attention.

Men, women and children were running about in every direction, panic-stricken. Passing down the street, now becoming crowded, were two express wagons. A man was stretched out in each. One had a mangled arm dangling, his face covered with blood; the other figure seemed all but headless, with one hand off. His leg must have been broken at the shin, as it was hanging over the edge of the wagon, swinging loose with the movement of the wagon. We could also see blood on the floor of the wagon.

As soon as we felt we could safely stand without fear of jolts, we dressed. I looked at my watch: it was a little after 5 a.m.[1]

We noticed, when we came back from the windows, that in the interim a large piece of plaster had fallen on my little boy's pillow. We felt thankful indeed that we had risen when we did. We fastened our satchels and left them, thinking the trouble was over and we would return after the room had been cleaned up.

Then we started for the hall. Horrors! The door would not unlock. We turned the key and shook the handle. It would not open. Then came to my mind a story I had read in *Harper's Bazaar* of a girl who had opened a door with a hair pin. I took my longest hair pin and tried. It worked.

Entering the good sized, carpeted hall, we saw large water pipes pouring water on the thick carpet, and a stream going on down the hall. On the fifth floor, the large skylight was in view and we saw that it had fallen in; pillars that had supported this were dangling over the well, and one corner of the ceiling was down. Plaster debris everywhere. Electric wires broken.

We wasted no time testing the elevator but made our way downstairs as others began to do; most of the guests seemed crazed with terror. In passing the different rooms, we noticed through open doors that furniture was overturned, windows shattered and broken crockery upon the floor. Some of the guests were congregating by the office desk. Most were still dressing. Some poor women were imploring the manager to save them.

Reaching the street, we mingled with the crowd which was moving this way and that. As we heard on all sides that another shock was expected, we made our way to an open square and sat down to think. We decided to make for Golden Gate Park[2] although it was several miles distant.

When we were starting off, a poor man and woman with three children came up to us. The woman had a tiny infant in her arms and wore little more than a wrapper shawl about her. She was bareheaded, hair unfastened, dishevelled, her bare feet in old shoes and the children and husband with no better covering. They begged that we tell them of a place of safety. When told that we were total strangers in a strange country, they looked at one another as though their last hope had gone. We then told them that we were going to try to walk to the park.

"Did we really think that was a place of safety?" And when we said, "Certainly, it must be," they wearily followed.

We spoke to members of families who were standing about dazed and fearful of moving from their little open space of temporary safety, for buildings of stone and brick were everywhere fallen or falling. We continued our tramp and noted that hundreds were now taking the same route. We found it an extremely long walk to Golden Gate Park and when we reached it, water was flooding the streets, the mains having been severed by the earthquake. Fire had broken out in some fourteen places simultaneously in the southern end of the city.

We wandered about the park and finally reached the children's playground, where there was a picturesque stone building. The caretaker and family lived there and supplied lunches and teas. The whole south side of the building was a total wreck and the poor woman told us that they barely escaped with their lives, by her presence of mind in breaking the windows nearest them and escaping with her little family that way. All other exits had been closed to them by falling masonry, and they had scarcely left the window sill when the roof fell in just as we now saw it lying.

We passed families sitting on benches, eating only a few crackers for their breakfast. Another had but a small jug of milk hurriedly picked up out of many possessions. A young father and husband was trying to soothe the grief of his wife and an older woman, evidently the mother of one of them. Their lips trembled and they could not speak. He would put his baby in the perambulator and then, in a hysterical manner, embrace first his wife and then the old lady, stroke their hair and try to speak calmly, but his breath would come and go as though he were faint. Then he would again take up the baby, and pace up and down, tears coursing down his cheeks.

Destroyed buildings in the San Francisco earthquake and fire, 1906.
Courtesy of S. Fallows.

We walked on and met four men coming towards us in haste and out of breath. Thinking to see over the whole city from the highest point on Strawberry Hill, we asked the men the right road to the top where the lake was. They threw up their hands in an excited manner and said that the whole lake was gone and closed in.

We wished to see this for ourselves, but there were so many miles of roads and by-paths winding in and out of this immense park, we thought we would get lost. We returned to the entrance gates, and saw that people were now entering in large numbers. Later we heard that that night no less than 20,000 were sleeping out in the open in the park.

We decided that if we were to be out all night we must endeavour to obtain our satchels for warm clothing. So we started on the long tramp back to the St. Nicholas.[3] When nearing it, we saw two youths in their 'teens driving a wagon with the words "PETS AND ANI- MALS" on the side. We hailed them and offered five dollars if they would take us to Jefferson Square.[4]

They agreed but within a block of Jefferson Square, they refused to go further. I persuaded one of the boys for two dollars and fifty cents extra to get out of the wagon and accompany me. I left the two children in the wagon, and seeing a patrolman guarding a line to keep people away from the fire zone — the roaring inferno could be seen and heard not far off — I gave him the names and addresses of the children in case I did not return.

He was doubtful if he should let me go further, but I said the youth was with me and we just wanted to get valises. Without debating the matter further, in the general confusion and noise, I rushed on with the young man to the nearby St. Nicholas.

The hotel was ominously deserted. When we reached the third flight up, my companion refused to go further. I urged him forward and finally we reached Room 514 on the fifth floor. He grabbed what he could carry and in frenzied haste flew down the stairs.

Gathering an armful of clothes and the remaining valises, I flew after him. Reaching the ground floor, the poor fellow almost collapsed from relief and fear. For, on running through the long corridors we heard plaster falling, creaking and cracking on every side. Just as we reached the wagon in safety, the inside of the hotel fell down. A narrow escape.

We soon reached the wagon and got into it again. Passing St. Ignatius Church and College, we noted that it was badly damaged, the whole front of the building having fallen out, debris covering the sidewalk and part of the street. We saw the Reverend Father Woods standing by the sidewalk surrounded by his parishioners. He was calmly addressing them, giving advice to this one and that.

While we were driving on through the crowded streets, and just as we were nearing Jefferson Square, a man drove up behind us in violent haste, shouting in a maniacal manner, his eyes blood-shot and staring. Violently crowding our wagon, he shouted for us to get out of his way. We being on the right side of the street, and its being crowded, the boys did not consider it safe to move to the wrong side

Destruction of the wholesale district of San Francisco (1906).
Courtesy of S. Fallows.

to please him, and paid no attention. Then he became infuriated and lashed his already frightened horse. He passed us and deliberately drove across our horse's head. All came to a full stop.

Jumping out with curses, he violently yelled at the boys that he was going to take our wheel off and kill them. He was commencing on the wheel, when some men in the passing crowd, grabbed him and turned his excited brain to his own business — got him into his own wagon and started him off. We then continued on our way.

On reaching the square, we found it was already overcrowded, with sick and injured being brought to it. The fire[5] by this time was gaining fast and the noise of raging walls of flame was horrifying in the extreme. Heavy detonations in various parts of town told of efforts to stop its progress by dynamiting buildings.[6]

Stranded fire-fighting equipment had been noted on many streets. Nearby stood a bright red pumping engine, with a large, shining metal boiler and pipe, smoke drifting from it. The huge, fearsome-looking black firehorses with cropped manes, rolled their big bloodshot eyes and nervously stamped and chewed their bits. The water supply had failed.

Seated in the crowded square, we made the acquaintance of an architect and his wife. They were intently watching the approach of the flames to their house, which was not very far from the square, they said. After awhile the wind veered and the flames began to move in the direction they indicated. It then occurred to them that they should first get some heavy clothing and blankets, as they would have to sleep out that night.

Before leaving, they gave us the small luncheon which they had brought. We were glad of it as it was the first we had had to eat since the night before. They asked us if we would remain where we were until they returned, promising that they would not be long as their dwelling was quite close.

They started off, calling as they went that they would be back in a very little while. We remained three hours watching the ever-growing inferno until we saw that the section of houses they had pointed out as their home, was in flames. We waited another hour, but we never saw them again. Our fear was great for their safety, and not knowing their names, I was never able to learn their fate.

It was now nearly five o'clock. Hundreds of more people had come into the already crowded square. The seething flames were so near that one could almost feel their hot breath. The failure of the architect and his wife to return brought home to us that we were strangers in a strange city.

We felt the need of some companionship; night would soon be coming on and we had neither food nor much cover. I looked about the sad scenes, wondering if I could spy a friendly face. But all were so pre-occupied with their own great troubles that I hadn't the heart to trouble them with ours.

Cautioning the children to remain on the seat where they were, I decided to walk slowly among the crowd to see if I could find friendly faces — some couple without children — not too busy with their own affairs. All were more or less engrossed, arranging their bundles and watching the approach of the flames; others sat with bowed heads.

Suddenly I saw upon one of the hundreds of bundles, three law books, in their unmistakable calf binding and red labels. My presence of mind then almost forsook me. *They* were friends! They were *home!* My house was full of them. Yes, the same titles — *Chitty on Contracts; Benjamin on Sale; Story* on Something or other, Equity I think. Tenderly, almost caressingly I picked them up, turned their leaves. "The same; yes, the very same!" I muttered. I hated to let them go, they were so comforting.

On laying them reluctantly down, I noticed that men sitting near were looking at me in a manner that brought me to myself again. I asked them if they knew who or where was the owner of these books. Some shook their heads pityingly. Then one, who until then had not paid attention to my question, spoke up briskly: "What? Them books! Don't you worry, lady; that's one of them damned lawyers." Turning wearily away, without comment, I awaited nearby to see if the owner would come.

Then, I thought from the look of the bundles, that he, too, might have a family, and we should not try to burden him. So I looked further, and saw a nice-looking couple apparently without family, sitting under one of the trees beside two bundles. Going up to them, I asked if they were alone. Yes, they had no children. I told them our names, where we were from and how we came to be there, strangers in a strange city.

They said they were a Mr. and Mrs. Brattan. (I was told later, that Brattan was the surname of a famed law writer ages before Blackstone.)

Mr. Brattan told us he was an official in some club, a tennis club I think. At any rate they were tennis players and, after the 'quake in

Wing City Hall, San Francisco, in ruins (1906).
Courtesy of S. Fallows.

the morning, they had dressed in tennis things for a walk to see what harm had been done, not dreaming of a vast catastrophe. By the time they had looked about, all they could save from their own home was in the two bundles beside them. We were heartily welcome to share with them.

After discussion, we all thought that before night the fire would probably get too close to Jefferson Square and we would run the risk of being scorched. A panic at night would be fatal even if we weren't burnt out. We therefore decided to walk to a very distant graveyard at the head of Eddy Street.

To us, the distance seemed without end, for San Francisco blocks are long and the hills steep. We stopped many times for rests. At last the graveyard was reached.

Mrs. Brattan then insisted on dividing four oranges with us. This was the first we had eaten since the night before, except for the crackers left us by the architect and his wife. Because we had been keyed up by the stirring events on all sides, I suppose we had never felt hungry, but now it was different.

We asked for some straw from a nearby stable, to cover the damp earth. We levelled the gravel a little to make a flat space, that we might not slip into the ditch nearby. On the straw I laid a canton flannel blanket which Mrs. Brattan had loaned me. We lay down for a rest, using as a cover Mrs. Brattan's table cloth (on her insistence) and our capes and overcoats. Mr. Brattan tied pajamas around his neck for warmth.

By this time several families were on either side of us. They were from houses near the cemetery, for all San Francisco was sleeping out that night. No house was safe for fear of what might happen.

They of course brought their bedding, but it isn't likely that many slept, because of watching the thrilling spectacle of a great city on fire. The furnace of enveloping flames could be seen over a constantly increasing number of districts and the deafening, roaring noise and cinders often reached us as the wind veered.

One old lady in a house nearby was an angel of help, for she not only went about reassuring people but she had her Japanese servant build a campfire in the open nearby and make hot coffee at intervals all night long, until four o'clock in the morning when water in that section of the city, gave out.[7]

Cinders fell on us so thickly that at first it seemed like raining.

CHAPTER 39

Escape

D aylight showed how rumpled we were, but no one paid attention. They were only too glad to be alive and so far beyond
the reaches of the fire.[1] People with improvised tents had filled the
graveyard since we had fallen asleep, for more had been coming in
all the time. Some broke into the vaults for shelter.

There was a general decision in the morning to go on to Golden
Gate Park, for the ever-burning fire had drawn considerably closer
to the graveyard and with a turn in the wind seemed to be headed
our way. It was feared that before another night, fire would have
surrounded the place.

Our hearts sank at the prospect. For us to move towards Golden
Gate Park would be tramping away from our objective, which was
now to reach the steamer for home as soon as possible, though we
heard on every side that the wharves[2] had been destroyed. Certainly the vast line of black smoke and fire seemed to extend for miles
and into that district. Still we determined to go to the wharves,

skirting as far to the left as we could to avoid the fire belt. When we told Mr. and Mrs. Brattan our decision, they shook their heads and tried to dissuade us, saying that the fire must have destroyed the docks.

We tried to get a conveyance[3] of some kind and went to a number of private stables nearby, but found that either their wagons were in the city or their horses had been killed or injured by fire while trying to give aid. Others again, had loaned their horses and they had not yet been returned.

At last I saw a man harnessing a team. I went up to him and offered some money and more on the strength of my bank letter of credit, to take us as near the ferry docks as the fire would permit.

He turned his bloodshot eyes on me, breathing heavily as he adjusted the harness. "No, madam!" he answered in curt, hurried sentences: "No money could induce me to go near that fire belt! We've gotter look after ourselves, woman! I have four families, my own people, to get out of here before dark, and to get them to the park as quick as I know how."

He busied himself with the harness. Then he exclaimed: "Hell is open — fire is coming. Look, woman, look!" And he stared wildly over his shoulder at great new clouds of dense black smoke that rose above the smoke bank.

We told him he was quite right. There was no use in arguing with him. We watched him from a little distance and noticed that he harnessed and unharnessed many times, while he glanced in our direction.

Feeling that he wanted to speak, I went up to him again: "I know you would only too gladly take us, if you could. We would help you, too, if we could."

"You are right, lady," he responded in almost a shriek, "God knows I would; God knows I would! And don't want any pay neither." With these words he sprang into his buggy, lashed his horses to a full gallop and tore over the hill without much regard for the line of the roadway.

View from Valley Street of the city ablaze (1906). Courtesy of S. Fallows.

Looking west on Market Street from 5th Street (the man on the ground may have been shot by soldiers). Courtesy of S. Fallows.

We then told our new-found friends, Mr. and Mrs. Brattan, that we must walk to the docks in the hope that the fire had not reached all of it. We took our satchels and started. When Mr. and Mrs. Brattan found that they could not dissuade us, they called after us words of good cheer and best wishes for our safety. We disappeared down the street on the long trek to the sea.

Each person whom we stopped to enquire the way, seemed to describe a different route. There were so many, and the fire seemed to be everywhere in that vicinity, however one might go. Some said that our march would be cut off by fire. Still, we determined to continue, taking streets as far to the left as we could.

We walked, it seemed to us, many miles, up hills and down. Sometimes on the sidewalks, more often in the streets because of the crowds in some places, all going in the opposite direction, apparently headed for Golden Gate Park. Some dragged trunks, tables, bedding, almost every imaginable thing.

Everywhere was desolation. Dead bodies lying here, injured there, blood spilled at some points where a collision or other accident had happened. Two men were shot nearby us. One was lifting his dead wife from the doorstep. He was immediately shot, as he was thought to be a stranger looting. Here was a three-storey house, with the first storey sunk in the earth to the second floor. In one of the streets, there were great cracks three feet wide at least. At another, which was cobble-stoned, the cobble stones were raised some four feet in the air.

The tramway double track was twisted in some places, to form a sharp elbow. Now and then we saw whole buildings of brick and mortar fallen in the street, except a chimney or piece of a wall, and it blocked traffic. One had to skirt around it carefully at the narrow passage ahead of the debris, which had been left or made by someone.

With some houses, the top storey had fallen away, exposing beds and furniture to the street. No building that we saw had escaped at least some damage. Nearly all were out of plumb, leaning like the tower of Pisa.

Here and there down the streets, little knots of people were making fires for a meal. Martial law reigned and no one could make fires in houses. At one street fire, a man was handing out coffee at fifty cents per cup and a loaf of bread for one dollar.[4] A foreigner ran at him and knifed his arm. In the confusion that followed, all food was taken from the cook.

We met cultured ladies,[5] hair dishevelled, wearing dressing sacks and house slippers, dragging furniture and trunks down the sidewalks, just as Japs and almost everyone else were doing. One old man was carrying with care, the legs of a stool. We asked him why he didn't bring some food or clothes; he would find them more useful, that chair legs would be of no use.

He looked up with a dazed expression, then at the legs and said: "That's so," and he sat down wearily on the stone steps of a house beside us, where we were resting.

"Where is your home?" we asked. With a vacant stare, he replied that he couldn't remember, but it was somewhere 'up there'," and he pointed beyond the fire lines. His mind was almost gone, poor fellow.

We passed the Crocker and Spreckels[6] expensive homes and wondered if they too would burn. They did.

On our way we met some soldiers on patrol; I think they were men of the California National Guard (state militia). Seeing us, they ran to us. Not to turn us back or stop us as we momentarily feared, but to carry our satchels which they did for several blocks, and in the politest and most friendly way. Then someone shouted, calling attention to smoke coming out of a chimney. They apologized for abruptly leaving us, fixed bayonets and ran, charging at the house to insist that the occupants put out the fire.

We tramped on, resting now and then on curbstones. Finally we reached a very queer section of the city. The houses were all more or less two- or three-storey and had not seen paint for many years; lace curtains were hardly holding together and black with age. The people around now seemed to be thousands of Chinese, Japanese,

Spanish, Italian, Mexican — all milling about or huddled together on the sidewalks or at street corners. Many, I thought, had the appearance of being dangerous characters. Had we been coming along a little later, I felt our throats would be cut for our clothes. This was the first time fear took hold of me.

We heard the sound and cry of another man shot, close by; by whom or what for, we couldn't see.

My tongue had suddenly become parched and seemed to be swelling. I stopped and told the children that I could go no further without water. Some foreigners were standing near. One had a fine cut glass, beautiful, silver-top claret jug in his hand. It was so out of keeping with the surroundings that I spoke to him, saying: "Water please . . . just a little."

He stared, looked at the others who were viciously watching a diamond brooch I happened to have on — attached to a rope gold chain around my neck — and a gold pin in the shape of a feather. These in the heat of travel had come in view. Jargon passed between them. And the fellow turned and went down some dirty steps under the wooden sidewalk. He returned with very cloudy water and, for fear it was not good, I merely wet my mouth and cautioned the children to do the same. We thanked them and hurried on.

We passed the most awful looking places one could imagine. Wagons and wagons loaded with people began now to pass us, as well as crowds on foot. The walks and streets were jammed. I cautioned the children to keep tight to my side for fear of separation, since I had more fear of these people than earthquakes or fire.

The dust raised by all this rushing, pell-mell traffic for the docks, for we were now nearing them, was fearful. At the other end of town, people were pressing to Golden Gate Park. At this end, they were rushing for the ferries to Oakland or to other small craft in the harbour.

One could scarcely breathe or see. In the noise of foreign jargon, a man, covered with blood, apparently having been injured by fire and falling timber, came tearing through the crowd, yelling wildly in some foreign tongue. This thinned the mass for a minute; then the crowd closed in again, nobody seeming to care.

At last, extremely tired, for we had tramped from about 6 a.m. to 3:30 p.m. on the long circuitous route we had taken, we came in sight of the docks. They had not been destroyed. Our troubles were over! At least, so we thought, as we exchanged smiles of success at having reached our goal.

Between the street and the wharves was a long paling. We hurried to the first gate. I told the gatekeeper our circumstances: how we had come to San Francisco to take the steamer for Victoria as provided on our through ticket; how we escaped in the disaster and had been walking all day to catch the *S.S. Senator,* which was to leave to-morrow for Victoria. I showed my tickets with the number of our state-rooms. Could we enter and go on now?

He listened attentively to it all, then answered sharply: "No, madam, you can't. The steamer does not leave until the 20th at 11 a.m. Today is the 19th."

We argued, the fire nearby might get to the docks and there would be no embarking to-morrow. We had a through ticket, with a couple of days stay-over privilege in San Francisco. We were strangers, with nowhere to go. The city was in flames.[8] What would a few hours difference make to the steamship company at such a time as this? We only asked shelter and a little food. We were famished and ready to drop from exhaustion.

"Can't help it, madam, you are no worse off than anybody else," and he absolutely refused to unlock the tall gates.

What were we then to do? To be out all night in the streets among the people who were now moving in the hundreds in the hot sun, smoke and dust, with neither money, food, drink nor shelter as yet, was a terrifying thought. For, aside from a little cash, I had only a letter of credit at the bank which I had been going to cash on the morning of the 18th.

We walked along the fence until we came upon an opening and got through. We saw some large steam launches. We asked the man

St. John's Church, San Francisco, after the fire.
Courtesy of S. Fallows.

in charge, who was shouting "This way to Oakland" if we might go
there. But his price was somewhat beyond the ready cash we had.

No, he must have his full price or we must stay ashore.

Finding the children places to sit on some large beams lying on
the wharf, and cautioning them not to move, I went off to see what
could be done, somewhat revived by the strong sea smell and by
being, at least, within the paling on the wharf and not challenged
for being there.

I met a policeman who said that he could do nothing. His duty
was to patrol along there and to see that no one got onto the
wharves or proceeded down the road into the fire belt. Seeing my
tickets, he evidently thought I had a right to be on the wharf, but
the problem of a boat leaving the next day, was beyond him. I tried

another gate keeper farther along but met with no better success; he had no power to let anyone on to the particular steamship wharf, much less on board the *S.S. Senator.*

I wandered about until I came up to a man wearing a wharfinger's or special police badge. I told him my troubles. His attitude was quite different. He looked shocked. "And you with a ticket, too! Well! Well! Lady, I'll fix you up some way. If we can't get you on board the *Senator*, you shall come with me to my home in Oakland, until your steamer leaves, if you will."

I thanked him heartily, and collected the children, who had never left the waiting place. We were escorted to the gate where we had been previously refused admittance. There still stood the guard who had said, "You are no worse off than anybody else." My escort sharply ordered him to open the gate; the man did so rather reluctantly, but as if he had better do it. We were taken to the wharf office to rest while he took up the matter with someone else. He soon returned, saying he had found a lady passenger who had been on the same steamer coming up with us, and wished to see us.

We went to where the ship was berthed and were met by one of the officers who insisted on taking us down to a hearty luncheon. There was no lady passenger who wanted to see us; it was just a clumsy seafaring man's way of trying to make me feel at home — I suppose thought necessary in dealing with ladies of 1906. It was all very kindly and gallantly meant, and we felt deeply grateful for this real human kindness.

The ship's officer then told us we simply must remain on his steamer for the night. When night came, he very gallantly gave up his cabin to us. We must have slept soundly, but now and then one or all of us heard sounds of fire-fighting, for blazing brands would alight on the roof of the long wharf or on the deck. The crew, as well as specials on the wharf who had been brought over from Oakland, worked like Trojans all night to check the spread of fire to the ship company's property.

Next day, no one connected with the steamers or wharf knew

Ferry building with the clock stopped at 5:15 a.m.
Courtesy of S. Fallows.

which ship was going to sail north. A peppery superintendent, with a very red face, came along gesticulating with his hands in a very nervous, abrupt manner, and said he couldn't help anything. It might be the *Topeka* or any other boat. The *Senator,* which was scheduled to sail, was quite out of commission: no provisions, no crew, nothing ready.

We were asked to wait on the *Santa Rosa* which lay beside the *Senator.* The officers on the *Santa Rosa* were also very considerate. A number of other passengers who also had tickets for the North, were on this vessel, waiting. All staterooms were filled; all hands, excepting an officer in charge, had gone off to help fight the fire, for the flames were now even closer, and the wind blowing more great pieces of burning stuff over the dock roofs.

Well might they be anxious, for there had been almost a panic at 3 a.m., we later heard, and it was said that the dock had actually caught fire. It was, of course, particularly inflammable and every effort had to be made to prevent a fire starting.

The *Senator* took on an emergency crew and hurriedly assembled provisions, from Oakland I believe. Once on board the *Senator,* we naturally went to the rooms that had been assigned in accordance with the numbers on our tickets. We had not been settled long before a raw hand went around saying that rooms were all to be changed. This uncertainty continued for a long time. Finally, as it grew late, one man came to me and advised us to retire where we were, that I was not fit to stay up, as he could well see and they dared not turn us out. "We'll cause a riot first and blame the company for ill management — lost heads," he added. But we wanted no fuss on our account and sat up; no change, however, was made, and we stayed there.

The lack of proper water supply and the poor provisioning of the ship became apparent to all before the voyage had proceeded far, but no one cared particularly as we were headed for home. But not quite as we expected or as out tickets said, for when we reached Cape Flattery,[9] we learned that the captain had decided to stop at Seattle instead of at Victoria. This was a keen disappointment to us as well as to some other Canadians. When we reached Seattle, we found that we would have to find our own means to Victoria.

I had not enough cash to pay the fare over, and was explaining the situation to the ticket office and about my letter of credit to a San Francisco bank, when a Canadian from Ontario stepped forward and asked to be allowed to advance the fare. In this way we returned to Victoria at last.

CHAPTER 40

Aftermath

When we arrived home, we found that my husband had been sending many wires to the authorities in the San Francisco Bay region, with a minute description of our persons and instructions to contact us immediately, and to get us safely to Oakland and on a train going north. If these three days of wiring had received any serious attention, it is remarkable that no officials caught up with us. But certainly none did, and reports from the south as to our being among the "missing," kept coming in, long after our safe arrival at Oakwood.

None of us was any the worse[1] for our experiences.

The children returned to school, my daughter going back to All Hallows boarding school,[2] at Yale, B.C., where, in 1907, she obtained one of her McGill certificates in music.

One day, Wong brought me the card of an unknown caller. I could not place the name, and was curious. Nor did I recognize him when we met. The caller introduced himself as the owner of the San Francisco skating rink. In some way, he had read a copy of the Victoria *Colonist,* which, under the following heading, had printed five columns of our experiences:

"EXPERIENCES OF THE GREAT 'QUAKE"
"Victoria Lady Describes Terrible Disaster at the Bay City."
"Very Exciting Scenes Witnessed." "A Narrow Escape from Death."
"All buildings are Badly Wrecked."[3]

That account I have given almost verbatim in the last two chapters, except that I stated in the newspaper account: "Some met at the rink, but the happiness and gaiety of the night before had turned to sorrow. The gay pavilion was turned into the deepest gloom . . . by agonizing cries of dear friends bending over their loved ones who had been carried to this temporary place of safety, both from the burning hospitals and from the streets. The frightfully wounded, mangled and dying were imploring God for mercy. Some relatives in their frenzy and despair at injuries to dear ones they could not alleviate, tore at their hair and clothing, and, with terror-blanched faces, flung themselves down on some of the ruins and fainted. Others remained and clung to their dead and dying. The fire travelled with such rapidity that many of the poor sufferers were burned with the building, being unable to get out all the injured in time."

"I have made a special trip here," my visitor explained, "to express my appreciation of your vivid account. *I was the owner of that skating rink.*[4] All that remains of it now are these tickets." And he handed me several tickets. (These were put in my book manuscript in the Archives.)[5] After a brief, pleasant call and also congratulating my husband, he left and I never heard of him again.

A war correspondent who happened to be in San Francisco at the time, and turned in reports for one of the press services, was also kind enough to praise my report.

On the other hand, when I was walking in town one day and

*Eunice Harrison, eighty years of age, walking with three
of her grandchildren in Victoria. Courtesy of L. Wilson.*

stopping to look in a shop window, I heard two men talking: "Yes, I read her account of the 'Frisco quake and fire. It was all made up, in my opinion; no woman could come through a thing like that."

I did not make myself known and contradict him. My account was all literally true and written down after I had been home a few hours — typed out by my youngest son, ten-year-old Herschel, on an old model typewriter there. Shortly afterwards, *The Colonist* printed it with only a few minor typographical slips.

But in 1906 women were just not supposed to be able to "go through" things like that. Now it is common place, with women standing the bombing of London as well or better than the men, and young women gladly serving in some of the most dangerous theatres of World War II.[6]

Mrs. H. Dallas Helmcken, mentioned earlier, who made periodic trips to live for awhile in California, sent me a fine collection of disaster pictures taken in the midst of the fire and these, with some other striking contemporary pictures, were also inserted in the Victoria Archives collection.

Victoria, not long after, had quite a bad fire, in which several blocks were destroyed. One of the buildings in danger was rented by us to a laundry. The man who got up on the roof to save it from the surrounding fire, later told my husband that, when he had got down from the roof, he met a group of people talking to a policeman. One was a woman of the demi-monde, whose house had just been burned down. She cried: "I had a place like this in San Francisco and it was burned down. I came up here to Victoria and started another. Now that has just burned down. This is God's judgment on me! I shall never do it again. I shall live a good life."

∼つ

In closing, I shall say a few words about the typical artistic activities of women of this period. These included wood carving, china painting, burnt work and music.

I did quite a lot of wood carving and china painting, as a hobby in my spare time. The unpainted china I got from England, and now and then it included pieces of Limoges.[7] After the designs were painted on the cups, saucers and other items of chinaware, I had them sent over to St. Ann's Academy, where they were burned in their kiln.

The craze for "burnt work" went to some length, as shown by the elaborately illustrated forty-four page catalogue of equipment and supplies, of the time, I now have before me. It is titled *The Art of Pyrography.*[8] This burning was done on selected soft wood or leather, by using a red hot point. The working outfit[9] consisted of a benzine bottle and bellows, or double rubber bulb, connected by rubber tubing: the bulb being at one end, the bottle in the centre, and the handle and point on the other end. With the foot or with the left hand, one worked the bulb constantly, while burning on the design with the burning point in the right hand. An alcohol lamp was also necessary for the heating of the point. These points were of platinum and ranged from $1.10 up to $8.00 apiece. They came in various sizes.

The catalogue lists three-ply basswood panels to be burned, on which were various outlines, as of women's heads, hunting scenes, horses' heads and dogs' heads. Some came in the shape of photo frames, at $60 per dozen, and some in the shape of tabourettes, work boxes and Dutch stools. Shirt waist boxes were $60 per dozen. Plaques sold at $97 per dozen. Tankards at $30. There were also checker boards, candle sticks and an almost infinite variety of other articles, including leather goods of a wide range.

I am afraid that this fad encouraged the perpetration of many atrocities, miscalled art, to which we all contributed. Worse than that, these articles when laboriously finished, either became an unwelcome addition to the furniture of obscure rooms in the house or were bestowed upon friends at festive occasions.

The manufactures of equipment and stock must have done quite well as the catalogue lists thousands of dollars worth of raw material over a wide line, all of course to be worked by the purchaser. Still, the fad kept some ladies who had nothing much to do, out of mischief.

I studied leather carving and the making of designs with a Miss Mills. The late Miss Mills[10] was English, short and plump, and in the 1900s had quite a studio in Victoria upstairs on Government Street next to the main branch of the Canadian Bank of Commerce.[11]

Miss Mills was no amateur but had degrees in her art and had done skilled professional work in England. Some of her design and work was done for the new Empress Hotel,[12] she told me. The hotel was preparing to open in 1907.

I saw Miss Mills at her studio, off and on, for several years, before and after the quake. It was a pleasure to study with her and perfect various designs to be used on copper, leather, wood or on china, and I have many of them now.

Miss Mills was once showing me a fine bit of laborious work she had done, when one of her students in the studio exclaimed: "But Miss Mills, you have designed Father Time standing still!" Whether it was the effect of Victoria or not, one couldn't say. But seriously, the whole intricate design was spoiled by this "Homeric nodding." A fleeting look of mortification came over her face, then she said quite simply: "What a blunder I made! I am glad you noticed it." And this from the artist who had so often corrected others — senior students almost as good as herself.

But my chief recreation indoors was music. I played the 'cello, viola and mandolin occasionally but not very expertly.[13] I should have been a lot better at the piano, as I had played ever since I was a small girl. No doubt I could be quite annoying with too much Beethoven, Mendelsohn, Mozart and Chopin.

Besides the modern piano in the sitting and music room, I still used the French piano my father had bought for me in France. It had come out just before the siege of Paris in the War of 1870.[14] This piano, which retained a fine tune with not much tuning, was something of a curiosity. I heard of only two others like it in B.C. It was a French Bord,[15] all black case, with ebony medallions, showing ancient Grecian figures in high relief. Brass candle stick holders were affixed to the piano, one on each side of the music rack.

The piano was highly polished and when the lights were low, and the red Morocco-covered music stool was firmly placed on a great black bear skin rug (all reflected in the piano) and soft old music was played, the effect was rather romantic à la the Second Empire.

I maintained my Oakwood home on Harrison Street for thirty

Eunice Harrison in San Diego, c. 1910.
Courtesy of L. Wilson.

years longer after returning from the San Francisco episode.

Later, my husband and I and the two children here referred to, visited other parts of British Columbia and also in Southern California again. In those succeeding years, we had numerous rather remarkable adventures and knew many interesting characters up and down the coast. But I close this book at 1906 as that is within the period to which my title *The Judge's Wife: Memoirs of a British Columbia Pioneer* refers, for from 1906 forward, the times can hardly be called pioneer.

Notes

Introduction by Jean Barman (pages 7–12)

1. The published memoir most directly comparable is by Emily Carr, born in Victoria a decade later in 1871, who depicted aspects of her childhood and adult life in *Klee Wyck* (Toronto: Oxford University Press, 1941); *The Book of Small* (Toronto: Oxford University Press, 1942), *House of All Sorts* (Toronto: Oxford University Press, 1944), *Growing Pains: The Autobiography of Emily Carr* (Toronto: Oxford University Press, 1946). Susan Allison's memoir, *A Pioneer Gentlewoman in British Columbia*, edited by Margaret Ormsby (Vancouver: UBC Press, 1976), treats mostly frontier life. Other newcomer women whose memoirs have been published wrote only at critical points in their lives, as with those edited by Kathryn Bridge in *Henry & Self: The Private Life of Sarah Crease, 1826–1922* (Victoria: Sono Nis, 1996) and *By Snowshoe, Buckboard and Steamer: Women of the Frontier* (Victoria: Sono Nis, 1998).

2. This account of Eunice Harrison's life is based on her memoir; information generously provided by Louise Wilson; her obituaries in *Colonist*, January 27, 1950, and *Cowichan Leader*, February 2, 1950; and Lionel Westover, "Last Judge of the Old Far West," *Canadian Bar Review* 9, 1 (January 1931): 24–32.

3. Death registration 50-09-001946, British Columbia, Division of Vital Statistics, BC Archives, GR 2951.

4. Eunice M.L. Harrison, "Pioneer Judge's Wife," *Northwest Digest* 7, no. 11 (November 1951): 4–7, 16–17, 19–20; 7, no. 12 (December 1951): 6–7, 14–21, 24; 8, no. 1 (January 1952): 8–12, 19, 23; 8, no. 2 (February 1952): 6–11, 14–17; 8, no. 3 (March 1952): 8–11; 8, no. 4 (April 1952): 6–7, 24; 8, no. 9 (September 1952): 6–7, 21, 23–24; 8, no. 10 (October 1952): 8–11, 24; 8, no. 11 (November 1952): 3, 18–21; 8, no. 12 (December 1952): 3, 19–21, 23–24; 9, no. 1 (January 1953): 8–11, 18–19; 9, no. 2 (February 1953): 7, 9–10; 9, no. 3 (March 1953): 7–8, 11, 14–18; 9, no. 4 (April 1953): 8–10, 14–18; 9, no. 5 (May 1953): 8–9; 20–21, 23–24.

5. Eunice Harrison, "Pioneer Judge's Wife," National Archives of Canada, R7574-0-2-E.

Chapter 1: Red Jackets (pages 17–21)

1. Joseph Seabrook: of Upper Canada, County of Middlesex, town of Caradoc, later London, Ontario. "Joseph Seabrook who settled in Caradoc in 1835 served against the Patriots [rebels] in the Rebellion of 1837–8," in *History of the County of Middlesex* (Toronto: W.A. & C.L. Goodspeed, 1889, reprinted 1972), p. 472.
2. The firing on Fort Sumpter took place April 15, 1861.

Chapter 2: "Ick Clune" (pages 22–24)

1. "Ick Clune": appears to be a Chinook phrase meaning "one [bundle of kindling for] three cents."
2. Gum stick: A kind of wood that is filled or impregnated with fir or pine resin found in old stumps or fallen trees, usually of the Douglas fir variety. One small piece is excellent for starting fires with damp fuel.
3. Inverted basket hat: These were made of cedar roots, softened by boiling. They were then dried and woven into baskets and other shapes, with geometric or animal patterns on the surface.
4. Smallpox: Around this same period in British Columbia, the Rev. Thomas Crosby writes of his visit to New Westminster and the Fraser area: "My next visit was...during the time when the country was suffering from a scourge of smallpox. The disease had been brought from Frisco, and was rapidly spreading among the Indians. Everyone felt interested in stamping it out. The government supplied me with a stock of vaccine and I passed down the coast of Vancouver Island, vaccinating all whom I could reach." He gives specific instances of the ravages made by this disease which he witnessed and tried to succour. From Crosby's *Among the An-Ko-Me-Nums, or Flatheads* (Toronto: William Briggs, 1907), p. 274. Dr. D.R. Hopkins, medical specialist in the disease of smallpox, writes: "Further north, a gold rush in British Columbia attracted 8 or 10 thousand men from California in 1862. They brought smallpox, which spread to the local Indian population.... The story of smallpox in late nineteenth century North America, therefore, is mainly the story of three widespread epidemics...1865–66, 1871–75 and 1881–83." D.R. Hopkins, *Princes and Peasants: Smallpox in History* (Chicago: University of Chicago Press, 1983), p. 274.

Chapter 3: Victoria and School Days (pages 25–29)

1. The *Enterprise:* An American vessel purchased by the HBC in 1862. For further details, see Captain John T. Walbran, *British Columbia Coast Names: 1592–1906* (Ottawa: Government Printing Bureau, 1909), p. 169. Also *The Reminiscences of Doctor John Sebastian Helmcken,* ed. D.B. Smith (Vancouver: UBC Press, 1975).

2. Victoria: in 1868 Victoria became BC's capital, replacing New Westminster.

3. The Songhees: An Indian tribe with a settlement on the shores of what is now Victoria. Dr. Helmcken mentions their appearance: "All the Indians had flattened heads — fearful foreheads, retreating backward. We saw babies undergoing the process...they did not seem to suffer. Perhaps it made them good." *Reminiscences of Dr. Helmcken,* p. 284.

4. Reformed Episcopal Church: This church consisted of Rev. Cridge and his congregation who had broken away from the Anglican Church because they did not favour the elaborate ceremonies used by Bishop Hills at Christ Church Cathedral. Sir James Douglas, writing to one of his daughters, explains briefly why he and other well-known Victorians left the Anglican Church: "Archdeacon Reece preached in the evening at Christ Church; his sermon gave great offence to the congregation, as he advocated ritualism. The Dean said a few words in dismissing the congregation, protesting against the doctrine, which has no warrant in scripture." Sir James Douglas to Martha Douglas, Dec. 3, 1872, BC Archives. A full exposition of this conflict is described by Susan Dickinson in her MA thesis "Doctrinal Conflict 1872–74 and the Founding of the Church of Our Lord in Victoria, BC" (1975).

5. St. Nicholas Hotel: This hotel is advertised in the 1868 *Victoria and District Directory,* published by E. Mellandine, thus: "St. Nicholas Hotel, Government Street, Fire Proof Building. J. Fried Proprietor. Visitors will find the rooms at this hotel most comfortable and elegantly furnished in Victoria and the charges most moderate."

6. The Ellas: The Ellas were Captain Henry Bailey Ella and Martha Beeton Cheney Ella, some of the first settlers of British Columbia. According to Martha Ella's diary, they were married July 19, 1855 at her uncle Blinkhorn's large farm in Metchosin. Henry Ella, born in London in 1826, first came to Victoria in 1851 as chief officer of the HBC sailing ship *Norman Morrison.* This ship made the remarkable trip, London to Victoria and return, by sail power alone. In the colony, Mrs. Ella delighted in colonial life: "...to churn and make...the butter...ironing all day...set the goose on 5 eggs...went to a dancing party on the *Trincomalee*...until 4 in the morning." Mrs. Ella's grand-

son, historian James K. Nesbitt, remarks: "She was a belle of the period, blushing with the coyest of maidens behind their fans, yet how capable she was as well. It is no wonder that she was destined to become one of Victoria's most gracious hostesses, equally at home in the drawing room of Government house or presiding over the wonderful smells of preserves and fresh bread in her own kitchen. She was a typical BC woman of her time and she led a full life." *The Diary of Martha Cheney, 1853–56*, ed. James K. Nesbitt, *BC Historical Quarterly*, vol. 13–14 (1949–50). The Ellas' beautiful pioneer home is one of the few colonial homes that exist today. A picture of this home, "Wentworth Villa," located at 1156 Fort Street, can be found in *This Old House* (Victoria: BC Heritage Advisory Committee, 1991), p. 72.

7. Lieut.-Governor Paterson: Thomas Wilson Paterson was a Liberal MLA, 1902–1907. His house is pictured in *This Old House* (p. 73) and was named "Sequoia." It is of Queen Anne style and constructed using local bricks for its outside walls. Paterson became Lieut.-Governor December 11, 1909. Paterson was also founder and president of the Victoria-Sidney Railway.

8. Sir James and Lady Douglas: Sir James (1803–1877) and Lady Douglas (1812–1890). Sir James, the first governor of British Columbia, retired in 1863 after a very full life, commencing as Hudson's Bay clerk and reaching the top position in the BC hierarchy and then the very highest position in the colony. When eight-year-old Eunice Seabrook met him he had been in retirement about five years. His wife, Lady Douglas, whom he married in 1828, was the daughter of HBC Chief Factor Connolly and a Cree woman. They had 13 children.

9. Dolly Helmcken: Youngest child of Dr. John Sebastian Helmcken and his wife, Cecilia, who was the eldest daughter of Sir James and Lady Douglas. Her full name was Edith Louise. Born on June 24, 1862, she was two years younger than Eunice Seabrook. She married William Ralph Higgins in 1889, but after his death in 1896, she returned to her father's house and cared for Dr. Helmcken for 52 years until his death in 1920. Dolly's care of her father is noted by D.B. Smith: "She was completely devoted to him, and, after his death, to his memory." *Reminiscences of Dr. Helmcken*, p. xxxi. Dolly was instrumental in having his home made a heritage building.

10. St. Ann's Academy (1858–1973): In June 1858, four Roman Catholic nuns from St. Ann's in Quebec arrived on the steamer *Seabird* at Victoria. Their first school was a log cabin, but in September 1871 the new brick convent school at Humboldt was opened (the present heritage building without the additions).

11. The Douglas and Helmcken homes: The Royal Victoria Museum now stands on the site of Sir James Douglas' house, while Dr. Helmcken's home, now preserved as Helmcken House, is nearby. Much later Douglas built a larger home in James Bay.

12. Dr. John Sebastian Helmcken: (1824–1920) He came from England and joined the HBC as a doctor in 1850. He was a much loved medical practitioner who was also interested in politics. He held the position of Speaker of the three Assemblies of the colony of Vancouver Island. The doctor also was president of BC's first medical society when it was formed in 1885.

13. Skookum: is a Chinook word meaning: "Very good, very strong."

Chapter 4: "Teignmouth" (pages 30–32)

1. Teignmouth: There is a town called Teignmouth in England in the West Country.

2. Mrs. Fellows' Finishing School: Mrs. A. Fellows was the daughter of Sir Rowland Hill. In England he had been the Postmaster General and had been famous world-wide for his work for the penny post. Edgar Fawcett mentions that Mrs. Fellows sang with others at a Christmas Eve celebration in Victoria; she appears to have been musically accomplished. See Fawcett, *Some Reminiscences of Old Victoria* (Toronto: W. Briggs, 1912), p. 127.

Chapter 5: A Summer in Granville (pages 33–35)

1. Bowman's stables: "W.G. Bowman, Livery & Sale Stables, Government and Broad, Victoria. Horses, wagons and carriages on hire." *Victoria Directory,* 1877–78, p. 393.

2. The *Etta White:* "Burrard Inlet in the sixties, seventies and eighties, had a fleet of amusing personality craft travelling across its waters with a host of colourful characters to guide them on their way. There was Navvy Jack's row boat; little *Seafoam; Old Union,* alias *Sudden Jerks;* Hans the Boatman's strange craft; the Hudson Bay's old *Beaver;* the *Etta White;* tugs *Maggie* and *Isabel* as well as the *Leonara* and *Senator* built at Moodyville." From Ruth Green's *Personality Ships of British Columbia* (West Vancouver: Marine Tapestry Publication, n.d.), p. 79.

3. Granville: "Vancouver, the growing and prosperous city on Burrard Inlet, owes its existence to the building of the Canadian Pacific Railway, of which it is the western terminus. Before the railway was constructed a small collection of houses was named Granville, but when it was decided that the Canadian Pacific Railway would make this point the terminus the village sprang into prominence and in 1886 the city was incorporated under the name of 'Vancouver' in honour of the man who ninety-four years before had explored and named Burrard Inlet." See Walbran, *British Columbia Coast Names,* p. 507. "In 1870 Gastown (the future Vancouver) was renamed Granville in honour of George Leverson Gower, Earl Granville, British Secretary of State for the Colonies. Granville Street and Granville Island are derived

from this naming." From G.P. and H.B. Akrigg, *BC Place Names* (Victoria: Morriss Printing, 1976), p. 112.

4. Moodyville was built on the present site of North Vancouver.

5. The Alexanders: "Richard Alexander, 26-year-old Scot, arrived with his beautiful wife to be Captain Raymur's assistant. Mrs. Alexander, who came to the colony on one of the famous 'bride ships,' became the social queen of the inlet, as Mrs. Raymur preferred to remain amid civilization in Victoria. Alexander had been one of the few to survive the gruesome overland trek from Canada to the Cariboo Goldfields." See Alan Morley, *Vancouver from Milltown to Metropolis* (Vancouver: Mitchell Press, 1961), p. 46. The same author relates other incidents in the life of these Alexanders. In 1872, Alexander started a post office in Raymur's Hastings Mill and used Canadian postage instead of American. In 1873, his wife gave birth to the first white child born in Gastown or Granville. Much later, Alexander was the manager of Hastings Mill.

Chapter 6: The Man in the Woods (pages 36–41)

1. Hastings: Named after Rear Admiral, the Hon. George Hastings, around 1866–1869. He was the second son of the 11th Earl of Huntingdon. Admiral Hastings was appointed Commander in Chief of the Pacific Station at Hastings Arm. His flag ship *Zealous,* equipped with twenty guns, was one of the earlier built Ironclads.

2. "Her Bright Smile Haunts me Still": The words and music can be found in *Heart Songs Dear to the American People* (Boston, Mass: The Chapple Publishing Co., 1909). It was written and composed years before by W.T. Wrighton. The opening verse is as follows: "Tis years since last we met,/ And we may not meet again;/I have struggled to forget,/But the struggle was in vain."

3. Burrard: Captain Vancouver named Burrard Inlet after Sir Harry Burrard, Bart, RN, who served with Captain Vancouver on the ship *Europa* in 1785 in the West Indies. More information on this very distinguished officer can be found in Walbran, *British Columbia Coast Names*, pp. 71–72.

4. Canadian pony: A very hardy breed of pony developed in Canada to withstand great fluctuations in temperature, particularly in Eastern Canada and in the interior of BC, in Alberta, the prairie provinces, etc. This horse has Morgan, quarter-horse and other blood and can survive on rough or coarse wild grasses with a smaller amount of grain than a less robust breed.

5. Indian war dance: Dr. W. Jilek makes a strong case for the healthful nature of Salish dancing, such as that described by Mrs. Harrison, including the trance dancing: "it is nevertheless true that all these functions also serve

as therapeutic as they ultimately promote the alleviation of anxiety in the individual and the collective." W. Jilek, *Salish Indian...Health* (Toronto: Holt, Rinehart and Winston, 1974), p. 106.

Chapter 7: A Strange Party on the *Matilda* (pages 42–44)

1. Dr. Patricia Roy, in *Vancouver an Illustrated History* (Toronto: James Lorimer and Company, 1980), shows sailing ships loading lumber in Vancouver as late as 1906.

2. *H.M.S. Shah:* Barry M. Gough calls this man-o-war an 1873 screw-frigate with a large iron-teak sheathed body. When Russia and Turkey declared war in 1877, Britain had to safeguard British Columbia as Russia might attack, Britain being an ally of Turkey: "Safeguarding these places [British Columbia and the naval base at Esquimalt harbour] was given high priority by the Pacific Squadron. [Rear-Admiral] de Horsey's flagship, the iron hulled 'Shah,' steamed from South American waters to Esquimalt, where on 4 August [1877] she joined four other Ships, the 'Opal,' 'Fantome,' 'Daring,' and 'Rocket.'" Barry M. Gough, *The Royal Navy and the Northwest Coast of North America 1810–1914* (Vancouver: UBC Press, 1974), p. 228.

3. In Lewis and Dryden's *Marine History of the Pacific Northwest* (ed. E. Wright, Seattle: Superior Pub., 1967) there is the mention of a ship with almost the same name, and it could be the vessel Mrs. Harrison visited: "The Hawaiian ship 'Mathilde' from Burrard's Inlet for Callao with a cargo of lumber was abandoned at sea" (p. 280).

Chapter 9: Romances and Tragedies (pages 49–52)

1. Fanny Palmer: In Lewis and Dryden's *Marine History of the Pacific Northwest*, pp. 223–228, she is listed among the passengers. *The Colonist* reported that Fanny Palmer "had a presentment of the dark Shadow...hanging over her. When she said farewell to several friends, she said she felt she would never see them again in this world...she wrote a note to a former schoolmate in which she expressed her belief that she would never return to Victoria" (*The British Colonist*, November 9, 1875, p. 3). Her father is listed: "Digby Palmer, Professor of Music, Fort Street," in Hibben's *BC Directory*, 1877/78, p. 314.

2. "The Capital Ship:" "In the company of 'The Flying Dutchman,' the 'Golden Vanity' and the other great ships of story and legend there will always be a small corner reserved for 'The Walloping Window Blind.' The verses are by the American master of nonsense, Charles Edward Carryl."

From *Fireside Book of Songs* (New York: Simon and Schuster, 1966, reprint of 1901 edition), p. 4. The opening verse is as follows: "A Capital Ship / A capital ship for an ocean trip / Was the 'Walloping Window Blind'; / No gale that blew dismayed her crew, / Or troubled the captain's mind."

3. *North Pacific:* "Many and various are the conjectures formed as to the causes that led to the destruction of Goodall, Nelson & Perkins' steamship *Pacific* in less than twelve hours after taking her departure from this port on the 4th inst. with a large number of passengers and a valuable cargo." The *British Colonist* speculates that she was a wooden vessel built quickly and well past her age, a very old ship. She had also been hit by another vessel, the *Orpheus*. (Incidentally the ship was the *Pacific* not the *North Pacific*.) Lewis and Dryden, when detailing the *Pacific's* tragedy, note that she was an American steamship going from Victoria to San Francisco, "her deck fairly black with people." Then follows a list of the crew including Miss Palmer, Sewell Prescott Moody and the survivor, Mr. Jelly: "Long will be remembered the year 1875....No greater calamity was ever visited on the people of this Coast than the loss of the steamship *Pacific*...a staunch, well-equipped ship floated near her [the *Orpheus*] and the Death wound was received while she was yet so near a port of safety" (pp. 223–24).

4. S.P. Moody: Sewell Prescott Moody, no relation to Col. R.C. Moody of the Royal Engineers, who Morley terms a brash young Yankee, came to BC around 1864. When Burrard Inlet Mills went broke, he bought it with Captain Stamp and J. Rogers. They made the mill a resounding success story. "Restless, energetic, scheming, sharp...there was a Yankee strain of Puritanism in him." His little milltown on the North Shore was known as Moodyville and it espoused temperance in a time of very hard drinking. Moody also stressed family men in his mill and urged them to build near their workplace. Moody was devoted to his Indian wife, states Morley. "When Moody drowned in the disastrous wreck of the 'S.S. Pacific' off Cape Flattery in 1875, he was universally mourned." Morley, *Vancouver from Milltown to Metropolis,* p. 27.

5. Mr. Jelly: Henry Frederick Jelly was a resident of Port Stanley, Ontario. He had been working on the CPR survey in the Rocky Mountains, helping to construct a way for the proposed railway.

6. Schooley: Tom Schooley was a gold prospector in 1858 in Yale when he was a youth of about eighteen. Some years later, in a drunken rage, Schooley shot his father-in-law, Mr. Foreman, who died the following day. Schooley was taken to prison, but, assisted by two guards, fled to the USA. He was later found, tried and hanged. See T.W. Paterson's "Happy Tom" in *The Daily Colonist,* December 3, 1974, p. 4.

Chapter 10: A Lantern Journey and its Sequel (pages 53–57)

1. Governor Nelson: Hugh Nelson, Lieut.-Governor 1887–92. Nelson is mentioned in Margaret Ormsby *British Columbia: A History* (Toronto: Macmillan, 1958, p. 307), as owning, among others, the Moody Sawmill. In the BC Archives, Victoria, BC there is the Ominica Roads Petition dated 1871 with Nelson's signature on it. He signed as the Member for New Westminster.

2. Frank Barnard: Barnard (1856–1936) was an industrial and transportation magnate elected to the House of Commons as Conservative Member for the Cariboo, 1888–96. His family roots started in the New World in Deerfield, Mass., USA in 1642. After the American Revolution, his ancestors escaped to Canada. Frank Barnard was born in Toronto on May 16, 1856, the eldest child of F.J. Barnard and his wife Ellen Stillman. In 1859 Barnard senior came to BC to take part in the Fraser River Gold Rush. Mr. Barnard later worked as police constable and ship's purser on Yale steamers. In 1862 he founded the Cariboo Express Co. and in 1866 the famous Barnard's Express. Young Frank went to the Collegiate School in Victoria, 1866–76, and completed his schooling with three years at Hellmuth College, Ontario. He entered military service with the Number Second Rifles, Victoria, 1874–77. On November 8, 1883 he married Martha Loewen, the daughter of Joseph Loewen, the owner of the Victoria-Phoenix Brewery. Frank Barnard ran a fleet of six ships in the Kootenays. He gained pioneer fame as the man to develop electric power in BC and reorganized the BC Electric Company in 1906. He became a world traveller but told everyone that no place could equal British Columbia. Condensed from John Osborne's *Miscellaneous Biographies* (Ottawa: Parks Canada, 1975), pp. 2–8.

3. Jack Gray: Born in 1853 in New Brunswick, he became a civil engineer. In 1888 he married Elinor Arbuthnot of Surrey, England. "They occupied an enviable position in social circles." See *BC: Pictorial & Biographical*, vol. 1 (Vancouver: S.J. Clark, 1914), p. 428.

4. Mr. Justice Gray: John Hamilton Gray was born in 1814 at St. George, Bermuda, a grandson of Joseph Gray, a United Empire Loyalist of Boston, Mass, who went to Halifax at the end of the American Revolution. After receiving his AB from King's College, Windsor, he was called to the New Brunswick Bar in 1837. After a distinguished career in NB, John Gray arrived in BC in 1876. Shortly thereafter he was elevated to the Supreme Court of BC, dying in office in 1889. John Gray was one of the Fathers of Confederation. In 1845 he married the eldest daughter of Lieut.-Col. Ormond, a direct descendant of the Lord Lieutenant of Ireland in Charles

I's reign. His wife Elizabeth and he had seven children. See *BC: Pictorial &*
Biographical, vol. 1, p. 327, et seq.

5. Jimmie Douglas: The only surviving son of Sir James and Lady Douglas.
For more details on his life, see Derek Pethick's *James Douglas* (Vancouver:
Mitchell Press, 1969).

6. Young Eli Harrison: His mother's (Mrs. Elizabeth Harrison) overland
trip together with her husband, Eli Harrison, Sr., is briefly dealt with by
N. de Bertrand Lugrin in *The Pioneer Women of Vancouver Island 1843–1866*
(Victoria: The Women's Canadian Club of Victoria, 1928). Eli Harrison's
father was Eli Harrison, Sr., who married Elizabeth Warburton.

Chapter 11: With the Covered Wagons (pages 58–65)

1. Prairie schooner: A long covered wagon used by the pioneers in travelling westward. In F. E. Herring's *Nan and other Pioneer Women of the West*
(London: Francis Griffiths, 1913), she tells of a fictional family crossing the
plains to California in the '49 Gold Rush. In her second paragraph, she says:
"Next morning their ox cart fell into line behind the more pretentious
bullock wagons (prairie schooners) with their white covers and mule teams"
(p. 9).

2. Sioux band: "The Dakota or Sioux are considered by historians to be
the most powerful of all the Indian races native to North America." D.
Robinson, Ross et al, *A History of the Dakota or Sioux Indians* (Minneapolis:
News Printing Co., 1904, reprinted 1967), p. 7.

3. Pipe of peace: "The old men of the tribe would start out first on foot.
They were always in front and we depended on them. They were experienced and viewed the lay of the land perfectly. If the start was made before
sunrise, it was beautiful to see the glow of the coming day. Then the old men
sat down to wait for the sunrise, while the rest of us stood around holding
our horses. One of the men would light the pipe, and, as the sun came over
the horizon, the entire tribe stood still, as the ceremony to the Great Spirit
began. It was a solemn occasion as the old man held the bowl of the pipe in
both hands, and pointed the stem towards the sky, then towards the East,
South, West, North and lastly to Mother Earth....The men smoked, after
which the pipe was put away.... After the ceremony was over, somehow we
felt safer to go on." Luther Standing Bear, *My People the Sioux* (London:
Wallace and Norgate, 1928). On page 25 there is a photo of the author,
Chief Standing Bear, a full-blooded Sioux, praying to the Great Spirit
through the pipe of peace.

4. Wake-si-ah: far away, in the far distance.

5. Fort Bridger: Originally in 1842 a fur trading post. Later in 1850, the
Mormons claimed the land on which the post was located. As the Mormons

were carrying on activities that annoyed all other settlers as well as the US Government, the US President sent in military forces and took Fort Bridger as a US Army post. The Mormon's practice of polygamy was condemned by government and citizens alike. It was only in 1890 that the practice of multiple wives was abandoned in order that the territory of Utah, mostly made up of Mormons, could gain statehood from the American authorities. See R.S. Ellison's *Fort Bridger: A Brief History* (Casper: The Historical Commission of Wyoming, 1931).

6. Commonwealth: After the execution of Charles I, Oliver Cromwell formed an English republican government in 1649 which he called a Commonwealth. Cromwell later assumed the title of Lord Protector. In 1660, Charles II was restored to the throne.

7. Carlyle's *Letters and Speeches of Oliver Cromwell:* Carlyle remarks that the term Butcher refers to Harrison's trade: "Thomas Harrison, for example, is called…'the son of a butcher,' which meant only that his Father, as farmer…had…in Staffordshire…fat cattle" (New York: Charles Scribner, 1899, vol. 1, p. 24).

8. Westover, Berkeley, and Brandon: These mansions or colonial manor houses and their vast estates on the James River in Virginia are described and pictured in Edith F. Sale's *The Manors in Virginia in Colonial Times* (Philadelphia and London: J.P. Lippencott, 1909), pp. 134–148 & 149–159.

9. See *Records of College of Arms*, London, England. Filed June 28, 1902 & December 7, 1931; and Fox-Davies *Armorial Families* (London, 1905), p. 663; (1929–30), p. 888.

10. Benjamin Harrison: (1833–1901) He was the 23rd US President, holding office from 1889–1893. He was a grandson of William Henry Harrison and a Republican.

11. William Henry Harrison: (1773–1841) A Whig and the 9th US President. He died after he had spent only one month as President. A general in the War of 1812, he defeated some powerful Indian forces and used his victory in his political campaign, under the slogan "Tippecanoe and Tyler, too."

12. Tippecanoe: The Indian chief Tecumseh was defeated at the Battle of Tippecanoe, Indiana, in 1811 by General William Henry Harrison and his USA troops.

13. William of Orange: (1650–1702) Considered by historians as one of England's most remarkable kings. William married his cousin, Mary Stuart, and they reigned together as joint King and Queen of England. See J. Miller's *William and Mary* (London: Weidenfeld and Nicholson, 1974).

14. Court sword: a sword worn with court costume when a person is presented to the King or Queen and the court.

15. Jane Welch Carlyle's letters: *Jane Welch Carlyle: Letters to Her Family:*

1839–1863, ed. Leonard Huxley (London: John Murray, 1924), p. 344, et seq. Jane to Helen Welch: "I was immensely glad the other day to receive Mazzini." Mazzini regaled her with stories of Garibaldi and himself fleeing for their lives.

16. Mazzini and Garibaldi: (1805–72) Italian patriot and founder in 1831 of the secret society known as Young Italy. The object of this group was to create a united independent republic in Italy. Mazzini and others were successful in bringing about a very short-lived republic in 1849. Garibaldi (1807–82) was an Italian patriot and soldier who fought against the Austrians in 1848–49 and preserved Mazzini's 1849 Italian Republic.

17. St. Louis Company of Saints: A group of Mormons in St. Louis, Mo. The Mormons were a new religious organization that called each member a saint. Joseph Smith told his followers that, in the 1820s, he had a vision in which he met Jesus Christ and God. He was told that no church was God's or Christ's and that Smith should start the true church. In another vision in 1830 the angel Moroni instructed Smith to publish the new revealed scriptures called *The Book of Mormon* from gold plates hidden in the earth. Smith was also told that he was the new prophet and leader of this new faith. At that time the Mormons practised polygamy as a religious belief, as a result of which the other citizens of America as well as the US Government became very hostile to this new religion and its followers. As a consequence, these followers and Smith were driven out of every state or territory they settled in, and finally in 1844 a group of non-Mormons killed Joseph Smith. The next leader, Brigham Young, was Prophet from 1847–1862. A great number of Mormons went to the territory that is now the State of Utah. There was much trouble and no hope of Utah ever becoming a State once the US passed a law against plural wives. Finally, in 1890 in order to gain Statehood for their new home, the Mormons decided to remove polygamy from their doctrines, and Utah achieved Statehood. Mormonism spread widely and today there are approximately eleven million Latter Day Saints.

18. Heber J. Grant: President of the Mormon Church in Salt Lake City, Utah until his death May 14, 1945. He was born in that city, of Mormon parents in 1856.

19. The Quorum of Seventy: In the Mormon church, the seventy elders who are designated as "travelling ministers unto the Gentiles...and the Jews." See also Exodus 24.1 and Luke 10.1.

Chapter 12: Mr. & Mrs. Eli Harrison, Sr. (pages 66–67)

1. Cocos Island: Territory of Australia consisting of 27 coral islands with three inhabited. They are located in the Indian Ocean southwest of Java.

There are tales of pirates and others who secreted treasure in the islands, but the gold has yet to be discovered.

2. Captain Gladstone: A reference to John Neilson Gladstone can be found in a note to a letter by his brother, W.E. Gladstone, to him in Gladstone's fourteen volume set of *Letters*. In 1823 Captain Gladstone was in the Royal Navy in Halifax, on *HMS Sparrow Hawk*.

Chapter 13: Marriage and a Royal Wedding Gift (pages 68–72)

1. St. John's Anglican Church: In 1880 this was the famous "Iron Church" then at the corner of Fisgard Street and Douglas Street where the present Hudson's Bay Department store now stands. In his book, *The Iron Church* (Victoria: Braemar Books, 1984), Stuart Underhill relates in minute detail the history of this unique church, its successors and its pastors. The outside walls had a framework of cast iron with interstices faced with corrugated plates, while the arch and the framework of the roof and girders of the aisles consisted of iron castings riveted together. All the church's iron structural parts were brought out from England on the barque-rigged *Athelstan* around the Horn to Victoria where two experts, also from England, supervised the church's erection on a foundation of timber and Salt Spring Island stone. Bishop Hill had accumulated gifts of over eleven thousand pounds sterling from Anglicans all over England to assist this project. Baroness Burdett-Coutts, the very wealthy religious enthusiast, donated many more thousands of pounds to help erect and furnish this church. St. John's Iron Church when completed could accommodate 600 worshippers and was considered the finest church north of San Francisco. The HBC bought the church's site in 1910, offering $150,000. St. John's Iron Church was then torn down and was replaced by a much larger church at Quadra and Mason Streets.

2. Rev. Percival Jenns: Rev. Jenns' marrying of the couple is recorded in a huge red leather book entitled "Marriages in the Diocese of Columbia, of St. John's Church, Victoria, 1879–1884." This book is located in the BC Anglican Archives, in a small building near Christ Church Cathedral on Burdett Ave., in Victoria, BC: "Number 125: Date: Nov. 24, 1880, Bridegroom: Eli Harrison, Jr., Condition: Bachelor; Bride: Eunice Mary Louisa Seabrook; Condition: Spinster; Witnesses: Thomas Lubbe, Anita Spain, Elizabeth Harrison, Annette Mary Seabrook; Officiating Minister: Percival Jenns." Elizabeth Harrison was the groom's mother; Annette Seabrook, the bride's mother. Thomas Lubbe is listed as a fur trader with his business on Yates near Wharf. Anita Spain is unknown. Rev. Jenns' life is well detailed in Underhill's book (see note 1). He was a Londoner from a well-to-do family, educated at home and then at university for holy orders. Bishop Hills

inspired the young minister to come to BC. Rev. Jenns was a man of many talents: a gardener at the church as well as woodworker and pastor, typifying the versatility of the early pioneers. He was a man of strong faith and morality. The grandchildren of the first pioneers have many stories of Rev. Jenns publically weeping over the sins of the inhabitants during his powerful sermons against sin and wickedness.

3. H.M. Queen Victoria: (1819–1901) One of the most famous of England's six Queens regnant. She came to the throne in 1837 and reigned until 1901.

4. Mrs. Eunice Bagster: Samuel Bagster married Eunice Birch in December 1797. She outlived him by 26 years, dying in 1877 at the amazing age of 100. In the *London Times* of August 27, 1877, page 9, there is a column about her death and also Queen Victoria's earlier visit to see her: "Her Majesty, with her usual kindness, drove over to Old Windsor early in July in order to pay a visit to one of her oldest subjects, and continued to inquire after her health to the very last" [Old Windsor was Mrs. Bagster's home]. The Bagsters' marriage was a life-long love affair as Mr. Bagster described in his memoirs: *Samuel Bagster of London 1772–1851*, with a foreword by the great Shakespearian actress, Dame Sybil Thorndike (London: Samuel Bagster & Sons, 1979), p. 135.

5. Mr. Bagster: (1772–1851) Eunice Bagster's husband (supra). He was the founder of the publishing firm of Samuel Bagster and Sons. He was born December 26, 1772. Educated at Rev. John Ryland's Establishment, Mr. Bagster became a bookseller and publisher in 1794. *The Dictionary of National Biography* devotes two pages to his work. The rare nature and expense of polyglot Bibles gave him the idea of supplying such books in accessible and inexpensive editions. Mr. Bagster also started publishing Bibles in many languages: English, French, German, Italian, Spanish, ancient Greek, modern Greek, Latin, Hebrew. He later added even more languages. In 1824 he brought out a polyglot grammar in thirty or more languages upon the principles of comparative philology. His 1827 Bible had 4,000 illustrative notes, 500,000 marginal references, an introduction and much more.

6. Fire: Mr. Bagster describes this fire of March 1822 which destroyed his business in Paternoster Row, on pages 175–82 in his *Memoirs* (see note 4). Mr. Bagster rebuilt his publishing business in an even better area of London, and Samuel Bagster and Sons Publishing Company became a far greater success than before and still flourishes to this day.

7. Yapp edges: Divinity circuit binding.

8. The opera bag: It is still in perfect condition and has been donated by the family to the Victoria and Albert Museum in London, England. A photo is included in these memoirs.

9. The London *Times,* August 27, 1877; *The Windsor & Eton Express,* August 25, 1877; *The Vineland Independent,* New Jersey, USA, September 20, 1877.

Chapter 14: Housekeeping (pages 73–75)

1. Museum building: This was the Parliament Buildings section closest to the Royal BC Museum but across the street. When the annotator as a child accompanied Mrs. Harrison to this Museum, a favourite spot with all the stuffed animals, birds and fishes, her grandmother pointed out the exact location.

2. Skookum: the dog Skookum had come from Teignmouth, her mother's home (i.e. that of Mrs. Annette Seabrook).

3. Electric street cars: These cars and electric lighting are extensively dealt with in Dr. Patricia Roy's article, "Late Nineteenth Century Technology and Municipal Enterprise," in *BC Studies,* no. 32 (1976–77): 79–92.

Chapter 15: The Tom Pool Murder Mystery (pages 76–79)

1. Tom Pool: Tom Pool, his Indian wife and their two half-breed children, a girl of ten and a boy of six, lived at Half-Way House in the vicinity of Pemberton Meadows in the Cariboo. He ran a farm and also had a general store. There is some information about this murder in "Who Killed Tom Pool was the Mystery of the Cariboo," by R.D. Cummings, *Vancouver Province,* August 1, 1936.

2. Chilcotin Indians: "Chilcotin" means "Inhabitants of Young Man's River." These Indians are Athapaskan-speaking tribes found around the headwaters of the Chilcotin River and Anaheim Lake district and from the Cascade Mountains to the west and the eastern area of the Fraser River. Their clothing was different from that of the other Indians they traded with, the Shuswap Indians. They wore moccasins, leather breech cloth or skirt, belt, robe, cap and leggings made from deer and moose hide. Their winter homes were earth-covered lodges finished with animal hides and brush. They were bolder than the Shuswap or Interior Salish and were known to be more turbulent. See Diamond Jenness's *The Indians of Canada* (Ottawa: National Museum of Canada, 6th edition, 1963), p. 361, et seq.

3. James "Scotty" Halliday: Mr. Halliday raised hogs and cattle and did other farming in Pemberton in 1879. He drove his animals on foot from Pemberton to the Cariboo gold fields market area. In April 1879 with his Indian helper, Sketch, he went to Lillooet for supplies and on his return stopped at Tom Pool's for some camaraderie, sending his Indian on ahead. Next day the Pool home was discovered burned down and Pool and his two

children dead in the remains of the fire. But bullets were also found in their bodies.

4. Jerry Woods: One of Tom Pool's neighbours, who was a witness in one of the many trials in this case.

5. Carey: Another witness and also one who was charged in the Pool trials, but later acquitted.

6. Red light districts: Several historians of early BC refer to red light districts in Victoria and in other parts of the province. One said the prostitutes were mostly from San Francisco. But there is hardly any historical detail on this subject. The lower end of Chatham Street near the ocean was said to be such an area but precise details are lacking.

7. Death flag: This was a flag put up on a house by the health authorities warning that a person or persons had died of the highly contagious smallpox. People were to keep away.

8. Uriah Heep: A character in Charles Dickens' *David Copperfield.* Heep is a villainous and cunning clerk who, by pretending to be a man of great humility, gets his employer into serious trouble and himself in jail.

Chapter 17: Interesting Callers (pages 84–89)

1. Amor de Cosmos: (1825–1897) Born in Nova Scotia as William Alexander Smith, he became an eccentric but powerful man in early BC. He was also a Freemason and brother Mason in Eli Harrison's Lodge. He became the second Premier of BC, 1872–74. Amor de Cosmos's name has been variously interpreted as "Love of the Universe" or "Lover of the Universe."

2. The Standard: A paper started in June 1870 by Amor de Cosmos. Earlier in 1859, de Cosmos was editor of *The British Colonist,* the second paper in the very early days of Victoria. The first was *The Victoria Gazette.*

3. Bishop Hills: Bishop Hills came from England and was the son of an admiral. He was given large grants to aid Anglican missions in the early colony by the philanthropist and wealthy religious enthusiast, Baroness Burdett-Coutts.

4. Sir John A. Macdonald: (1815–1891) Sir John A. Macdonald was the principal architect of Canadian Confederation and was Canada's first Prime Minister, 1867–73, and then again in 1878–91.

5. Sir Matthew Baillie Begbie: (1819–1894) was born in Scotland, the eldest son of Col. T. S. Begbie. Educated at Cambridge (BA 1841; MA 1844), he was called to the bar in 1844. He went to the Crown Colony of BC in 1858 and was appointed judge there. He is best known for his preservation of law and order in a wild and exciting gold rush country. He was also known as "The Hanging Judge." In 1870 he was appointed Chief Justice of BC and

died in office in 1894. He received a Knighthood from Queen Victoria in 1876. There are a number of biographies.

6. Chief Justice McColl: (1854–1902) He was one of the lesser known early pioneer Judges. Angus John McColl was called to the Ontario Bar in 1875. In 1882 he arrived in BC and went to New Westminster where he became a partner of G.E. Corbould. In 1896 he was appointed a Supreme Court judge and in 1898 succeeded Chief Justice Davie, dying suddenly in 1902 in Victoria.

7. Chief Justice Theodore Davie: Mr. Davie was Premier of BC from 1892 to March 2, 1895, but when his term was finished he was appointed Chief Justice of the Supreme Court of BC, thus following Judge Begbie.

8. Dr. Robie L. Reid: Dr. Reid, who died February 6, 1945, was the Masonic Grand Historian from 1931 to 1945. On June 18, 1942, he presented to the Grand Lodge of Free Masonry a number of items, one of which was material belonging to Eli Harrison, Sr.

9. General Pike: Albert Pike was born in Boston, Massachusetts, December 29, 1809. Becoming a teacher in 1831, he went with some trappers to Little Rock. Pike edited a paper there and studied law. He served in the Mexican War and when the Civil War broke out he led a force of Cherokee Indians under the Southern banner at the Battle of Pea Ridge. After the war, General Pike practised law in Washington, DC. He was acclaimed an early American poet after he published *Hymns to the Gods*.

10. Gilbert Malcolm Sproat: (1834–1913) Mr. Sproat was born in Southern Scotland of a large farming family. He was educated at a grammar school, Haddon Hall, and later at King's College, London. Sproat came to Vancouver Island in 1860 as an employee of Anderson and Company, ship owners and ship brokers. This firm had a sawmill in Alberni to export spars and lumber for ships because of the blockade caused by the US Civil War. Sproat married Anne Wigham, December 23, 1862, and they had three children. He was appointed a Magistrate in Alberni in 1863 and in 1871 became BC's first Agent-General. He served on several Commissions concerning Indians. Leaving government service in 1889, Sproat relocated to Kamloops until 1898 and then moved to Victoria, finally dying there in 1913. Sproat wrote much on the early Indians. In 1869, he published *Scenes and Studies of Savage Life*, a study based on the Indians he had met on Vancouver Island's West coast. Charles Lillard republished the book as *The Nootka: Scenes and Studies of Savage Life* (Victoria: Sono Nis, 1987).

Chapter 18: A Trip Through the Wild Interior (pages 90–107)

1. Mr. McIntosh: A horseman, miner and farmer for years in the area Mr. Harrison describes.

2. Hill's Bar: In the gold rush of 1858 on the Fraser River, the first bar which gave great promise to the veteran gold miners from all over the world was given the name Hill's Bar. Not only was this the richest bar on the Fraser but it was also occupied by the most violent miners. A bar was a sandy flat that was found in the river bends.

3. Ned McGowan: McGowan was born in Philadelphia in 1813 of Catholic parents but later gave up religion. He held a job as Town Clerk in Philadelphia, then married and had four sons. He was elected as a US Representative after campaigning as a Democrat. McGowan tried to have imprisonment for debt abolished in 1830–40. After becoming a Police Superintendent, he was later suspended for fighting. McGowan then went to San Francisco and in 1850 was elected a judge of the Court of Quarter Sessions there. According to one authority, McGowan did not get along with the Vigilantes and they determined to destroy him. Along with another man, he was charged with the murder of John King but was later acquitted. Then when he wrote what he thought about the Vigilantes, he was sued for libel. The Vigilantes drove McGowan out of San Francisco, and he fled to the BC gold fields. His vindication in court through his acquittal of King's murder did not help him in BC, because Bartlett, the editor of the *Victoria Gazette,* was an American who had run the *True Californian* and who immediately repeated all the abuse the Vigilantes ran in the California papers about McGowan. For further information about this exciting period in pioneer history, see John Myers' *San Francisco's Reign of Terror* (New York: Doubleday, 1980).

4. The Vigilantes: Citizens in San Francisco who took the law into their own hands to punish miners and others in the various gold rushes.

5. John King: John King was manager of Adams and Company bank in San Francisco until it failed in 1855, when he started a newspaper, *The San Francisco Bulletin.* He filled his paper with much sensational and libelous material. At this time there were eight daily newspapers as well as two in German, in San Francisco.

6. Bunch grass: This grass is mentioned as long and sweet. Cattle and horses fattened on it as noted by R.C. Mayne, RN, FRGS, in his book, *Four Years in British Columbia* (London: John Murray, 1862), pp. 108–109.

7. Lytton: In 1862 Lytton had about a dozen huts, a saloon, a large court house, an express office, and two HBC buildings reconverted to a magistrate's abode. See *Four Years in British Columbia,* p. 109, note 6.

8. Sir Edward Bulwer-Lytton: (1803–1873) A man famous in the history of British Columbia. He became Colonial Secretary in 1858 while the gold rush was at its zenith in British Columbia. He instituted a new British Colony so that BC could have control over its minerals. There would be law and order, free trade, and there would be a Colonial government. The region, previ-

ously known as New Caledonia, was now to be designated "British Columbia," a name chosen by Queen Victoria herself. One of the reasons why Colonial status was hastened was because some USA politicians and others cast envious eyes on BC and its new gold discovery and wanted to annex the territory for America.

9. Rev. J.B. Good: (1833–1916) Rev. John Boothe Good's Indian Mission at Lytton was quite famous. H.P. Wright, Archdeacon of Vancouver Island and Chaplain to the Forces, First Class, wrote in *British Columbia Mission* of his visit to the Lytton Indian Mission run by Rev. Good: "One of the most remarkable Missions known to our Church" (1877). One of the Rev. Good's amazing talents was his rendering of the Anglican Offices of Marriage, Burial, etc., into the language of the Thompson Indians. His translation into Nitlakapamuk can be found in the BC Archives.

10. Spence's Bridge: A very well-known early bridge. The road between Spence's Bridge and Lytton was completed about 1864.

11. The Cascades: The Cascade Range runs from Northern California through west central Oregon and Washington to British Columbia, where it is termed the Coast Range. These mountains are of volcanic origin, and have many high peaks such as 14,410 foot Mt. Rainier.

12. Forty-Niners: People who joined in the world-famous 1849 gold rush to California. Vast numbers of gold seekers from all over the globe flooded into California heading for the banks of the Sacramento River. Songs and lyrics were composed to tell of their adventure and way of life in the California gold rush.

13. Fort Hope: In the famous 1858 gold rush to the Cariboo, Governor Douglas found it imperative to prevent miners from squatting on the gold rush area. He contacted the Colonial Office and announced to the miners that Fort Hope and Fort Yale, former Hudson's Bay Company posts, would be made into towns. Douglas told the miners that town lots in Fort Hope and Fort Yale could be bought by them on installments until the whole price was paid. The miners would thus own lots on which they could build cabins or houses.

14. Anglican Sisters: They founded All Hallows school for Indian girls and later included Caucasians.

15. The Duke and Duchess of Cornwall and York: The Duke was the second son of Edward the Seventh, born in 1865. The Duchess (1867–1953) was Princess May of Teck. The couple were married at St. James Palace, July 6, 1893. When the Duke and Duchess came to BC in 1901, Vancouver gave them a magnificent welcome and reception. They ruled as King George and Queen Mary from 1910 to 1936, when King George died.

16. Political feeling: This high feeling between the Federal Government

and BC may refer to the fact that the BC Government under Walkem told the federal Government in Ottawa that BC would leave Confederation if the promised railway was not built, one of the terms of BC's entering the union in the first place. (Dr. Ormsby comments that the political situation at this time in BC is very confused and little understood by modern day historians).

17. Jackass Mountain: The first group to consider a road into the interior of BC was the town council of Yale in 1860. They were Dr. Max Fifer, Yale's HBC Chief Trader Allard, and two elected road builders, Hugh McRoberts and William Power. One of their main requests was that a bluff by Jackass Mountain be tunneled. This mountain got its name after a jackass loaded with mining tools and supplies lost its footing and fell to its death.

18. Accused Indian: Mr. Harrison is careful to omit all identifying names.

19. Kamloops: Originally an HBC post, Fort Kamloops, in the late 1870s was more a transportation depot than a mining centre, according to H.H. Bancroft in his *History of BC: 1792–1887* (San Francisco: History Company, 1887).

20. Cache Creek: Also a transportation centre rather than a gold mining location.

21. Brigade Trail: Dr. Ormsby mentions that, in 1862, 1,000 miners used the Old Brigade route which preceded the more famous wagon road. This trail and two others had been started in the earliest HBC times in BC and by 1847 "the last fur caravan passed down the old brigade trail" (Ormsby, *British Columbia*, p. 91).

22. Wagon road: In 1862 James Douglas requested the Royal Engineers to start the first part of this road from Yale to Boston Bar and 9 miles to Spence's Bridge. Built by the Royal Engineers and public contractors, the wagon road ran some 400 miles.

23. Mule Deer: Now considered one of BC's most populous big game animals. It has large ears and forked antlers unlike white tailed deer.

24. Clinton: Originally an Indian village given the name of Sprague. In 1863 it was re-named Clinton, after Henry Clinton, Duke of Newcastle.

25. Lillooet: This town in the Cariboo gold area had a roadway to replace its old 1858 trail built by Royal Engineers, Marines and civilians.

26. The Chasm: Often called Painted Chasm, a box canyon over 1,000 feet deep at its south end and one-quarter of a mile wide. Its sheer walls blaze with colour, the effect of weather on its mineral rocks. It contains chabazite, heulandite, analcite and opal. The modern road is part of the original Cariboo road.

27. Lac La Hache: A small community on a lake by the same name. The first store there was run by Isaac Ogden, grandson of an HBC man.

28. 150 Mile House: An important junction in the time of the wagon road.

Freight and passengers changed for stages to the Keithley Creek goldfields.

29. Harrison-Lillooet road: In 1859 James Douglas made a contract to send 260 men on the *Umatilla* to start construction of the Harrison-Lillooet road. It took a number of months and the road was not a good one but it was sufficient for the large number of mule trains heading for the gold fields and returning with their cargo of the bright metal.

30. Soda Creek: The town took its name from a nearby creek that bubbled up like soda water as it rushed past a lime formation, in its bed.

31. Alexandria: A former HBC post, Fort Alexandria was the end of navigation in the Cariboo. In 1860, one ton of goods from Alexandria to Victoria cost $825.

32. Australian: This ranch was started in 1863 by the Downes brothers, three men who had come for gold but decided instead to homestead and farm and sell their produce to the gold miners. Later they sold to other ranchers.

33. Kersley Ranch: Charles Kersley took out homestead rights here in 1867 and built up a large cattle, horse and grain ranch.

34. Quesnelmouth: Simon Fraser named this place after his third helper in his historic canoe voyage. After 1900, the town was called "Quesnel."

35. Lightning Creek: The gold rush to this creek opened in 1861. "The total product of this creek in October 1876 was $500,964." See Bancroft, *History of BC,* p. 507. Three years later it must have yielded less. Bancroft remarks that the US consul said there were about 15,000 miners in BC in 1862, 75% from California, Washington and Oregon. In 1862 the three main gold areas were Williams, Lightning and Lowhee creeks. In this Cariboo area, less than 50 miles square, it is said that gold worth $30,000,000 to $40,000,000 was recovered from 1862 to 1882 from half a dozen main creeks. The settlement of Lightning Creek is now a ghost town.

36. Stanley: In the early gold rush days of 1862, Stanley was a town crowded with bars, saloons, hotels, shops, and, according to Mr. and Mrs. Wright, "hurdy-girdy girls and unwashed miners."

37. Williams Creek: When the road along Lightning Creek was finished in 1865, Williams Creek was found to be rich in shallow gold deposits. The creek was named by William Dietz, a German prospector. Later, deep drilling to 80 feet or more produced much gold until 1882. *Richfield:* The new town on Williams Creek, was the site of government buildings for the area. It was one mile from Barkerville. *Cameron Town:* This place takes its name from James A. Cameron who found gold there a mile downstream shortly after Billy Barker discovered the yellow metal. *Barkerville:* Billy Barker, who came late to the Cariboo, employed a new method of mining. Instead of panning, he felt he should dig deep. Finally when he had excavated to 52

feet, he found the gold sitting on the bedrock. Other individuals and companies also dug deep in this area called Barkerville, and the Diller Company in one day brought up 200 pounds of gold (2,400 troy ounces). Multiplied by $16 (gold was $16 an ounce then) that comes to $38,400. (In 2002, gold is approximately $460 an ounce so that one day's take today would be $1,104,000!) So much tunneling by so many in Barkerville no doubt produced all the tailings Mr. Harrison speaks of in the town when he was there in 1879, three years before the richest gold strikes. In 1962 Barkerville was restored to its pre-1880 days and made a provincial historic park, featuring well-known characters in period costumes, boardwalks, saloons, etc.

38. Bald Mountains: These mountains are made up of metamorphic clay slate through which are found broad strips containing gold-bearing quartz. But they are only a small part of other such mountains and areas with the same composition. The early writers who describe these gold-bearing mountains and areas are Murchison, Forbes, Hector, Bauerman, Selwyn and Dawson.

39. The "Colonial" and the "Driard": Harry Gregson regards the Colonial Restaurant at 95 Government Street as one of Victoria's better cafés in the 1858 to 1880 period. It was run by Sosthenes Driard who was very corpulent and had asthma. The Driard Hotel was very well appointed and could accommodate 350 people in its fine dining room. It was opened in 1872 by Mr. Driard and was later enlarged and improved but went into decline after the Empress Hotel opened in 1908. Before that time, the Driard was considered the best hotel north of San Francisco. See H. Gregson, *History of Victoria, 1842–1970* (Victoria: Victoria Observer Publishing Co, 1970), p. 20.

Chapter 19: Edging the Precipices (pages 108–115)

1. Judge: Mr. Harrison was appointed Judge in the Cariboo and Lillooet area in 1884 and served there until 1889 when he was made a local Judge of the Supreme Court for Nanaimo County: "County Court judgeships should not be confused with those of similar name in England and in Eastern Canada, for his jurisdiction was far greater in every way, with an appeal directly to the Supreme Court of Canada, and his territory covered thousands of miles...." See "Last Judge of the Old Far West," in *The Canadian Bar Review*, vol. 9 (1931), p. 28.

2. Hon. Mr. Justice Walkem: George Anthony Walkem (1834–1908) was born in Newry, Ireland, Nov 15, 1834, the son of Charles and Maran Walkem. The family moved to Canada in 1847 where Mr. Walkem's father was appointed surveyor on the staff of the Royal Engineers engaged in the survey of Canada to the USA border. George was one of ten children. He studied

law and was called to the Bar of Lower Canada in 1858 and Upper Canada in 1861. Coming to BC in 1862, Mr. Walkem was refused entry to the Bar as, according to the authorities, BC had no power to do this. Even when the Colonial Secretary said Walkem could be called to the Bar, Judge Begbie refused, as he had a strong dislike of Walkem. Walkem was elected to represent the Cariboo in 1864 in the Colonial Assembly. He finally became a BC lawyer and in 1881 requested Sir John A. Macdonald to make him a judge. He was appointed in this capacity in 1882. For further information, see John Osborne's *Miscellaneous Biographies* (1975), p. 166.

3. K.C.: King's Counsel is an honourary title given by the Federal and Provincial governments to distinguished court room lawyers or barristers.

Chapter 20: Departure Bay (pages 116–119)

1. Nanaimo: This town started when coal was found there in 1852. James Douglas, then Governor of the Crown Colony of Vancouver Island, went to appraise the coal and had the area taken over in the name of the Hudson's Bay Company. Miners were sent in and houses built and the place was called Colville. In 1862 its name was officially changed to Nanaimo, sometimes spelt "Tsanaimo." By 1862 there were over 500 whites. Coal was shipped at an annual rate of 18,000 tons, mostly to San Francisco. At the World's Fair in London of 1862, six tons of Nanaimo coal were on exhibit. Patricia Johnson notes that an 1887 directory (two years before the Harrisons came to Nanaimo) lists several opera houses, not including those at Wellington. No doubt, even with 18 hotels Nanaimo did not equal the larger city, Victoria, the capital. See *Welcome to Nanaimo* (Burnaby: Trendix Publishing, 1974), p. 84.

2. Train: In 1878 when Lord Dufferin, the Governor-General of Canada visited Nanaimo, he was met by many people who informed him that Vancouver Island would leave Canada unless a railway was built on the Island. In 1882, the Marquis of Lorne when in BC asked the coal millionaire, Robert Dunsmuir, if he would construct such a railway. P. Johnson notes that Dunsmuir, with railroad financiers Huntington, Hopkins, Stanford and Crocket of San Francisco, built the railroad, receiving the agreed land grant and $750,000. The first section of the railway was completed in 1886 when the so-called "last spike" was driven at Shawnigan Lake by Sir John A. Macdonald, but the tracks did not reach Victoria until 1887 and Esquimalt until 1888.

3. Judge: Mr. Harrison was appointed resident Judge of Nanaimo County Aug. 13, 1889 (Nanaimo Archives AR7/11). Nanaimo County included a number of other cities: Duncan, Chemainus, Ladysmith, Parksville, etc.

4. The Dunsmuir house: The Harrison family was renting this house until their own home was built. (However, later they chose to erect their new home

in Victoria, not Nanaimo.) "The new Dunsmuir home at the Bay was the grandest yet and appears to have been kept as a summer residence after the James Dunsmuirs moved to Victoria a decade later." See Lynn Bowen's *The Dunsmuirs of Nanaimo* (Nanaimo: The Nanaimo Festival, 1989), p. 27.

5. James Dunsmuir: (1851–1920) The eldest son of Robert and Joan Dunsmuir founded the coal and industrial empire on Vancouver Island and elsewhere. There were ten children in his parents' family. James Dunsmuir married Laura Surles of North Carolina and they produced 12 children, 10 reaching adulthood. With the Dunsmuir money from the coal discovery on Vancouver Island and the investment of this money in shipping and other industry and trade, James Dunsmuir became a world famous millionaire. His brother, Alexander, born in 1853, was the first white child born in Nanaimo. Later he ran the Dunsmuir business interests in San Francisco.

6. Young child: One of the incidents that this might relate to is the fact that James and Laura Dunsmuir's third child, Joan Olive White Dunsmuir (1880–1884), died in the Dunsmuir Departure Bay house as did their sixth, Alexander Lee Dunsmuir (1886–1887). Mrs. Harrison's second of her four sons, Victor B. Harrison (1884–1972), stated that many of the Dunsmuirs were Spiritualists and that one in particular who went to live in England and corresponded for many years with Mr. Harrison, was a devout Spiritualist and sent him many Spiritualist papers and other such material on this particular topic.

7. Gowey: He was one of Mrs. Harrison's Chinese servants. She would employ young Chinese men straight from China and supervise their training so well that several of them were requested to serve at Government House.

Chapter 21: Bess (pages 120–121)

1. Phaeton: A light, four-wheeled, open carriage drawn by one horse.

2. Mrs. O: Mrs. Onderdonk, the wife of the well known railway executive and businessman in the early years of British Columbia.

Chapter 22: The Eastern Thakur (pages 122–125)

1. Social call: Victorians designated certain hours of the day as those for social calls. However, the context suggests that this was not an "At Home" visit.

2. Tobacco: Mr. Harrison was a chain smoker and also used pipes excessively. It took a toll upon his life and greatly affected his lungs, causing his death some 20 years before Mrs. Harrison's. He took to tobacco to relieve

the intense pressure and anxiety he felt during his long trips in the wilds of the Cariboo. His judicial duties required that he make these circuits in an age that lacked the great highways and modern automobiles of the 21st century.

3. Court: In pioneer days many offices, stores, and other businesses and legal facilities stayed open during the evenings.

4. Mr. Justice John Foster McCreight: (1827–1913) Born in County Tyrone, Ireland, he was called to the Irish Bar in 1852 and went to Melbourne, Australia. He came to BC in 1860, practising law in the two most western BC colonies. McCreight was BC's first Premier, 1871–72. In 1880 he was appointed to the Supreme Court of BC and served until 1896. *The History of the Grand Lodge of British Columbia, AF and AM* (Vancouver: Grand Lodge, 1971) states that McCreight was the first Senior Grand Warden (p. 117).

5. Mr. Justice Henry Pering Pellew Crease: (1823–1905) He was born in Cornwall, son of a British naval captain. He came to Canada in 1849 after his call to the English Bar. At Lake Superior, Crease worked with a survey and exploring party, then returned to England to run a large Cornwall tin mine. This work helped him later to understand BC miners, it was said. He came to BC in 1858 and was called to the Bar of both Colonies. Crease was appointed Attorney General in 1861. He was elevated to the Judgeship in 1870 and retired in 1896. Returning to Ontario, Crease died there in 1905.

Chapter 23: Riding the Unfinished Trans-Continental (pages 126–133)

1. March 29, 1888: The date when the E. & N. Railway finally reached Esquimalt. The so-called "last spike" was in 1886.

2. Barrister: this chapter goes back to the year 1883 when Mr. Harrison was still a barrister before he was made a Judge.

3. Transcontinental C.P.R.: The Canadian Pacific Railway required a great amount of preliminary survey work due to the vast size of British Columbia and its mountains. The historian H.H. Bancroft notes that between 1871 and 1878 the Dominion of Canada spent $3,250,000 for explorations and surveys in BC before the chief engineer at last decided that the C.P.R. line through BC should lie along the valleys of the Thompson and Fraser Rivers and terminate at Burrard Inlet.

4. Mr. Onderdonk: (1848–1905) Andrew Onderdonk was a member of an old New York family. A Dutchman who came to New York in 1672 was his direct forebear while his mother was English, a Trask, from Boston. After completing the massive sea wall and docks in San Francisco, Onderdonk was intrigued by Canada's efforts to begin a transcontinental railway. He wanted to take part in the action and submitted tenders to the Federal Government.

Onderdonk was awarded the contract to construct the railroad through the Fraser Canyon. He rushed to Yale, had a beautiful home built for his family, built a sawmill, engine and repair shops able to produce railway cars and wired for a large labour force mainly from San Francisco. Later, he imported 2,000 Chinese from Hong Kong. Mrs. Onderdonk, a very capable woman, supervised the new hospital.

5. Emory's Bar: Onderdonk assembled in 1881 all that he needed to erect a blasting powder factory between Emory and Yale. This factory, including a maze of bins, tanks, and immense jars, when completed employed 16 men and was able to produce 1,200 pounds a day of the highest grade of explosives then available.

6. The Chinook: a warm, drying wind that blows down from the eastern slopes of the Rocky mountains at different times causing a quick thaw.

Chapter 24: Early Water Rights (pages 134–138)

1. Harrison, Anderson and Seton Lakes: Harrison River and Harrison Lake were named after an early HBC employee. Anderson Lake was named after Alexander Caulfield Anderson, chief trader of the Hudson's Bay Company. Anderson was born in Calcutta, March 10, 1814 and after education in England joined the HBC in 1831.

2. Pavilion mountain: This place was named "Pavilion" because of a flag or pavilion that flew over a dead Indian Chief's grave. The death of this Shuswap chief almost started a war. The Indians believed that their chief's death was caused by a curse put on him by HBC Chief Factor, Samuel Black, at Fort Kamloops. The late Chief Tranquille's nephew sought revenge. He went to Samuel Black's HBC Post and asked meekly if he might stay overnight as he was sick. Always hospitable, Black allowed him to come in. But as soon as Black turned his back, the nephew gunned him down. The nephew was shot as soon as caught while trying to elude his captors. The threat of an Indian war was then over.

3. Fountain: Fountain is eight miles above Lillooet on Fountain Creek and is a remarkable growing area.

4. Wire cable: W.J. West in *Stagecoach and Sternwheel Days in the Cariboo* (Surrey: Heritage House, 1985, reprint from 1955) states that a heavy ring-bolt is fixed in the canyon wall at a point most favourable for attaching the cable to pull the steamer up through the very strong current at the foot of the canyon. The cable is then strung along the wall and attached to the ring-bolt. The capstan is then set in motion and the start is made to pull the steamer through the rapids.

5. Gold: The Minister of Mines' report in the Sessional papers in the

BC Archives states that the total gold yield between 1858 and 1884 was $48,672,128. This estimate averages a gold yield of $1,900,000 a year. However, by 1884 this gold had fallen to an amount of $736,166 a year.

6. Harvey Creek: Named after the miner George Harvey who went to Harvey Creek in 1861, built sluices to recover the gold, and became very wealthy.

7. The Forks: Considered today as one of the finest ghost towns in BC, this town lies at the junction of the Cariboo and Quesnel Rivers. It was on the original gold fields trail and a stopping place for the miners. The Royal Engineers had surveyed it in 1861 for the purpose of a supply camp or centre for all the towns, camps and miners' groups in the gold fields.

Chapter 25: The Finding of the Strange Disk (pages 139–143)

1. Hazelton: W. Mason and T. Hankin were sent out by the HBC in 1852 to start HBC trading posts in this area of the Skeena and Watsonquah Rivers, but during 1868 the HBC stores were moved to Port Simpson because the furs in the former area were not as good. Hankin left the HBC and settled near the old posts in a flat region on the Skeena River. There were so many hazel trees growing there naturally that this place was called Hazelton.

2. Dr. Johnson's dictionary: Some writers consider this 1755 *Dictionary* to be the first lexicon that was a pleasure to read. Lexicographers regard the work as the first systematic study of the English language.

3. Kispiox: A Gitksan village situated on the area between the Skeena River and the Kispiox River and ten miles from the Indian settlement at the entrance of the Bulkley River. The word "Kispiox" means "loud talkers" in the Gitksan language.

4. Forbidden Plateau: A Comox Indian legend relates that the warlike Cowichan Indians threatened to kill the Comox Indians and take away their women and children. To protect their families, the Comox men sent their wives and children into hiding in this area as it had plentiful fish, game and roots for food. After their war with the Cowichan, the victorious Comox went to the Forbidden Plateau but could not find their women and children.

5. Peace River: A river 1,065 miles long which rises near the Finlay River in the Rocky Mountains in BC, near 55 degrees North, rushes through the mountains and pours northeast into Slave Lake, near Lake Athabaska in Alberta.

6. Northern Buddhism: Two main branches of Buddhism are the Northern or Mahayana called the Great Vehicle and the Southern or Hinayana termed the Little Vehicle. The former was found in Northern India, China, Japan and Mongolia, etc, while the latter flourished in Sri Lanka, Burma, etc.

7. Bell and dorje: These are religious instruments used in the many rituals of the Northern Buddhist priests. Abbé Huc mentions these as well as the censers and incense that were part of many religious ceremonies he witnessed in Lhasa and other parts of Tibet.

8. Atisha: In 1042 CE the Indian Mahayana monk, Atisa or Atisha, arrived at Lhasa, Tibet. He was instrumental in providing a reformed Buddhism in Tibet which did not include the old animist Bon religion that emphasized black magic and human sacrifices.

Chapter 26: Translations of the Disk? (pages 144–147)

1. *Book of Changes:* The *Tao Te Ching,* said to be written by Lao Tze in the Chou Dynasty (1122–249 BCE). But even today with the latest in scholarship, the author and the date are still not definitely settled. It is anti-Confucian, stresses humility, and speaks disparagingly of an over-emphasis on the mental faculties.

2. Taoist: Followers of the *Tao Te Ching.* These range from strict otherworldly ascetics living in solitude to everyday people engaged in worldly life. There is a vast range of methods used in following Tao or the great unknown spiritual principle.

3. Lao-Tze: His birthdate and death are still unknown and there is much conflict among those who are experts on this great Chinese philosopher. Some say he was just before Confucius; others that he was far, far earlier. His followers revere him as an Immortal and an emanation of the primordial Tao.

4. Confucius: Scholars agree that his birth date is sometime between 600 BCE and 551 BCE but as yet there is no exact date. He died after a life of great scholarship and duty to the state; he left many disciples who practised and preached his doctrine of the perfect morally upright scholarly and intellectual gentleman. Confucius appreciated elegance, beauty, good breeding and good manners, and extolled these qualities in his *Analects,* as well as the highest morality.

5. A work: This is a reference to Madam Helena Petrovna Blavatsky's book *Isis Unveiled,* published in 1876, that became an overnight best seller. Her writings have now been consolidated into a 15 volume set edited by Boris de Zirkoff, and entitled, *H.P. Blavatsky, Collected Writings* (Los Angeles: Wheaton, 1957–1983).

6. Chou dynasty: Recent scholarship has assigned the Chou (or Zhou) dynasty to the dates 1050–221 BCE. There is a Western Zhou and an Eastern Zhou, the former covering the period of 1050–771 BCE and the latter 770–221 BCE. See *The British Museum Book of Chinese Art,* edited by Jessica Rawson, et al (London: Thames and Hudson, 1992).

7. The Higher Triad: The fifth translator, the only one whose name has not been lost, was the late Mrs. H. Henderson of the HPB Library, Victoria, BC. (The HPB Library is now in Toronto, Ontario). She is here referring to an Eastern northern Buddhist doctrine about man's nature. He is said to have seven sheaths, the Higher Triad being in Sanskrit terms, Atma, Buddha and Manas: the Spirit, the spiritual soul, and the higher mind. The other four elements are the Lower Quarternary: Prana, Linga Sirara, Kama Manas and Kama Rupa, which represent the physical body, the life or vital principle, the astral body and the seat of animal desires and passions, respectively.

8. Temple of Heaven: The T'ien-T'an or Temple of Heaven is located in the outer city of Peking or Beijing. It is unique in its architecture and represents the supreme achievement of traditional Chinese structures. It was built in 1420 as a place of heaven worship for the emperors. The temple is a lofty cone-shaped structure with triple eaves, the top of which is surmounted by a golden ball. The base of the building is a triple-tiered circular stone terrace more than 63,000 square feet in area. The roof of the hall is deep blue, similar to the sky. The structure is 125 feet high and contains no steel. The four central columns represent the four seasons. The center of the stone-paved floor is round, containing a round marble slab which displays the design of a dragon and a phoenix — traditional symbols of king and queen.

9. Ming dynasty: (1368–1644 CE) "Ming" means brilliant. This dynasty was founded in 1368 by General Zhu Yuanzhang, a leader of rebels who lived in Nanjing. His background was very unusual as he was an orphan and a Buddhist monk novice. He defeated the last inept Mongol rulers and proclaimed himself emperor. This was the first time since 1127 that a Chinese dynasty had governed the whole of China.

10. Manchus: In the 17th century, the Ming dynasty was defeated by the invading Manchus. The Manchus then took over and founded the Quing dynasty (1644–1911). These people were all Manchurian tribesmen related to the Jin dynasty of the 11th century. The Manchu emperors were enthusiastic patrons of every form of Chinese art and culture. They fostered a very high scholarship.

11. John Delisle Parker: (1884–1962) Born in New York City, Parker was educated in England from age nine. His father, the American Consul there, encouraged his interest in art. Parker studied at Croydon Art School and later spent five years in Paris at the École des Beaux-Arts, the Sorbonne, the Académie Julian and the Académie Grande Chaumière. He went to the USA in 1931 and had a studio in Broadway. Being interested in US history, he made oil paintings of persons and events in the American revolution that were accepted by the Valley Forge Museum of American History. He travelled all over the East and in Africa. After living and painting in Paris from 1926 to 1935, Parker came to Vancouver to settle permanently. He met Emily

Carr and praised her work highly. In 1937 he had a one-man show in the Vancouver Art Gallery. His painting "The Old Carr House" belongs to the Vancouver Art Gallery's permanent collection. He wrote a column for the Vancouver papers, and Lawren Harris of the Group of Seven commented favourably on his work. In fact there is an exhibition folder by the Vancouver Art Gallery April 3–April 22, 1951 with a list of 43 paintings and notes on the artist by Lawren Harris. Parker's painting of the Buddhist monk's junk at Nootka during his supposed visit is among his many works. His military paintings and other productions can be found in the Vancouver Art Gallery, UBC, the Officers' Mess, Kingston, Ontario, the City of Odessa, Ukraine and many other collections in the US, Canada and elsewhere.

Chapter 27: All the Families Were Not Large (pages 148–150)

1. Bagster: Bagster Roads Seabrook (1865–1950) was born in New Westminster and went to Victoria with the family in 1869. His middle names "Roads" was after an English ancestor said to be a distant relative of the empire builder, Cecil Rhodes. The name has nothing to do with any Dutch cognomen, as a free lance writer in the *Colonist* once suggested. Bagster Seabrook became the general manager of Albion Iron Works Ltd. in Victoria, the largest engineering plant north of San Francisco. Later he went to the USA and developed several of his inventions. See "Energy and Ability Are Harnessed By This Inventive Son of BC," by L. Bell-Clemmens, *Vancouver Daily Province,* March 2, 1946, for an account of his life.

2. Niece of a BC financier: She was Elvira A. Crosby of Markham, Ontario. Her uncle was the financier, Alfred C. Flummerfelt, prominent in mining, development and business. His home at 906 Pemberton was a show place of old Victoria for years.

3. Ivan: Joseph Ivan Holloway Seabrook (1866–1966) had a very adventurous life and died at age 100 in Langford, BC.

4. Klondike: This place was the goal of the major gold rush of the 20th century. The peak of the rush was 1900 but from 1900 to 1973 10 million ounces of gold were produced. The name was derived from the Klondike River, a 100-mile-long tributary of the Yukon River, joining it at Dawson. In 1896 Gorge W. Carmack and two Indian helpers made a rich gold strike here and the news caused 100,000 people from all over the world to rush to the Klondike. Bonanza and Eldorado Creeks were the richest. Now the area is a tourist attraction.

5. Rosa Bonheur: (1822–1899) A French painter of animals, born in Bordeaux, France, Bonheur was taught by her father, an artist, and by Leon Cogniet of Paris. Her animal paintings were declared amazingly accurate.

Bonheur was a regular salon exhibitor from 1841 to her death. Her painting "Ploughing in Niverais" won the 1st-class gold medal in Paris in 1848. Because she smoked cigarettes, wore men's trousers, and kept a lioness in her art studio, Bonheur was considered very unconventional. In 1894 she became the first woman to be invested with the French Legion of Honour.

6. Gibson Girl: Charles Dana Gibson (1867–1944) was an American artist. His pen and ink drawings of girls in *Collier's Weekly,* to illustrate the well-known "Adventures of Mr. Pip," typified the ideal American girl of that period.

7. Harrison Fisher: (1875–1934) An American artist and book illustrator. A sample of his driving girls can be seen in Meredith Nicholson, *The Main Chance* (Indianapolis: Bobs-Merrill, 1899), p. 1.

8. Peter Secord Lampman: The home at 1630 York Place, Oak Bay, pictured in *This Old House,* was originally designed for Judge Peter Secord Lampman in 1905 by Rattenbury and built in 1907–08.

Chapter 28: The Case of the Crooked House (pages 151–153)

1. Large school room: It is well-known in the family that Mrs. Harrison herself tutored the children when they were quite young if there were no school nearby in the area or if the school was too rowdy. When the family moved to Victoria and were not far from private schools, all the children were sent to these schools (girls and boys then had separate private schools) as day pupils not boarders — with the exception of Bernice who was a boarder.

2. Clive Phillips-Wolley: (1854–1918) His full name was Clive Oldnall Long Phillips-Wolley. He wrote many books, both novels and non-fiction, about big game hunting in British Columbia, gold rush stories, the Stikine River, the route to the Klondike, travel (*Trottings of a Tenderfoot*) and especially featured BC as a sportsman's paradise (*A Sportsman's Eden.*) He took a very extreme view of Imperialism, one that Mrs. Harrison and her friends did not approve of. Here is an example of what Mrs. Harrison probably means by his extreme views: "There have been none like us, nor any to tame our pride." From Sir Clive Phillips-Wolley's poem "The Sea Queen Wakes," written about 1896.

3. Russo-Japanese War: Considered by historians as the most surprising war of the 20th century. It took place in 1904–05 between Japan and Russia. Japan, an Asiatic rising power, defeated one of the great European empires, Russia. (Dr. Patricia Roy has commented on this war: "The fact that Russia was an European nation made its defeat shocking to Western eyes.")

Chapter 29: The New Parliament Buildings (pages 154–159)

1. New Parliament Buildings: These buildings (the present ones) replaced the "Birdcages" as the earlier structure was called. Premier Theodore Davie and cabinet voted $600,000 for a better building. They made a world-wide request for drawings and designs from architects. Of the 67 plans received, 5 were put on the short list. Rattenbury's architectural designs were accepted as the best to express the importance of the British Empire's most westerly Canadian province.

2. Francis Mawson Rattenbury: (1867–1935) Mr. Rattenbury was born in Leeds, England. Trained in his uncle's well-known firm of architects who specialized in the Queen Ann style, he came to BC in 1892 and started his own firm on Granville Street in Vancouver. He built many of the fine homes and other buildings in BC. He became quite wealthy but also accumulated enemies. In 1925 he married his second wife, Alma, who had been a famous nurse in the First World War. Rattenbury was fifty-eight and Alma around thirty. A world wide-scandal erupted when their chauffeur, a teen-aged youth, fell in love with Alma and shot Rattenbury in their magnificent home in England. The murder trial of Alma and her lover filled all the papers. Alma was acquitted but the chauffeur was given a life sentence.

3. Blackstone: (1723–1780) Sir William Blackstone was a famous English jurist. His world famous *Commentaries on the Laws of England* had an enormous influence on jurisprudence, particularly in North America.

4. One photo: There is a photograph in the Archives that is no doubt a copy of the one Mrs. Harrison refers to, which is included in the text.

5. Lieut.-Governor McInnes: (1840–1904) Thomas Robert McInnes was born in Nova Scotia of parents who had come from Scotland. His father had been a sea captain but switched to farming in Canada. Thomas McInnes went to Truro Normal School and then graduated at Harvard as a doctor. He practised medicine in Chicago and was a surgeon in the American Civil War. In 1866 he moved to Ontario and married Martha E. Webster. After becoming mayor of Dresden, he moved to New Westminster in 1874. McInnes was mayor of New Westminster in 1877 and 1878. He continued his medical practice and headed the BC Insane Asylum. After his election to the House of Commons, he was later appointed a senator in 1881. McInnes became an Imperial Federationist. In 1898 he was appointed Lieut.-Governor of BC. His two sons became lawyers and practised together in Nanaimo, BC.

6. Judge Bole: (1845–1915) W. Norman Bole was the eldest son of John and Elizabeth Bole of County Mayo, Ireland. He received private tuition in Ireland and was called to the Bar in 1873. Mr. Bole went to the USA, then Quebec and finally New Westminster in 1877 and was admitted to the bar

there. He was the first lawyer to locate permanently on the mainland. In September 1889, he was made New Westminster's County Court Judge and local judge of the Supreme Court in 1891. He married in 1881 and had two children.

7. Mr. Justice Crease: (1825–1905) Mr. Crease was the eldest son of Captain Henry Crease of the Royal Navy and his wife, Mary Smith. He married Sarah Lindley and they had 3 sons and 4 daughters. He came to BC and in 1858 was the first practising barrister there. After becoming elected to represent Victoria in 1864, he was later appointed attorney-general. He was appointed a judge of the Supreme Court in 1870 and retired from the bench in 1896. A very interesting biography of his wife, Sarah and himself and family is *Henry & Self*, by Kathryn Bridge of the BC Archives (Victoria: Sono Nis, 1996).

8. Lord Herschell: (1837–1899) Born in England and called to the bar there from Lincoln's Inn in 1860, he was appointed Solicitor General in 1880 and appointed Lord Chancellor of England in 1886. He worked on law reform and law codification. In 1899 Lord Herschell died suddenly from a fall, leaving a wife and children.

9. Chief Justice Archer Martin: (1865–1941) Mr. Martin was born in Hamilton in Canada West, as Ontario was then known. He graduated from Trinity College in Ontario and was called to the bar in 1887. After coming to BC he was called to the bar in 1894. In 1898 he became a judge of the Supreme Court, in 1902 a judge in admiralty, and in 1909 an Appeal Court judge.

Chapter 30: Camps (pages 160–164)

1. Thomas A. Edison: (1847–1931) A famous American inventor who was mostly self-taught. He held the patent to over 1,000 of his inventions. The second of Edison's inventions was the phonograph (1877), which used tin foil for a record. By 1898, however, he had refined the record and the material he used to such an extent that the music and words which the machine emitted from the record were clear and natural and no longer tinny.

2. Bowler: Bowler was a 19th-century British hatter. He constructed the derby or bowler: a hard, round, curly-brimmed hat, usually black.

3. Norfolk jacket: A loose-fitting, single-breasted shooting jacket with box pleats and belt.

4. *Harper's Bazaar:* A 19th-century upper-class fashion magazine.

5. Whig: This was a nick-name for Claude Harrison, Mrs. Harrison's third son, because he had such a large crop of wavy blonde hair. He died in 1986 at age 100.

6. Todd's camp: Todd was Bagster's son-in-law. He was a one-time Victoria mayor and a member of the well-known Todd industrial and salmon canning family of BC.

7. Bret Harte: (1836–1902) An American writer who was inspired by 19th-century mining camp life in California. His most famous books are *The Luck of Roaring Camp* (1868) and *The Outcasts of Poker Flat* (1869).

Chapter 31: Broken Hulks and Broken Lives (pages 165–169)

1. The Gorge: The inner arm of the sea just outside Victoria.

2. *Dora Sieward:* The 98-ton sailing schooner owned by Rithet and Co. and mentioned by Peter Murray in *The Vagabond Fleet* (Victoria: Sono Nis, 1988) together with other schooners in the fur sealing fleet.

3. *Ainoko:* A schooner of Capt. Grant's sealing fleet that went to the Bering Sea and the Pribilof Islands. Other ships of Capt. Grant were the sealing schooners *Penelope, Beatrice, Vera* and *Arietis.* These sailing ships and many others engaged in the fur sealing trade are described in detail in the pamphlet "The Memorial of the Canadian Sealers Respecting their Interests and the Quebec International Conference, 1898" (8015 BC Archives). The brochure also includes the petition of the undersigned owners and agents of the British sealing vessels. *Inter alia,* it states that in 1894 there were 65 schooners representing 4,292 tons valued at $643,800, employing 807 whites and 903 Indians, making, with wives and families, at least 8,500 dependants. The prices paid for the furs in Europe brought in an average of $750,000 annually. Many people therefore experienced great hardship when the treaty between the USA and Great Britain stopped this sealing.

4. Captain Grant: A pioneer Victoria sea-faring man who owned many sealing vessels and made a very good living for himself, his family and relatives until the seal hunt was prohibited by the USA and Great Britain Treaty.

5. Victoria Sealing Company: A group of sealers who incorporated a company at the Federal Government's request to better facilitate their gaining rightful remuneration from the USA government for giving up their fur sealing rights and livelihood. As a result of Mr. Audette's report, however, instead of receiving their rightful compensation, they were expressly excluded from the USA monetary settlement. The Company and its members tried for many years to receive recompense but never succeeded. This is another example of the injustice experienced by some of the early pioneers when dealing with the Federal, the British and the USA governments of that time.

6. Commission Report: There are many volumes in this Commission, its report and commentaries, filling more than a shelf in the University of Vic-

toria McPherson Library under the topic of Fur Sealing in the Bering Sea and the Pribilof Islands. The result of the Commission is summarized very succinctly by Mrs. Harrison.

7. Premier Brewster: Harlan Carey Brewster had been a sailor and cannery manager. He was premier of BC from November 23, 1916 to March 1, 1918, dying March 1, while in office. Brewster had been an MLA for Alberni from February 1907 to 1912.

8. "Jarndyce v. Jarndyce": This case, found in Charles Dickens' novel *Bleak House*, was the author's brilliant attempt to show how useless, costly and futile the law often is.

9. $12,000: A judge's pension in those days was very small and, with a large family, it was necessary to have other income. There was no judge's widow's pension either. This very large deficiency caused Mrs. Harrison's later and declining years to be fraught with great hardship. However, she lived with her youngest son and his wife and family on a 100-acre wilderness ranch that had many fruit trees and a good garden. She enjoyed great love and care from the family and good food from the ranch, while she was adored by her grandchildren. She was always interested in spiritual matters and, though she writes nothing about this side of her life, it was a mainspring in her existence.

Chapter 33: Early School Days (pages 175–177)

1. The Collegiate School: Founded in Victoria about 1861 by Bishop Hill, it was modelled on the great Public Schools of England and stressed sound training — moral, mental and physical. It was second in establishment to St. Ann's.

2. Corrig College: A boys' boarding and day school in Victoria, the oldest private school in BC conducted "entirely on the English Grammar School system." It provided training in practical, commercial and professional education. As its prospectus states: "It aims at providing for the sons of the best families in the Province and adjoining State of Washington those advantages which are likely to accrue from residence in a simple, quiet, Christian and Gentlemanly home, and from association with pure, obedient, well behaved and industrious comrades." Boys were prepared for commerce, the law, medical, military or naval services and the universities. The school was noted for its strict corporeal discipline, the rod being used frequently.

3. Staff-Sergeant Clarke: Trained the Cadet Corps in the School. For nine dollars, a cadet was given "a uniform, puttees, service cadet cap and shoulder strap badge." Rifles were lent and there was an indoor and outdoor rifle range and a drill hall.

4. Dr. J.W. Church: came to Victoria in 1891. He studied at King's College and at the University of Durham, receiving a first class in theology and philosophy at Cambridge. He became Headmaster of Corrig College and prepared pupils to matriculate for the Universities of Toronto, Manitoba and McGill, as well as Cambridge. In 1896 Dr. Church married a local lady, Miss Emily Wilson, daughter of Mr. William Wilson.

5. D.W. Higgins: was the publisher of the *Daily Colonist* in the latter part of the 19th century. He led a full life as alderman and finally Deputy Premier of BC. His house, one of the first in Rockland Avenue, is at 1501 Fort and still stands today as a heritage house in the Victorian Italianate style.

6. Angela College: is still standing and can be seen at 923 Burdett Ave. It was built in 1865 by John Wright in the Gothic Revival style. It is named in honour of Baroness Angela Burdett-Coutts and was run as a girls' college by the Anglican Church. Lady Burdett-Coutts donated large sums to aid Anglican private school education in BC, and this was one of her favourite projects. In 1903 the school closed and the building became a hotel. Now it is a retirement home for Roman Catholic nuns, who acquired the place in 1959.

Chapter 35: The Peculiar People (pages 188–195)

1. St. Alice Hotel: In 1887 *The Colonist* states that the St. Alice Hotel was a large, cosy, well-built hotel warmly furnished, the dining room being the finest on the coast. Instead of being numbered, the rooms were given the names of cities, i.e., London, Paris, New York, Baltimore, etc. Customers considered the hotel and its surrounding outdoor area to be better than a similar hotel in Switzerland. The hotel grew its own vegetables and kept milk cows and chickens to supply its own table. *Harrison Hot Springs:* Harrison Hot Springs at Harrison Lake and the Lake itself were named in 1828 by Governor Simpson of the Hudson's Bay Company. He chose the name Harrison from his friend, Benjamin Harrison, Deputy Governor of the HBC from 1835–1839. Harrison was a Quaker who was such a philanthropist that he served as treasurer of Guy's Hospital in London, England for fifty years without pay. The Indian name is Pookpahkohtl. The Hot Springs were first written about in the *Victoria Gazette,* December 30, 1858.

2. Transcontinental: This is the famous Canadian Pacific Railway linking Eastern and Western Canada.

3. Shawnigan Lake: This lake is on Vancouver Island west of the Malahat highway between Victoria and Duncan.

4. Hairy giants: These are called Sasquatch and there have been many books written about them, such as John Green's *Sasquatch* (Seattle: Hancock House Publishing, 1978); John Napier's *Bigfoot! The Yeti and Sasquatch in*

Myth and Reality (New York: E.P. Dutton & Co, 1973); *Manlike Monsters on Trial,* edited by M. Halpin and M.M. Ames (Vancouver: UBC Press, 1980).

5. Abominable snow men: The Bigfoot or Sasquatch are sometimes compared to the Yeti or abominable snow man of the Himalayas. "Sasquatch" is the North American Indian name for the wild creature, while "Yeti" is the Nepalese name for the same. These strange creatures have been recorded in BC at least as far back as 1884 when the *Colonist* reported that a strange beast was captured near Yale by Costerton of BC Express and his men. This creature, which they named "Jacko," was covered all over with hair about an inch long. It was only 4 ft. 7 in. tall, however, and weighed 127 lbs. (Perhaps a baby Sasquatch?) The noise it made was between a growl and a bark. Its favourite food included milk and berries. "Jacko" is said to have died on his way to England while he was being taken there by a BC scientist.

6. There has been much speculation for many years now that a race of people existed on the Pacific Northwest coast who predated contemporary Native cultures. The sculptured stone seated human figure bowls found along the Fraser river at some distance from the coast have been alleged to be the work of an earlier people. See Wilson Duff, *Anthropology in British Columbia,* no. 5 (1956). The recent discovery of the skull of "Kennewick Man," which is somewhat Caucasian in appearance, as well as stories of early Chinese voyagers to the coast have continued to fuel speculation.

7. Midiwiwin: An Ojibway (now spelt "Ojibwa") secret society like the secret Cannibal Society and other secret cults of the Northwest Coast Indians.

Chapter 36: "Sealing Wax . . . of Cabbages and Kings" (pages 196–207)

1. "Sealing Wax...of Cabbages and Kings": A quote from Lewis Carroll's *Alice in Wonderland* meaning a mixture of unrelated subjects.

2. Commissioner: A judge is appointed to investigate some problem relating to Federal or Provincial institutions and to give a ruling. See *Royal Commissions and Commissions of Inquiry et al,* by M.C. Holmes covering the period 1872–1942, BC Archives, 1945.

3. Public Inquiries Act: A BC Act allowing Commissioners to investigate injustices or other problems in Provincial or Federal institutions.

4. Gilbert and Sullivan: Sir William Gilbert (1836–1911), the playwright, collaborated with Sir Arthur Sullivan (1842–1900), the musician, in comic operas of great success such as *HMS Pinafore, The Mikado, Trial by Jury, Iolanthe,* and many others.

5. Police magistrate: Judge Harrison was appointed on December 15, 1894 to inquire into the charges against Mr. J.P. Planta, a police magistrate at Nanaimo. Mr. Planta waived his salary and instead retained the costs he

ordered people to pay in court. This was illegal. He was found guilty on 231 charges. Judge Harrison handed in his 20-page report February 26, 1895.

6. Enquiry into conduct: Judge Harrison was appointed Commissioner January 15, 1898 to investigate charges against Warden Armstrong and Guard Callbeck about the appropriation of prisoners' money. The charges were substantiated and the men found guilty.

7. New Westminster Fire: Appointed October 26, 1898, Judge Harrison made his report January 31, 1899. Mr. Harrison found that the water reservoir was not kept completely filled, as it had to be, because of lack of finances. This lack of sufficient water hindered the firemen and others in combating the fire and resulted in the great conflagration that caused much damage in New Westminster, September 10th and 11th, 1898.

8. E. & N. Railway: Judge Harrison was appointed October 12, 1900 as Commissioner to deal with the claims of settlers who were living on land that had been given to the E. & N. Railway. He found the settlers held surface rights only to their land and delivered his report in January 1901. The settlers thus could stay on the land, and live there, but anything such as coal, found under the land, belonged to the E. & N.

9. New Westminster jail: Judge Harrison was appointed Commissioner July 24, 1901 and submitted his report September 4, 1901. He dealt with charges of neglect of duty, violation of rights, ill treatment of prisoners and immorality. He found all charges substantiated except the one of alleged immorality.

10. Duke and Duchess of Cornwall and York: They later became, in 1910, King George the Fifth (1865–1936) and Queen Mary (1867–1953), his Queen Consort. They had five sons and one daughter.

11. New house: Three plans of this Judge Harrison House by Samuel Maclure, the famous architect, remain extant. The house was finally torn down by later owners in the 1960s and there are now four large apartment buildings on the one acre.

12. Trams: These were electric street cars. For more information, see "The BC Electric Railway..." by Dr. P.E. Roy, *BC Studies*, no 16 (Winter, 1972–73): 3–24. In Vancouver, trams started January 27, 1892.

13. Tally-ho's: Horse-drawn carriages. Brochures on these are in the BC Archives.

14. "The Dardanelles": A narrow strait between Europe and Asiatic Turkey. The narrow Fort Street in Victoria was named after this well-known place.

15. Samuel Maclure: Mr. Maclure's father, John Maclure, was one of the Royal Engineers who came out with Captain Moody. He was born in Scotland in 1831. When John Maclure came to BC he was already married to his

wife Martha from Northern Ireland. They had five children. Samuel Maclure was born in 1860 and raised in Matsqui, BC. A talented artist, he was sent to the USA to study art. Later he met Daisy, the daughter of a Victoria clergyman. Forbidden by her father to marry Daisy, Samuel eloped with Daisy in 1889. To be worthy of his wife, Maclure decided to become an architect, and a good one.

16. Mesher: One of Samuel Maclure's many architecture students that he trained when he became famous. Maclure houses were eagerly sought after and acquired by persons all over BC, Washington State and elsewhere. He practised his profession from 1890 to 1929 when he died.

17. Victoria taxation: In the Depression of the thirties, many of the old Victoria families lost their treasured homes due to excessive Victoria property taxation. The Crease home, for instance, went for taxes and the Truth Centre acquired the large home and grounds.

18. Eldest daughter: Eunice married John Coote in London, Ontario in 1904, and they took up residence in that city. Mr. Coote's father, from Northern Ireland, ran a large, successful business building carriages and breeding famous horses that won many prizes.

19. Thomas Jefferson (1743–1826): He was the 3rd President of the USA, born in Virginia and a life-long politician. He was also a Renaissance man in his extensive interests, literary and otherwise.

20. $2,000 could build a fine home then.

21. One of the boys: The boy was her third son, Claude, who also owned the Irish Setter.

Chapter 37: Going South (pages 208–213)

1. Kipling: Rudyard Kipling (1865–1936), a world famous author and poet, wrote much about India where he was born and about the other countries he lived and worked in. Some of his well known works are *The Jungle Books, Plain Tales from the Hills, Soldiers Three,* and *Kim.*

2. A. Todd: Alpheus Todd (1821–1884) was born in London, England and at age eight accompanied his family to Canada. Refusing his father's demand that he attend Upper Canada College, Todd decided to make a very realistic map of the streets of York by walking them. This map so impressed the Legislature that they bought it from the eighteen-year-old Todd and gave him a job in the Legislative Library. He became established as a scholar at age nineteen with the publication of his book on Legislative Rules. His magnum opus is the book mentioned by Mrs. Harrison. Later it was condensed by Spencer Walpole. Sir William Anson declared that the book was the finest ever published on that subject, while G. Barnett Smith regarded it as one of

a kind. The second edition, edited by Todd's son, was published in 1894 by Longmans, Green, London.

3. Sword: The sword was given to one of the Harrison ancestors who had distinguished himself at the Battle of the Boyne (1690) in which William of Orange and his army successfully defeated James II.

4. The young boy was Herschel, aged ten, and the girl, Bernice May, aged thirteen.

5. Older children: Mrs. Harrison had six children. In 1906 the eldest, Eunice, was married and living in London, Ontario. The eldest boy, Paul, was a young lawyer in Whitehorse, YT. The next two — Victor and Claude — were law students. Mrs. Harrison's children are now all deceased: Paul died in 1949, Victor in 1971, Eunice in 1975, Herschel in 1978, Bernice in 1977, and Claude in 1986 (in his 100th year). Years later, the young boy Herschel who accompanied his mother in this amazing disaster, became the annotator's father.

6. *S.S. Queen:* The Pacific Coast Steamship Company's *S.S. Queen of the Pacific* was added to the fleet in 1882. She ran to San Francisco and was 1,697 tons. In 1890, "Of the Pacific" was dropped from her name.

7. Lick House: A famous San Francisco landmark built by the very wealthy James Lick, a philanthropist. It was swept away by the terrible conflagration following the earthquake.

8. Palace Hotel: An observer noted that soon after the earthquake "the hotel was a mass of flames." G. Thomas & Max Witts, *The San Francisco Earthquake* (New York: Stein & Day Publishers, 1971), p. 126.

9. Father Woods: In a rare book in the BC Archives — *The First Half Century of St. Ignatius Church and College,* by J.W. Riordan, S.J. (San Francisco: H. S. Crocker Co, 1905) — written one year before the world famous earthquake and fire, there is a brief mention of Father Henry Woods, a teacher of elocution at the College. He also put on plays with student actors. Most of Shakespeare and other plays such as *Richelieu* were directed by Father Woods at the school.

10. *S.S. State of California:* This steamship was built in Philadelphia and arrived in San Francisco, May 8, 1879, in charge of Captain Lachlan. "A handsome steamer of rakish lines, she maintained a reputation for speed well into her old age, having set a record for a round trip from Puget Sound to Nome in 1901." Lewis and Dryden's *Marine History of the Pacific Northwest* (cited earlier). She was on the San Francisco run until 1913 when she was lost in a violent storm.

11. *Umatilla:* This ship carried the San Francisco to Puget Sound to Victoria trade. *Senator et al:* fine steel passenger ships constructed by the Union Iron Works of San Francisco for the Pacific Coast Steamship Co. They were

single screw vessels of about 2,432 tons with two single-end Scotch boilers, and with extremely tall funnels. *Indianapolis:* Bought on the Great Lakes by the Puget Sound Navigation Co, she was built by Craig Shipyards of Toledo, Ohio in 1904. She registered 765 tons. Her horsepower was 1,500 and she could proceed at 16 knots cruising speed. In 1906 she was assigned to the Victoria-Seattle run. (She was operating in the Puget Sound area as late as the 1960s.) *Avalon:* A wooden steam schooner of 881 tons operating in the same area as the above ships.

12. *Pickwick: Pickwick Papers* (1837), by English writer Charles Dickens (1812–70), made its author famous overnight.

13. *American Notes:* Written by Charles Dickens after his visit to America. Macready was a famous Shakespearean actor and friend of Dickens.

14. Tingley: Katherine Tingley was a Theosophist, successor to William Q. Judge, one of the founders of Theosophy with Col. H.S. Olcott and Madam Helena P. Blavatsky in New York in 1875. Mrs. Tingley went to Point Loma in the later 1900s and built a community there whose aim was to practice the Theosophical virtues in everyday life. For more information on this daring and in many ways successful achievement, see E. A. Greenwalt's *California Utopia: Point Loma: 1897–1942*, 2nd & rev. ed. (Berkeley: University of California Press, 1978).

15. St. Nicholas Hotel: In 1906 this was a large, handsome hotel on Powell Street, fronting on Union Square. When the earthquake came it was left a ruined shell. See Charles Morris, *The San Francisco Calamity by Earthquake and Fire* (Citadel Press: New Jersey, 1986, reprint of 1906 edition), p. 27.

Chapter 38: A Strange Awakening (pages 214–223)

1. Five a.m.: "Time hung poised at 5:12 a.m. At that moment the earthquake came" (*San Francisco Earthquake*, p. 61). An eye-witness observer commented: "Again and again the trembling of the earth passed by, three quickly repeated shocks, and the work of the demon was done. People woke from their beds to find themselves flung to the floor, many of them covered with fragments of broken ceilings, many lost among the ruins of falling floors and walls, many pinned in agonizing suffering under the ruins of their houses, which had been utterly wrecked in those fatal seconds....Those seconds of the reign of the elemental forces had turned the gayest, most careless city on the continent into a wreck which no words can fitly describe" (*San Francisco Calamity*, p. 27). The magnitude of the earthquake was at least 8.3. Since the earthquake occurred a mere eighteen minutes before sunrise, visibility in the street would be good. At that time the eastern sky would be very bright.

2. Golden Gate Park: "Near it and extending to the Golden Gate channel is a presidial military reservation containing 1,480 acres....To these open spaces, to the suburbs in every available direction, the fugitives streamed in thousands, in tens of thousands, finally in hundreds of thousands....There were many persons with scanty clothing, women in underskirts and thin waists and men in shirt sleeves. Many women carried children....It was a strange and weird procession that kept up unceasingly all that dreadful day and to the night that followed as the all-conquering flames spread the area of terror" (*San Francisco Calamity*, p. 8). "In the seventeen minutes following the earthquake, nearly 50 fires were reported in the downtown area of the city, Not one fire bell clanged. The Fire Department's central alarm system housed in a building in Chinatown, had been wrecked. The first jarring shock of the earthquake broke 556 of the 600 wet-cell batteries that operated the system. A mile away from where the system lay in shambles, the man who had installed it was dying" (*San Francisco Earthquake*, p. 78). "It is said that fully 100,000 persons, rich and poor alike, sought refuge in Golden Gate Park itself, and 200,000 more homeless ones located at the other places of refuge" (*San Francisco Calamity*, p. 106).

3. St. Nicholas Hotel: "In much of the Hayes Valley district, south of McAllister and North of Market Street, the destruction was complete. From the Mechanics' Pavilion and St. Nicholas Hotel opposite down to the Oakland Ferry the journey was heartrending, the scene appalling. On each side was ruin, nothing but ruin and hillocks of masonry and heaps of rubbish of every description filled to its middle the city's greatest thoroughfare" (*San Francisco Calamity*, pp. 44–45).

4. Jefferson Square: "At Jefferson Square were camped thousands of people of every class of life" (*San Francisco Calamity*, p. 106).

5. The fire: John Barrett, the *Examiner* newspaperman who watched the earthquake, sent the following telegram to New York and all the world on April 18, 1906 at 2:20 p.m.: "The city practically ruined by fire. It's within half block of us in the same block. The Call building is burned out entirely, the Examiner building just fell in a heap. Fire all around us in every direction and way out in the residence district. The City Hall dome stripped and only the framework standing. The St. Ignatius Church and College are burned to the ground. The Emporium is gone, entire building, also the old Flood building. Lots of new buildings just recently finished are completely destroyed. They are blowing up standing buildings that are in the path of flames with dynamite. No water. It's awful. There is no communication anywhere and entire phone system busted. I want to get out of here or be blown up" (*San Francisco Earthquake*, pp. 121–122).

6. Dynamiting buildings: Brigadier General Funston and his USA Federal

troops were called out to take charge. To try to prevent the incredible spread of the raging fires, the General used dynamite. He said later: "I doubt if anyone will ever know the amount of dynamite and gun cotton used in blowing up buildings, but it must have been tremendous, as there were times when the explosions were so continuous as to resemble a bombardment" (*San Francisco Earthquake*, p. 135).

7. Water: "In San Francisco, the rumble in the streets came mostly from fire engines racing over cobblestones, seeking the unobtainable: water." Of the twenty-three cisterns each (holding up to 100,000 gallons) were dry and had no effect in stopping the inferno. The supplementary salt-water system...was no more than a tragically unrealized dream" (*San Francisco Earthquake*, p. 105).

Chapter 39: Escape (pages 224–234)

1. Fire: "The air was stifling, the heat intense, people plodded on mechanically. The scope of the disaster seemed to have exhausted the senses" (*San Francisco Earthquake*, p. 199).

2. Wharves: "Many of those who sought the ferry on that fatal Wednesday met a solid wall of flames extending for squares and lengths and utterly impassable" (*San Francisco Calamity*, p. 89).

3. Conveyance: Only at exorbitant prices, such as $50 a day, could a teamster, horses and wagon be procured. Fifty dollars was the minimum price. The police and military seized teams at gun point if the owner refused to turn them over. See J.R. Wilson's *San Francisco's Horror of Earth Quake and Fire* (Philadelphia: G.W. Burton, 1906), p. 120, et seq.

4. Coffee and bread: The usual price of coffee was five cents and bread two loaves for five cents.

5. Ladies: Dr. Ernest E. Fleming relates: "The women were in their night robes; they made a better appearance than the men....The street was a rainbow of colours in the early morning light...in many cases never meant to be seen outside the boudoir" (*San Francisco's Horror*, p. 163).

6. Crocker and Spreckels: Crocker was a leading banker and a man with many interests in commerce and railroads, as well as hydro-electric concerns. His home and banks were destroyed. Claus Spreckels, the sugar king founder, had his home on Van Ness Ave totally wrecked while the home of J.D. Spreckels, one of his sons, located at Pacific Avenue and La Guana Street, and one of the most magnificent mansions, crumbled and went down "like so much spun sugar out of a wedding cake" (*San Francisco's Horror*, p. 163). In spite of all this destruction to their property, the Spreckels family donated much money and aid to help San Francisco in the disaster of 1906.

7. Flames: "The fire that consumed so much of the city...was the greatest conflagration in the recorded history of cities...even exceeding the famous 1871 Chicago fire....Approximately 514 city blocks were destroyed" (*San Francisco's Horror*, p. 163).

8. Cape Flattery: a high point of land jutting out at the northwest extremity of Washington State at the entrance to the Strait of Juan de Fuca.

Chapter 40: Aftermath (pages 235–241)

1. Any the worse: This may be a Victorian understatement. Mrs. Harrison's youngest son, Herschel, told the annotator many times that the terrible experience he had endured during the earthquake and fire, and the terror undergone by himself, affected him adversely for the rest of his life.

2. All Hallows School, Yale, BC: In 1884, Sisters from All Hallows Anglican Convent at Ditchingham, Norfolk, England, started this private school, first for Indian girls in the old Yale Anglican parsonage. The school's academic and cultural fame spread and in 1890 a new building was added for white female boarders. According to school inspectors such as Archdeacon Woods, the school proved one of the highest caliber in religious studies, academic subjects, manners, gentility and deportment. Dr. Barman writes that in the early 1900s: "All Hallows became fashionable...and attracted daughters of prominent local figures." The Depression caused the school to close, and the Sisters returned to their Convent at Ditchingham, England. It was the only school in Canada at that time teaching girls and young women, both white and Indian. See Jean Barman, "Separate and Unequal: Indian and White Girls at All Hallows School, 1884–1920," in J. Barman, N. Sutherland and J. D. Wilson, ed. *Children, Teachers and Schools in the History of British Columbia* (Calgary: Detselig, 1995), pp. 359–74.

3. "Experiences of the Great 'Quake": Mrs. Harrison's full page article appears in *The Victoria Daily Colonist*. The editor remarks: "The following interesting letter regarding her experiences during the recent earthquake and fire at San Francisco was written for *The Colonist* by Mrs. Harrison, who with her daughter and little boy, 10 years of age, returned a few days ago from a visit to Mexico and Southern California." See *The Victoria Daily Colonist*, Tuesday, May 1, 1906, pp. 7–8.

4. The owner: The owner ran his skating rink under the name of the San Francisco Co., at Market and Eighth Streets, in San Francisco.

5. Archives: In Mrs. Harrison's 91-page large scrapbook filled with her own handwriting explaining all the different documents, historic letters from historic figures to her husband, etc., there is a card that is evidently the ticket she is referring to here. On the ticket is the following:

San Francisco Co
Requests the pleasure of your attendance
At the opening of the New Central Park
Skating Rink, Market & Eighth Streets.
SAT OPENING AP 7, 1906
Present this card at the door.
Admit gentlemen and ladies.
This scrapbook is in the BC Archives, under No. WA H24H.

6. World War II: From other notes and material it is clear that Mrs. Harrison wrote this portion of her memoirs during World War II, probably in 1942. Mrs. Harrison always kept up to date with historic events and she saved many clippings about the bombing in England. She had her Bagster Bible relatives in London and elsewhere at this time.

7. Limoges: A city in Haute-Vienne, in Western France, famous since the 13th century for its very fine porcelain.

8. "The Art of Pyrography": There are a few booklets published at the turn of the century about pyrography in the archives of Yale University and the University of Illinois. No others can be located so far. One of the former, Maude Maude's *A Handbook of Pyrography* (London: Dawbarn & Ward, 1899), describes this art in detail, with many illustrations. The author appeals strongly to women: "Clever lady workers will find it an endless satisfaction as a means of translating their most evanescent fancies."

9. Working outfit: Frost & Adams of 37 Cornhill, Boston, Mass., put out a catalogue, *Pyrography Supplies,* describing and including illustrations of the bulbs, platinum points, etc., with their 1899 prices. A lady artist in Victorian garb gracefully reclines on the front page, to attract other ladies, no doubt.

10. Miss Mills: In Henderson's *BC Gazetteer and Directory,* 1905, there is listed a Miss M.L. Mills having an art studio at 54 Government Street, with her home at Chevin, Oak Bay, BC.

11. Canadian Bank of Commerce: In the same directory of the same year, the Canadian Bank of Commerce is located at 50 Government Street, corner of Fort and Government, with George Gillespie, Manager.

12. Empress Hotel: In 1904, Victoria city passed a by-law giving the CPR certain tax exemptions to build a tourist hotel, the Empress Hotel. This famous building was designed by the well-known Victorian architect, F. M. Rattenbury, and was completed by January 1908 at at cost of $1,600,000. To produce the effect of an old English Hall, 7-foot-high panels of stained English oak were used. Every chair had embroidered on its back the symbol of Victoria, a sprig of holly. The Hotel of 1908 did not have the present additions.

13. Expertly: Despite Mrs. Harrison's poor opinion of her playing on

numerous musical instruments, many old timers as well as family members can attest to the superb quality of her renditions of the great classics. The deprivations of World War II, following the Depression, left her with only the flute to satisfy her musical interests.

14. Siege of Paris: In 1870 France's war with Prussia ended in her defeat at Sedan with her Emperor, Napoleon III, taken prisoner. A Republic was declared but the National Guard in Paris started a siege of the city with differing political factions.

15. French Bord: Antoine-Jean Bord (born Toulouse 1814, died Paris 1888) was a French piano maker. In 1843 he invented the Capo Tasto, a metal bar which exerts downward pressure on the strings, increasing resistance and improving sonority. In 1846 he also patented a double-escapement grand action. By 1934 the business was taken over by Pleyel. On September 22, 1996, the annotator found a rare Bord piano in the drawing room of the Dodd Heritage House in Saanich, 41239 Lambrick Way. This one is exactly like the one Mrs. Harrison describes.

Index